Truvenge™

THE KRIYA PROJECT

STEPHANIE THIRTYACRE
DAVID KLEIN

Truvenge™, The Kriya Project
ISBN: 978-1-7362363-5-2

Prologue

There are some people in this world that deserve their comeuppance. And there are some people in this world who have the means to dish out this justice in defense of those who cannot defend themselves.

Then there are people - good people - men and women who would use their last days or months to see that bad people in the world are punished appropriately and held accountable for what they've done to others. Each feels a burning urge to correct the wrongdoing they have witnessed over a lifetime; sins that were never properly addressed by legal systems that all too often seemed to protect the guilty and prosecute the innocent; wrongs that remained beyond the reach of any system of equity.

Impending death forces each of us into a re-examination of our lives, and of the world in which we have lived, and still live.

Individuals approaching life's end may wish there were an organization to whom they could turn, in their final days, to mete out prescribed punishments to those self-centered transgressors who've trampled on the rights of others: the violent, the greedy, and those bearing ill will toward humanity.

Righteous people given terminal diagnoses might relish the thought that their ultimate acts could contribute to a kind of karmic justice - justice that the legal system all too often fails to address or is unable to achieve. In taking on this mission, they would seek to bring balance to an often cruel world or add balance to a life not lived as fully as desired.

Balance is essential, for there must be balance in all things.

Determined individuals, however, cannot function alone. Justice can be complicated, and costly. There must be a bigger entity behind each seeker of justice, of balance; one that supports its volunteers and assists them in their assigned tasks.

Would you be surprised to learn there exists just such an organization?

It is, perforce, a secret organization; one whose business it is to collect personal bounty warrants; to plan and monitor appropriate retribution, then to reward those deserving participants for assignments satisfactorily completed and deeds well done.

On the outside, this organization appears to be just another charity; a non-profit that offers scholarships and grants, receives and distributes donations, and which creates the kinds of connections that many people need in order to feel they are living - and will have lived - worthwhile and fulfilling lives, while receiving some small degree of recognition and appreciation. Having earned significant benefits and wealth, there are many who believe in "giving back," as it were....

Others, however, may value their connection with this organization not for themselves, but for those they love and care about and want to see prosper in their absence.

This is the story of The Kriya Project, heart and soul of a very small and very private charitable organization, incorporated under tax law as the Truvenge Foundation.

It is better known, however, simply as, Truvenge.

Table of Contents

Chapter 1 - Erik Walker, Truvenge, and the Kriya Project

Standing at the window in his office, a man known as Erik Walker sipped his coffee slowly as he watched the sun rise over the city. On the desk behind him papers were stacked in neat piles, piles that seemingly grew in size and number with each passing day.

There are so many petitions! He sighed, glancing at the desk and thinking, Yet so few can be found who are willing, or able, to take them on and see them to completion. As increasing numbers of people are referred to Kriya for help, we'll urgently need extra hands. Many extra hands. The question is, where to find them?

Deep in thought, he stroked his chin, then took another sip from his cup.

To describe the man as tall, dark and handsome was an understatement. Tall and slim, but well-muscled, with a shock of black hair, a clean-shaven 'forever-young' face and penetrating, crystal-blue eyes, his looks and suave manners continued to serve him well, both personally and professionally. Age had lightly painted the hair on each side of those startling blue eyes with a comforting dash of white. With time, Nature had relieved him of the need to dye his hair to inspire the confidence that his young face failed to bestow. He'd found, early in his career, that wealthy people more readily opened their checkbooks when they felt comfortable with him, and were able to relate.

Erik Walker was well-known in the high-paying executive world of charitable fund- raising, and it was especially noted that whenever he'd left one charity to take a better-paying position running another, still more prestigious foundation or charitable entity, his contributors loyally followed him. Not surprisingly, most of his contributors were women, or supportive companies run by women. The men were usually their husbands.

His devastating good looks drew women to him like flies to fly paper, and always had. And, particularly with his older female admirers, Erik drew their money along with them as he subtly persuaded them to follow him from job to job.

While staring out the window at the city, slowly sipping from his cup and musing over his dilemma, the door to his office opened slowly. Sharply aware no visitors had been announced by his administrative assistant, Erik turned, scowling, to confront the person walking into his sanctum sanctorum – his office. Visitors were only rarely allowed entrance. He preferred to meet them in the conference room.

A young woman with whom he was unfamiliar walked into his office, and stood defiantly in front of his desk. His assistant, April Mathis, followed behind her, twisting a handkerchief nervously as she stopped in the doorway, watching for his reaction. April's eyes pleaded with Erik as she told him in a trembling voice, "Th- this is Miss Felicity Brooks. Ms. Brooks. She insisted on seeing you immediately, and I – I think you will want to hear what she has to say." Quickly exiting, and firmly pulling the door closed behind her, April vanished,

"Are you Mr. Walker?," the rather plain-looking woman asked, holding a stack of files to her chest. She was dressed professionally, but simply, and the fitted dress was appropriate for the warmer weather they had been experiencing in recent days. She wore no makeup, which Erik found unusual.

He sized her up visually, as he would any woman. Imagining how her large brown eyes might appear if properly made up, and how her full lips would look if glossed with color, Erik realized the shapely but simply attired woman before him was actually quite attractive. Or could be.

"Yes, of course. How can I help you?," Erik replied, as stepped over to the round meeting table by the window. He placed his cup of coffee by one chair and, pulling out the chair next to it, gestured for her to take a seat.

The woman smiled and instead drew out the chair opposite his, then sat down facing him.

Ah, an independent woman, Erik thought. Defiant. He liked that. He liked to wrap that kind of woman around his little finger, and viewed her independence as a challenge to his charm.

Undaunted, Felicity began, "Mr. Walker, I was referred to you by Sarah Knight, at City Central Hospital. And I understand the need for . . .," she paused. "Shall we call it discretion? I was led to understand that your organization deals with some unique cases with her hospital, offering some, how shall I say it . . . interesting opportunities . . . to some of their terminal patients who are otherwise still in relatively good health. Patients with family members who are still dependent on them, though not directly. Patients with no . . . with no life insurance, whose savings will likely be depleted by their medical needs".

When Erik quizzically raised an eyebrow at the extent of her knowledge, the woman blurted, "I'm sorry, I failed to properly introduce myself. My name is Felicity Brooks. I'm the head social worker employed by University Hospital near City Central. Sarah and I had met before, professionally, and we encountered each other again during a break at a three-day seminar on 'Economic Management of Health Crises: Preserving the Family.' She and I really hit it off and I learned about the Kriya Project from her, over lunch the next day. It struck a chord, primarily because I have several such patients." The woman had set her files on the table, and now leaned back in her chair, hands clasped over her midriff, and nodded at the files.

"I've brought you a few prospective employees. Volunteers. Whatever you prefer to call them. They're good people, with a wide variety of business and vocational skills and experience. But because of how employment is these days, when each got their diagnosis, things started going downhill from there. After a while, their treatment schedules became 'problematic." Small employers generally don't offer disability benefits, and most can't carry a non-productive employee for more than a few months. These people have families; people who rely on them. But all of their money goes into treatment, and toward prolonging their quality of life as long as possible."

As Felicity spoke, Erik reached over and flipped open a few files, pursing his lips and frowning slightly as he read through the first few pages of each. "And these people are confirmed terminal?" he asked, looking up at the woman.

Resting her hands in her lap, she gave him a nod. "All are confirmed. Diagnosed terminal, or pending test results for a probable terminal illness. And in financial need. They all want to leave something to their families - if only to bury them and pay off their bills, or care for a disabled relative when they are gone. Should I expect you'll send someone to speak with them fairly soon?"

"These patients... are they strong enough to return home?"

"Well," Felicity frowned. "Most of them. There are a few in those files who are still of sound mind, but their bodies can't support them. If family cannot take them in and provide care, they will have to go to a convalescent center or an intermediate- care nursing home."

"To work for Kriya, they'll need privacy, and they must have the ability to maintain a secure laptop in their living space. That pretty much eliminates those prospects – except, perhaps, if they can do research online. They'll need access to a printer, though some stuff can be emailed. And someone will need to be routinely available to pick up what they print, and mail it here or send it by courier. No personal visits, please. For those who are only able to read, but have sharp minds and can plan, we may be able to use their ideas; but there's not much we can offer them in terms of work. We do require a degree of physical agility, or artificial mobility at a certain level."

He flipped through the files again, stacked them and nodded. "Right. I'll read these more closely over the next day or two, and see what I can do. For those who can work from home in privacy, and who are mobile, there might be something we can offer."

Erik rose. "Well, thank you for your time, Miss Brooks. Leave your contact information with my assistant on your way out. I'll be sure to take a good look through these files to determine if any of these people are the type of person we're looking to employ on a freelance basis, if we have appropriate work for them. I may call you with questions. And, of course, to set up any meetings."

Felicity smiled and rose from her chair, smoothing out her dress. She held out a hand. Erik took her proffered hand, then placed his own hand atop hers for a double handshake. Smiling warmly, he held her hand a moment longer than he needed to as he said in his deep baritone, "A pleasure meeting you, Ms. Brooks."

"And you as well, Mr. Walker. I'll be sure to come by every few weeks, should I come across anyone who might be of interest to you," Felicity replied, retrieving her hand from his grasp.

"I look forward to it." Erik walked Felicity to the door, stepping out to tell April to get Ms. Brooks' contact information, then nodded a 'goodbye' in Felicity's direction. April promptly opened Mr. Walker's address program on her computer, and typed in Felicity's information with long, polished nails. As her fingernails clicked on the keys, Felicity looked down quickly at her own professionally short, clear-polished nails and briefly wondered if Erik Walker preferred long nails on women, or if he could appreciate her no-nonsense manicure.

Seated once again behind his large and impressive mahogany desk, and backed by a tastefully filled bookcase, Erik rested his elbows on its surface and leaned his head against his hands. He breathed in deeply, then exhaled and sighed audibly. He remained in that position for nearly a minute, then attacked the stack of files Ms. Brooks had brought him.

"Some of these do look promising," he muttered, picking up his coffee to take a sip. It had grown lukewarm during his conversation, but he did dislike waste, so he drank it anyway, then buzzed April to bring him a fresh cup.

Setting Felicity's files to his left, he pulled the larger stack of job files toward him and flipped through petition details he had practically memorized, rereading them as often as he had, when searching for just the right individuals to be the particular "justice effectors" he needed to handle the often complicated requirements of each case. Despite his excellent memory of each, Erik went through all of the job petitions stacked on his desk, one by one, assessing the qualities knew would be demanded for success.

As he reviewed the details, he could not help but wonder what he had to work with, now that he had some new terminals interested in whatever work he could offer, if they qualified, that would enable them to provide for their loved ones.

Flipping through the many pages that cried out for action, for justice, for retribution, Erik decided that there were also far too many frivolous requests - requests that simply should go into the shredder.

Too many were small jobs, or missions that could never be planned in a manner that would satisfy the disgruntled complainant or provide a worthwhile result. "Some of these are just . . . petty," he grumbled, "and merit absolutely no action." The shredder was not an option, of course. Each petitioner deserved at least a personal letter returning their petition and explaining that "The Kriya Project is unable, at this time, to satisfy the petitioner's request due to lack of personnel appropriately equipped to deliver justice for the grievous wrong done, on a level with which the petitioner would be satisfied."

That reason was flexible enough and vague enough to apply to every situation Erik and the Bodhi had thus far found too insignificant, or too petty, distasteful, or dangerous for Kriya Project to undertake. Once accepted, and a commitment made, it was the Bodhi's requirement that each plan be carried to its resolution. No one whose petition had been accepted was to be left disappointed. The Kriya Project had, over the previous three decades, won a reputation for delivering each agreed- upon form of justice competently, and to the satisfaction of every aggrieved petitioner.

Vengeance was the "product" that the Kriya Project unfailingly delivered. And that commitment to its petitioners was basis for the name this specific charitable arm of the Bodhi's private foundation bore, a name based on their perception of the deep- seated human need for justice - as opposed to true revenge - for significant financial, physical or emotional injury, and outright abuse. The Kriya Project formed the core of the Bodhi's humanitarian works.

For that reason, the Kriya Project's encompassing charitable 501(c)(3) had been named 'Truvenge.'

The Truvenge Foundation itself operated to avenge pervasive societal neglect or abuse of certain populations through programs that offered housing assistance and food vouchers, family and individual counseling, drug and alcohol interventions, and social worker follow-up visits, referrals, and case monitoring. But it was the Kriya Project, above all, that was near and dear to the hearts of the Bodhi – the organization's mystical founders, and its active directors.

When Erik deemed that he had appropriately weeded out those cases that would achieve little or no merit for anyone but the petitions' applicants, he decided to go out for a bit of lunch, and invite Tracey to accompany him. She had earned a little time away from the office, he decided, and it was a beautiful day.

He buzzed April and asked her to come in and get the pile of rejected petitions, and to immediately start working on letters to the applicants, so they could be sent out that afternoon.

Erik stood from behind his desk to stretch, then walked over to the window. He chuckled.

Since accepting his position as Executive Director and President of Truvenge Foundation, Erik was constantly astounded by the insignificant level at which many holders of grievance – those perpetually feeling wronged in some manner by someone, or by *everyone* - desired the most severe and painful retribution for a perceived harm; while others, those truly harmed and unwitting victims of malice aforethought, including medical error, carelessness, gossip and rumor, or actions initiated by others that cost them their reputations, forced them into bankruptcy, deprived them of one or more limbs, destroyed their health, robbed them of physical capacity, cost the life of a loved one, or otherwise wreaked havoc with their lives – were far more charitable.

He also found it interesting that those most harmed only rarely initiated their own petitions for vengeance, while those least harmed always did.

April sailed in, got her instructions, and whisked the rejected petition files to her desk, freeing Erik to phone his daughter and arrange for her to meet him at his favorite restaurant. He only hoped Tracey wouldn't have dyed her hair some bizarre color over the weekend, or show up sporting the omnipresent earbuds she often defiantly refused to remove, or wearing some gawd-awful outfit that would garner stares.

When she did appear at Chez Robert, however, Erik was pleasantly surprised to see her hair was neatly combed and still its normal winter shade of golden brown, streaked with sun-lightened blonde strands. Dressed appropriately, she'd smiled at him, then sat and immediately removed her earbuds, tucking them into a pocket of her handbag. She was a pleasant conversationalist over lunch, and had complimented her father's choice of restaurants without gushing sarcastically or making faces. Tracey was turning into an excellent employee, and Erik had praised her. Always reserved with her father, she seemed to appreciate his words. Their meal together was an unusually pleasant one. Tracy was working on an assignment, and so ate quickly and had to leave, but left Erik immensely pleased he had treated her to an enjoyable lunch at a restaurant she could not likely afford on her own, even after her recent promotion and significant raise.

Driving back to the office, Erik thought about his relationship with Tracey.

She had always been difficult. She was her mother's daughter in every way - even looked like her. Tracey and her mother had been very close, and ever since her mother's disappearance Tracey had barely spoken to him, and was usually disrespectful or sarcastic when she did. Erik attributed her improved attitude to the position he had created for her at the suggestion of the Bodhi, who had apparently ascertained certain skills and potential in his daughter that he had missed. Where she had been hostile to him, and visibly bored with the work he had asked her to do, her new position with the foundation seemed to light a fire under Tracey, and resulted in a miraculous change in attitude. His compliment to her, as they were leaving, was genuine. She'd made a 180-degree turn, and was proving invaluable in working the requisite investigations, developing and coordinating plans, and supervising their execution. Erik had wanted her to know he had noticed the change, and got a smile from her for his efforts.

This opportunity for the two of them to work with Truvenge Foundation, and the Kriya Project seemed heaven-sent. After his wife's unsolved disappearance, suspicion had fallen - as it always does – on the man closest to the woman in question, whether husband, or boyfriend, or neighbor.

Erik had been their first suspect.

The local news reports had been ugly, filled with commentary noting odd timelines, inexplicable choices, and interview responses that were characterized as implying guilt. The publicity drove suspicion even higher than seemed warranted, and soon a half dozen TV stations were digging deep and exhibiting skepticism about his alibis.

Although the police had concluded their investigation of Erik within a few weeks and told him they were satisfied he was not involved, the national charity that employed him was not so benevolent.

The Board of Directors, to their credit, had not acted hastily. They'd met with him on several occasions to discuss the widespread television, radio and newspaper publicity about the case, which had drawn immense media interest. They expressed their concerns over the multiple videos of him leaving the police station after questioning, trying to avoid cameras, and asked him a number of uncomfortable questions, all the while assuring him that they understood that spousal suspicion was normal police procedure in these cases, and following investigation, would surely be dropped.

Wouldn't it?

Board members met repeatedly with Erik over the days and weeks when police and members of the public were actively searching for Marilyn – or for her body – and fretted at every meeting that the press frenzy had not abated as quickly as expected. Members "took the pulse" of their largest contributors and monitored the inflow of donations as news crews dogged Erik's footsteps and questioned the neighbors, his previous employers, and the therapist who had helped him quit smoking, and who'd treated him some years earlier during a bout with depression.

News crews across the nation followed the story avidly. He'd been cursed by the absence of other local, state or national news of import to distract from the plethora of reports highlighting Erik's prominence in his community, and speculating endlessly about his wife's unsolved disappearance.

Reports of Marilyn's perplexing vanishment had even made the national news. Talking heads interviewed anyone who held an opinion on the case, including, of course, many of the individuals who'd actively participated in the search of nearby neighborhoods and adjoining woods, lakes and streams, as well as those who knew absolutely nothing, but had merely been standing around to watch SCUBA crews search the watery depths for a body or any possible evidence. Yet, eager for their own 15 minutes of fame, were more than happy to pontificate about his wife's tragic disappearance when handed a microphone, as if they'd been life-long family friends.

Reporters even managed to locate a few contributors to the foundation Erik headed at the time, and quizzed them on-air in a video clip featured prominently at the top of the six o'clock news, asking whether they would continue donating to a charity they were listed as supporting, when its President was under suspicion for the possible murder of his missing wife

That was the straw that broke the camel's back, so to speak. The Board Chair called the next day to advise Erik that, despite his excellent performance, he was being let go since it was apparent to "some members of the Board" that his situation was tarnishing the reputation of the charity. That, in turn, could jeopardize fundraising. The Chairman assured him Board members empathized with his situation, and therefore intended to honor the 'golden parachute' he'd negotiated when first employed, despite his particular situation not being recognized in its terms. But he would have to be let go.

Good thing they didn't fight his negotiated severance, Erik thought, because the settlement was rather substantial, and that money had made it possible for him and his daughter to head north and start to rebuild their lives in the Big Apple: New York City.

He never a questioned how the Bodhi had found him to make their offer. He had no doubt they had been searching for a new Executive Director, and his stellar reputation for fundraising had attracted their attention.

Erik disregarded the fact he'd been fruitlessly sending out resumes for a month and a half without a bite, tapping contacts for information about who might be considering a move, and even contacting charities he'd dismissed in the past as too small and insignificant to meet to meet his salary (and ego) requirements. His industry contacts had either failed to respond, or declined meetings on the thinnest of excuses for being unable to fit him into their suddenly busy schedules. As he searched to find a new position, Erik realized the publicity about Marilyn's disappearance had reached into virtually every corner of the country and was whispered throughout the fundraising community, marking him as an undesirable hire.

Charitable work was all he'd done for over 20 years, and it paid very, very well, at his level. So transitioning to a for-profit organization as a novice to the business world, and obtaining an executive position at an acceptable level of pay was simply not feasible.

Erik had never had a problem finding work, since applying for his first job in his chosen profession. Headhunters generally came to him, and usually with several opportunities for him to choose from, at any given time. To be on his own, fruitlessly sending out resume after resume without even an acknowledgement of receipt, was truly a humbling experience.

When the letter arrived offering him an interview for the position of Executive Director at Truvenge Foundation, he noticed that it was signed strangely, in triplicate, with three identical signatures overlaid, one atop the other, in perfect alignment – executed by one or more persons who identified themselves simply, as "The Bodhi." An affectation, perhaps?

Their succinct letter invited him to arrange travel as soon as possible and respond to the interview invitation by speaking with their foundation representative, who would handle arrangements. Erik was given a name and phone number to call that individual direct, along with a contact deadline. Since the position would require a move to New York City, Erik gratefully assumed the foundation was probably led by foreigners who didn't concern themselves with the U.S. nightly news. Excited, he promptly called to arrange the interview and was pleased to learn Truvenge would pay for his round trip flight from Florida to New York, and back. He flew up the next day.

Upon his mid-morning arrival at the impressive office building that housed the Truvenge Foundation, Erik was greeted warmly, and was shown to a nicely furnished room where he could refresh himself, work or watch television, and even nap, if desired, while awaiting the hour of his appointment. The bathroom was outfitted with clean towels, a hair dryer, electric shaver and aftershave lotion. His every need was seemingly accommodated, and there was a limited menu available from which he could order a snack, or light lunch. He skipped a snack and requested an early lunch - a Cobb salad and an iced tea. Removing his jacket, tie and shirt to keep them fresh for the interview, he ate lunch in his undershirt. He had not slept well the previous night, so after calling the concierge to arrange a wakeup call, Erik napped for a bit, covering his eyes with a cool washcloth.

When his interview time arrived, he heard light tapping on the door and was escorted to the business suite where he was to be interviewed. He was surprised to note how uncharacteristically nervous he was.

The lighting in the large room was muted; furnishings were simple. A small tray holding a two water glasses and a half-filled carafe was positioned between two comfortable leather chairs arranged in front of a long, pierced-wood Indian screen that consisted of nine panels. A modular sofa in beige leather filled one corner, with a low square table of some exotic wood serving as a coffee table, nestled in the crook of its Vshaped junction. The broad table-top held a number of large volumes and a stunning, oriental-appearing arrangement of fresh flowers. Incense filled the air with a light scent of sandalwood.

As his eyes slowly adjusted to the dim light, Erik noticed three shrouded figures positioned at intervals behind the screen. It unnerved him that he'd been silently observed as he'd made himself comfortable, blowing his nose and clearing his throat in anticipation of "The Bodhi" walking into the room to take the chairs arranged closest to his.

The figures remained so still that perhaps – Erik could only hope - they were actually the statues they appeared to be.

His prospective interviewers, however, had been sitting silent and motionless, observing him. Once he was settled, he - they - whoever it was, or however many there were behind the screen greeted him in a single, layered voice that immediately called to his mind the Asian twins from the original "Godzilla," although these multiple voices were deeper in tone, softer in pitch, and more resonant in delivery.

He'd smiled on hearing the united voices, then dropped the smile and returned their grave salutation, expressing gratitude for the opportunity to meet with them for the interview, and his hope that he'd be found suitable for the position.

On later giving it some thought, Erik decided the multiple voices speaking to him in unison were created by just one of the individuals, with the special effect of multiple voices speaking together achieved through clever use of a voice modulator.

The interview extended a good two hours before the Bodhi wrapped it up by extending an immediate offer of employment, and set the terms of that offer. If Erik were not prepared to make an immediate decision, he was welcome to return to the room where he'd waited for the interview, to take a few hours and ponder their terms, then decide. If he accepted, paperwork would be handled that same day. His actual start date could be negotiated with the representative who had handled his travel plans. But the Bodhi made it clear that they required a decision from him that very day, or they would continue their search.

He was less than pleased with the starting salary, which was lower than his previous compensation. But he figured he could work on upping the figure later, once he was on board as Executive Director. He didn't hesitate to accept the position. It was a big step toward repairing the tremendous damage that had been done to his professional reputation by the police investigation.

Erik was absorbed in thought on his flight back to Tampa, pondering the enigmatic presence of whomever it - or they - were, those three odd individuals who had just hired him. He could not help but wonder why a same-day decision was required, given his need to relocate. They wanted him to start as soon as possible; however they understood that a degree of delay would be necessary to make arrangements for the move.

Who had held the position previously, and why did they leave? Asking those questions had never entered his mind, in great part because he was so flummoxed by their questions.

The interview had seemed more like a session with a psychiatrist than a business interview, and many of the Bodhi's questions had left him stammering and grasping for answers. Erik grew so certain the interview was a disaster and there was no way he would qualify, that when the unusual trio extended their offer he shamelessly jumped at the opportunity, for fear they might change their minds.

Realizing the move would allow him to escape continue police attention, and remove him from unpleasant issues he wished to forget about, Erik accepted the offer without hesitation.

The representative he'd met with following the interview seemed to have a good deal of authority, so he broached his concerns about the adequacy of his initial salary, since it was less than he'd expected. In response to his query he was told not to worry, and was then promised a nice raise would be his, once he knew the ropes and understood what was expected of him.

Erik was never asked why he was interested in a position at far lower pay, nor the reason he'd left his previous position. And he'd volunteered nothing. He figured he would handle those questions when, and if, they arose. His biggest fear - that police investigation of wife's disappearance, which had dominated the headlines and national news for weeks, would be brought up at some point and require an explanation, proved entirely unfounded.

Accepting the Bodhi's offer meant leaving the city where his wife had disappeared. And that was good enough for Erik.

Tracey's response had not been so sanguine. "You are moving us out of Tampa? Out of state? How could you? Really, how could you do that! What if Mom's sustained some kind of head injury and lost her memory? What if she's in a hospital somewhere, and doesn't know who she is? What if she was kidnapped?" She was shrieking by that point, and accusing him of abandoning her mother.

Calming the girl had taken a good deal of time and patience. Erick explained to his daughter that he needed to work if they were to survive, and if she wanted to finish her finals for the AA degree she was so close to achieving. The investigation had left him a marked man, and this was an opportunity for him to work again and restore his career.

He also assured Tracey that he was obliged to tell Tampa police if he left town, and provide his whereabouts. He could now inform them he'd be leaving to take a position in New York City that he'd been offered by the Truvenge Foundation, a charitable organization, and would be the Executive Director.

Tracey was distraught about the move, but Erik tsked at her fears and dismissed her objections. He assured her the police detectives assigned to Marilyn's case would be given their new contact information as soon as they found a place to live. He had been cleared, and TPD detectives assigned to the case had their email addresses and cell phone numbers. *If* there were any news, he would surely be contacted immediately, and they would naturally fly back if anything were to change.

There was no need to stay, but the young woman stubbornly held out hope her mother would be found.

A wry smile flickered across his lips. "Kids," he muttered, "are *always* a problem."

Chapter 2 – A Hard Day's Work

Over the course of the afternoon, Erik worked to sort through the files and papers he had on his desk. Rejecting a significant number of petty petitions, as he had after Ms. Brooks' departure, left a much more manageable stack to look through.

"Let's see…," he muttered, setting out a few of the files on his desk that Felicity Brooks had brought to him.

This was always his least favorite part of his work: vetting petitions; evaluating skills, measuring character. On the barest of information, Erik was charged with estimating an individual's physical condition and stamina, plus his or her ability to handle stress and operate under extreme pressure. It also meant getting into the finer details of what each job might entail, working from the facts of the case, the information in the personnel file, and a strict adherence to the preliminary plans that Erik and the Bodhi had developed for each.

There was always a Plan 'A' and a Plan 'B,' plus an emergency fallback plan. Sometimes the necessary skills were the same for both 'A'; and 'B'; more often than not, however, the personal skill sets required were quite different. That frequently necessitated a second, practiced crew to be on standby for plan switches, or last- minute tweaks to an existing plan. The quantity of unknowns and degrees of potential risk in every plan served to magnify the number of matches that had to be decided upon, and at the ready. Ultimately, every plan had to be reviewed for suitable matching involving the who, the what, the why, and the where.

As for the how each plan was devised and developed – well, that took place over several visits with the Bodhi. Then Erik would review the stacks of files, selecting and matching applicants with jobs appropriate to their skills and characters. Timelines were drawn up, and the entire package was presented in toto to the ultimate "deciders" - the Bodhi.

Erik still found dealing with the Bodhi an unsettling experience.

Tracey seemed to get along with them much better than he. And it was Tracey who had informed him of their true nature, and what their name stood for - explaining to him with feigned, elaborate patience (and an eye roll) that the word 'Bodhi', in the Indian languages of Sanskrit and Pāli, meant "awakening" or "enlightenment." She'd told him, "In Buddhism, Dad, Bodhi stands for the final Enlightenment that ends the cycle of transmigration of the soul and leads to the ultimate spiritual end: to Nirvāna, the name Buddhists call the spiritual release that provides an end to all suffering. The soul then accomplishes full Awakening – which means "perfect knowledge" – and I guess that is as close to divinity that we can get: an illuminated and enlightened intellect. That's the state of enlightenment that the Buddha, the Prince Siddhartha, ultimately achieved.

"Sheesh, Dad! I would have thought you'd have at lease checked out Wikipedia to find out a little bit about something you clearly don't understand. Haven't you realized your employers are from *India*? It's no wonder you can't figure them out!" Tracey had then lowered her voice and muttered, just loud enough so he could hear, "Sometimes, I honestly feel you're afraid they've figured YOU out." At that, the young woman had turned abruptly, and flounced out of the room.

Proud at having put Dad in his place, Erik thought, chuckling as he recalled the event. The Bodhi were, without a doubt, highly intelligent. But possessed of "perfect knowledge"? He chuckled again. Yet her explanation had left him with the uneasy sense the Bodhi knew far more about him than they ever let on . . .

Tracey, in her new position as Kriya Project's Chief Detective and Planner, had also begun meeting with him and the Bodhi as they mapped out strategy. This was a development that Erik actually found comforting, as though her presence shielded him to some degree from their intense scrutiny.

They generally worked as a team on no more than three (3) cases at one time, due in part to available staffing, and in part to the lack of an adequate number of physically or intellectually capable "terminals." The Bodhi lent great credence to numerology - the power of numbers - and insisted on limiting everything in their domain by the numbers 3, 6, and 9.

Erik found that positively bizarre.

Truvenge Foundation employees were limited to no more, nor less, than 93 employees at any one time, with 39 of those full-time employees $(3 + 9 = 12 = 1 + 2 = 3)$ assigned exclusively to the Kriya Project, and the three active Kriya Project teams. Kriya Project employees included six (6) evasion-trained drivers (all of whom were also superb stunt men and women); 18 researchers $(1 + 8 = 9)$ split amongst the three (3) "justice effector" teams; and three (3) costumers – one for each team. Each costumer was also a makeup artist. There were three (3) master carpenters; three (3) mechanical engineers; and six (6) skilled character actors – male (3) and female (3)

– all on call, and pledged to secrecy. Everyone in the organization had to sign a non-disclosure agreement – an NDA – each year at their annual review. The majority of Kriya Project employees had worked with the Kriya Project for years – some for decades - and all were immensely loyal to the Bodhi.

The other 54 employees served in various roles in the Truvenge Foundation itself, led by an Executive Vice President who reported directly to Erik and the Bodhi. Erik maintained a formalized oversight role over the social service functions of Truvenge Foundation; his primary role, however, was as Truvenge Foundation's executive administrator.

Except for his finite role with the Kriya Project there existed a 'Chinese wall' – an insurmountable but artificial barrier that restricted communications and information exchanges between the Truvenge Foundation and the Kriya Project. Erik was, first and foremost, the 'face' of the entire organization, and its primary fundraiser.

Only the three (3) Executive Administrative staff dealt in any way with the Kriya Project: Erik, who was both Truvenge's Executive Director and President (the latter a fairly recent title - a promotion, of sorts), his Executive Administrative Assistant, April Mathis, who had been in her position for over 20 years, and Tracey, who - because of her personality, inquisitive mind, and a natural aptitude for solving puzzles and mysteries - bore the recently bestowed title of Chief Inspector and Planner for the Kriya Project.

It was Tracey's role to work undercover and ferret things out, to think on her feet and manage the execution of each of the plans, to monitor the training of terminals, and their performance as they worked to effect justice.

Her responsibilities included helping them succeed in their tasks, avoid dangers, and to resolve or evade whatever problems and incidents might arise with a case.

Her title was justified by her recently awarded AA degree in Criminal Justice, as well as her innate skills and talents, ferreted out and identified by the Bodhi in their early contacts with her. Tracey was a natural for the position, and she loved the work. Her long hours usually kept her out of the office and away from her father. It kept her mind functioning intently, gave her a status that opened many doors, and conveyed to all a sense of her absolute importance to the Kriya Project's ongoing mission. The position allowed her to work on her own schedule and allowed her to spend a great deal of time with the Bodhi.

Lastly, of course, the three (3) Bodhi acted in the role as the Board of Directors; the ultimate decision-makers. Theirs was the last word on everything.

They were Indian Mystics, who − interestingly - spoke, thought, and worked in unison. That ability absolutely fascinated Tracey, even as it unnerved her father.

The Bodhi ran The Truvenge Foundation like any other foundation: raising funds, developing a public presence and contributing to the community in which they were headquartered, providing necessary services and distributing monetary awards to worthy causes. They farmed out much of the basic foundation work of their organization to three (3) private and well-managed social service organizations that provided caseworkers in three distinct areas: Family evaluations, disability assessments, and therapeutic referrals; family and individual counseling and follow- up; and emergency financial, housing, and food assistance. These social service organizations were dedicated primarily to the Truvenge Foundation and reported directly to the Executive Vice President who was responsible for the smooth operation of these programs and who then reported directly to Erik and the Bodhi.

But it was the Kriya Project that was truly near and dear to the Bodhi's hearts. They defined their mission on this earth as delivering precisely-tailored karma to avenge what earthly institutions could not. Ultimately, the function of the Kriya Project was to provide karmic justice to those petitioners deserving of it. While the teaching they ascribed to instructed believers that karma was an energy exchange that was as spiritually instructive as it was materially effective in restoring the internal and external balance between good and evil. Karma could be either punitive or rewarding and restorative, depending on the situation and character of each individual. The Bodhi just saw to it that karma arrived sooner, rather than later, in the lives of the aggrieved, or the deserving.

Tracey had occasion to inform her father, during one of their rare lunches together, of the meaning of the word 'Kriya' and of the events that had led to the institution of the Kriya Project by the Bodhi.

"Kriya," she had explained, "means 'completed action' in Sanskrit. It is an action leading to an ultimate manifestation of something – like seeds lead to plants in bloom, or – or an initial thought or desire leads to a commitment that then leads to its manifestation, through intention - or through the physical action necessary to make something manifest."

"Manifest?" her father inquired, raising his eyebrows skeptically.

"Yes. Manifest. Manifesting, in the spiritual sense, is the creation of something that you desire to own or gain for yourself, or want to happen, through a focused *intention*. Thoughts are powerful. We all create our own reality - the world around us – through our intentions, and our will. Everything is energy, constantly vibrating - including this table, this plate and fork. When your vibrations match with your objective, you draw it to you. Haven't you heard about the Law of Attraction, Dad? Don't tell me you've never heard of it!"

For a moment, Erik stared at his daughter blankly. Then he attempted a feeble joke to change the subject: "Right now, young lady, as you can see, I am busily *manifesting* this terrific pasta dish that I *intended* to order. It was, in fact, the reason we came here. Watch now, as I *draw it* to my mouth on the end of this fork …"

She sighed, rolled her eyes, and shook her head. "Of course not."

He went on, "Mmmmm. Mystically good. I feel that I am feeding my soul."

"Cut it out, Dad! I am serious. And so are the Bodhi! Truvenge – that beautiful foundation that employed you – us - was created by the Bodhi's joined intentions to do good."

Tracey then went on to explain, "Kriya, for whom the Project is named, was a beautiful Indian woman who lost her husband and four young sons in battles waged by an avaricious and heartless prince. One day, when passing through the marketplace, the prince spotted Kriya selling her wares and was so transfixed by her beauty that he stopped his entourage and motioned to his guards to seize her for his pleasure. When Kriya saw the prince's guards approaching her, she understood immediately what was happening, for that prince had a wicked reputation for defiling powerless women who caught his eye.

She was determined to deny the prince his wish, so Kriya ran to the stall of a man in the market who was a kerosene merchant. She grabbed a lantern he kept burning as a form of advertisement to draw buyers to his stall, and she doused herself with the burning kerosene. Her soaked garments immediately ignited, and she was consumed in flames. Thus did Kriya keep her vow not to be taken by the prince – the man responsible for the deaths of her sons, and of the husband she desperately loved. It was a great tragedy, and whether factual or not, the tale has been kept alive in the oral traditions of India. Hence, the Bodhi created the Kriya Project in her honor, as a means to right the kind of wrongs for which there is no other justice."

Erik nodded to show understanding, but his first reaction was to congratulate himself that Tracey had actually called him 'Dad.' Perhaps that meant things were improving between them. Her attitude had certainly improved.

They'd been estranged since Tracey was 14 – her mother's influence, no doubt - and on reaching adulthood at 18 she'd refused to acknowledge him as her father any longer, both privately and in public. Since then, she'd persistently addressed him as "Erik." Whenever he'd confronted her in the past about this, she'd grown hostile and demanded that he *prove* to her that he was her father. How? By taking a paternity test, of all things!

Tracey claimed there was absolutely nothing about her that resembled him, which was true. Erik was tall and lean; Tracey was short and moderately plump. He had coal black hair, an olive complexion and piercing, crystal blue eyes. She had pale skin with a sprinkling of freckles, rosy cheeks, tawny blonde hair, amber brown eyes, and was a tomboy with a well-muscled physique, like her mother. She loved sports, swam, and played tennis like a pro. Erik eschewed sports, but enjoyed dancing, good Scotch, and playing poker.

Where Tracey was an extrovert, open and honest in all her dealings, like her mother, Erik kept a tight rein on his emotions and was extremely private – although he could quickly turn the charm on, or off as easily as flipping a light switch.

And Erik's demeanor was perpetually serious – almost somber; his sense of humor was virtually non-existent. Tracey often joked that Erik would have made an outstanding funeral director. She was his opposite – generally good-humored with a perspective on life that saw humor in everything.

"You've gotta laugh at life, or you're gonna cry," was her favorite saying, although she could not, for the life of her, recall where or when she'd first heard the phrase. Perhaps she had invented it, in a flash of brilliance? She hadn't a clue. It was most likely her innate reaction to the sad tale her mother had recounted again and again over the years, a sad tale of poor decisions made in her youth, and of a miserable and loveless marriage she could not leave.

Erik knew his wife despised him. And he blamed her for Tracey's disaffection and alienation, as well as the girl's sudden but persistent refusal to consider him her real father – an idea that he knew Marilyn had planted in the girl's young mind.

Water under the bridge, he thought.

Erik usually took most of what Tracy said with a grain of salt, but he knew that she had been spending increasing amounts of time with the Bodhi, while he found himself spending less time in their presences. She was now contacting the Bodhi on her own to discuss various details of the cases she was charged with investigating and handling. Grudgingly, he found himself giving increasing weight to whatever she spoke of, particularly when it involved those things she was learning about the Bodhi. Tracey approached them with a fresh curiosity of which Erik was incapable. He had to admit – if only to himself – that curiosity was not in his character.

"And Kriya is also a yoga discipline that requires both energy and breath control," Tracey was saying, while picking at her pasta with her fork. "The Bodhi told me it is a comprehensive spiritual path that could benefit me greatly. You learn breathing techniques and exercises to increase concentration, and bring calmness and joy into your life. The Bodhi said they could refer me to an excellent Kriya Master.

"What do you think, Dad? I would love to start learning yoga. You'd probably be a little less stiff, yourself, if you could bring yourself to try it."

Tracey was still talking. Focused on his meal, and thoughts of Felicity Brooks, he'd missed her last few sentences, but couldn't admit to her that he had not been listening. Fortunately, he was good at faking attention. She never seemed to notice when he had zoned out during a conversation with her.

His meal finished, he cut her short. "If you are not going to eat that, let's get it boxed. You can warm it up for dinner. I have to get going. Lots to accomplish this afternoon." Tracey nodded and surrendered her half-eaten pasta to the waiter to box, and gathered her things.

End of subject. Erik was ready to leave, and that was that.

But it backfired on him when she waltzed into his office a week later. "I am so excited – and the Bodhi are so excited for me. I am going to start with my Kriya Master this Friday."

"Your who?," Erik asked.

"I told you last week at lunch, Erik." She was back to that, he thought. Calling him Erik again. So much for fatherhood. He sighed.

"I told you the Bodhi would hook me up with a Kriya Yoga Master to teach me. They did. I met him today. Babaji Neelakantan. He is amazing! He is a disciple of Paramahansa Yogananda, the Kriya Master who wrote "Autobiography of a Yogi" in 1946. Yogananda lived in Los Angeles in the 1920s, '30s and '40s. That is where his remains are. Yogananda was told by Mahatvar Babaji, who appeared to him in a vision, that his life's mission was to introduce Kriya Yoga to the West. And that is what Yogananda did from 1920 to 1952. That is when he departed his body and transitioned, attaining the yogic state called mahasamadhi.

"Mahatvar Babaji was a great 'siddha' *who lived for centuries* in the Himalayas - a siddha is a holy man who has meditated and studied under great masters to attain the ability to overcome human limitations and teach at great distance. Babaji continued to work for the spiritual evolution of all humankind. That is who Babaji is named for. Babaji's grandfather was V.T. Neelakantan. He was a famous journalist and was one of two individuals chosen by Babaji to disseminate the practice of Kriya Yoga throughout the world.

"Babaji dictated three books to his grandfather, V.T., who then had them published. When Babaji, my Yoga Master, was born he was dedicated to the study and dissemination of Kriya Yoga. Do you know that Paramahansa Yoganada wrote that, during his missing years, Jesus the Christ – that's what he called Him - traveled to the Himalayas on the Silk Road that traders used in their journeys to the mysterious East, and that he studied Kriya Yoga? When his ministry gathered a following, Jesus also taught Kriya Yoga to his disciples!"

"Hey, slow down, slow down, Tracey," Erik declared, laughing. "I know you're thrilled about studying yoga with this Babaji guy, but I have things to do. If the Bodhi want you to take yoga, good for you. It will probably help you slim down a little. That's what you're trying to do, right?"

Erik had shooed her out of his office at the time, without giving the yoga idea another thought. She was an adult now, and earned her own money. If that was how she chose to spend it, well, who was he to stop her? But there was no way he could be persuaded to try it.

He found himself staring out the window at traffic, watching the tiny cars and delivery trucks maneuver on the street several stories below his office.

Enough fiddle-faddling!, Erik thought, brusquely shaking himself out of his reverie. Enough of this nonsense! I'm wasting time, when I need to get a move on!

There was work to be done, and he reminded himself that he had a late-afternoon appointment with a prospective donor.

Erik buzzed April to brew some coffee and bring him a cup, and dove into the justice petitions, file by file.

The first petition Erik read through that afternoon had promise – it involved a regional insurance tycoon who had grown rich cheating his health insurance clients out of money they were owed and desperately needed to prolong their lives and enjoy greater comfort, or perhaps find a doctor who could provide a cure.

The insurance magnate owned a company that sold policies to blue color tradesmen and their families, but set each policy up so that all benefit checks were sent to his company office. His staff would then cut a new check to the client, the doctor or hospital – after deducting an additional "service fee" on top of the legitimate commissions his company and its agents earned. He saw to it that the unearned fee was skimmed off the top of each benefit payment as a percentage, before sending the reduced insurance proceeds to his client-victims or their medical providers. Victims of his scheme came from all over the region. More than a few were union members, blue-color men, secretaries and workers who were beneficiaries of large union policies that paid large commissions. But that was never enough for the tycoon, or for the union leaders with whom he split his 'fees' in order to acquire and retain the business.

Clients and union members were left with medical bills they never anticipated, and often had difficulty paying. Quite a few even passed away over the many years he'd been in business, due to the negligence and intentional deception of his company that left them with too little reimbursement to continue costly treatments. Many others who died had their estates attached for medical payments the deceased should never have had to pay, so that their heirs suffered.

The situation appealed to Erik. It was a kind of "class action" approach to vengeance, with the Kriya Project's search for absolute justice tied in with the general practices of an industry Erik disliked, rather than a case of specific malice aforethought. Erik could actually empathize with these clients, since he had fought his own battle to get his therapist's bills covered by his employers' insurance companies when working for several foundations over the years. This particular petition had been submitted by a man who was an accountant for the insurance tycoon, and had figured out his employer's scheme. The job had possibilities, Erik mused. But the case was potentially quite large and would require a great deal more research. There were many extenuating factors to consider.

Erik decided it was not a pressing case, and figured Tracey could dig into that one a little further, once things slowed down a bit and she had more time on her hands. After a thorough job researching the situation she could present her findings to him, and they could then approach to the Bodhi. They might be interested after all.

The second petition Erik reviewed was a more targeted case with a clearly-defined 'wrong' that called out to be vindicated. Although there would never be a shortage of individuals to fall prey to this sort of nefarious and predatory business practice, Erik observed that, in this instance, a single individual had been deeply affected. The man's clever idea – his innovation - the invention of a lifetime - had been stolen by someone on whom he'd depended to provide the necessary services to support his efforts. As a result of nefarious tactics, his dreams had been destroyed.

Now, *this* is a petition we can all sink our teeth into, Erik thought. He kept reading the supporting material, engrossed.

The CEO of the particular candy manufacturing company the inventor had approached when he first dreamed up the product, had agreed to run some prototypes. They hastily drew up a tentative agreement with fairly liberal terms. The CEO, George Fitz, was skeptical of the new candy's success, but agreed to produce a few hundred cellophane sacks of the sweet treat that were to be sold from a modest display in a small, but popular caramel corn shop in a location with good walk-in traffic.

After all, he figured, the inventor had admitted to being on a tight budget, and had limited resources with which to continue production if the candy didn't sell in volume, right away. George Fitz further calculated that most inventions in the highly competitive candy market were loser ideas that never gained traction, or treats that became fads that quickly faded, or ideas "before their time" that the market was not yet prepared to accept. In other cases he'd encountered, manufacturing the product was not cost-effective, and sometimes the sweet treat was impossible to produce and distribute profitably in the manner envisioned by its creator. Whatever the reason, successfully bringing a new candy to market in a highly competitive business with many copy-cats was difficult - if not impossible.

The CEO of the contract manufacturing confectionary company never once imagined that they would wind up utilizing their excess manufacturing capacity to produce a candy creation that would rapidly take hold and become a highly popular and affordable delicacy - due, in great part, to the superior marketing efforts of its creator.

The once-skeptical manufacturing CEO had begun production during a lull in its own candy business, and subsequently watched the clever candy product that the contract manufacturer's new customer and eventual victim had invented and launched on a shoestring, grow to great profitability through the "can-do attitude of its creator and the novelty of his idea. Their initial business contract had been drawn up casually, and liberally, on a single piece of paper - as befitted an idea the contract manufacturer was absolutely certain would fail.

Sales of the inventor's candy grew exponentially; however, the manufacturer found his company was increasingly devoting more resources to the popular candy's production without participating in the candy's soon-to-become-enormous profits. Rainbow Gummy Drops proved to be a multi-million dollar idea.

Greed soon entered what had been an amicable relationship, one that – while greatly profitable to the George Fitz Candy Company – was nowhere near as profitable to the manufacturer of the treat as it was becoming to its inventor and marketer. The original CEO, George Fitz, who had struck the manufacturing deal with the candy's inventor, a man named Quirky Lewis - passed away suddenly, leaving his business to his eldest son, Jason Fitz. The young man recognized that the huge increases in sales of Rainbow Gummy Drop candies – now manufactured in a variety of flavors - had subsumed their own candy production and forced the factory into a costly expansion and purchase of new and more sophisticated candy-making machinery, with no change in the original agreement, inked years earlier.

Jason Fitz brought his concerns to the company lawyers, who pointed out the weak position of the candy's inventor, who had allowed the contract candy manufacturing company to retain all recipes for the manufacture of the multi-flavored gummy drop, while retaining only the Trademark. Between them Jason and the corporate attorneys developed a scheme to take over all aspects of the original candy. The inventor was the original trademark owner of the candy marvel, and the devious CEO was told how he could force Lewis into surrendering the product trademark to the contract manufacturing company for but a fraction of what it was worth.

And how was that accomplished?

The initial production agreement was a casual contract created in an atmosphere of trust between two men years earlier, and never updated. Now that one of the two men was deceased, and the manufacturing company was in new hands, it was seemingly an opportune time to rectify the situation. George's son, Jason, learned that the agreement between his father and Lewis now had to be rewritten, since his father was deceased. A new contract would have to be drawn up, written in a manner that would acknowledge Jason as George's son and the heir of his deceased father's company, chosen to inherit the leadership responsibilities. The prior agreement, while executed in good faith, could not protect the inventor from the planned theft. And operating in good faith, Lewis had not individually protected his candy's recipe formulas, or demanded and retained copies of the flavor formulas that were often jointly developed. As a result, the lawyers suggested the contract manufacturer could maintain that the flavor formulas in fact now belonged to the company. And the original bare-bones agreement signed between George Fitz and Quirky Lewis did not protect Lewis from the contract manufacturer deciding to compete directly with him, merely changing the candy's name. By threatening to withhold and modify the sweet treat's numerous formulas, already in the possession of the contract manufacturer, and simply renaming the candy and marketing the product as their own, the contract manufacturing company felt capable of cutting the inventor out of his own business entirely, without a cent. Without the formulas, Lewis could not even take his product to another contract manufacturer to produce.

Therefore, Jason, as new CEO of the contract manufacturing company, could then "magnanimously" offer the inventor an alternative: A bitter pill.

That bitter pill was what Jason Fitz subsequently proposed to Quirky Lewis in a hastily called meeting with the inventor: Accept the contract manufacturer's offer of a set amount of compensation paid out over a term of 15 years, in return for selling the trademark. Or refuse, and lose everything.

The meeting had been called for midday on Friday, and lasted well into the afternoon. Lewis had been faced with the prospect of making a life-changing decision within the stringent three-day deadline they provided, which included that Friday. The meeting took place in the afternoon, and the candy's inventor was thus left with no time to hire an attorney, or even find one to provide telephone advice on a Friday afternoon. With nowhere to turn to get his product manufactured, no access to the candy formulas that had been modified multiple times over the years, and no funds to hire a law firm to take on what was now – thanks to his product's success - a megalith of a company, the victim had little choice but to sign away his trademark rights, for a pittance – less than one tenth of its value at the time, based on sales, and paid out over 15 years, which further reduced the value of the offer.

The Rainbow Gummy treat was now raking in millions, and the contract manufacturer had felt justified in its treatment of Quirky Lewis since it now devoted the major portion of its business to producing the novel candy invented by the petitioner, while still making approximately the same amount that his father had originally charged per pound of candy, since neither party had ever moved to have the original contract rewritten once the multi-flavored treat proved to be a raging success.

Defeated, the inventor surrendered his trademark – the only asset he actually held, and the contract manufacturer proceeded to rename the company in line with the trademark it now held, devoting itself solely to production of that one candy line, and reaping multimillions.

Erik read the petition twice, then sat back to think about it.

Though this job might involve more time and resources than the preceding case he had perused, and would provide justice to a single recipient, Erik felt the damage inflicted was severe enough to disturb the Bodhi's sense of fair play.

It certainly disturbed Erik's sense of fair play. He could identify with someone whose dreams and ambitions had been thwarted. He had to admit that devising retribution in this case was an exercise that would deeply intrigue him. He decided to make this one a priority.

There was always that first petition involving the unscrupulous insurance broker that he had kept to one side, because a public example needed to be set in order to discourage repetition and convince others who might be inclined to follow in his unethical footsteps, that actions have consequences.

Erik grimaced as the thought crossed his mind of the unavoidable hypocrisy this position forced him into, on a daily basis. Then he quickly dismissed it. Unpleasant actions can, and often do, have the most unpleasant consequences; Erik knew all too well that avoiding those consequences could be a full-time job.

Compartmentalization, however, had always been his forte.

The next few petitions were unexciting, so Erick kept reading, hoping for at least one more petition that would grab his interest, and that might also appeal to the Bodhi.

At last he came across another grievance filed on behalf of a group of elderly individuals and young couples that struck a chord with him. It involved the many victims of a contractor who repaired and remodeled houses, but who always skimped on materials while advertising pretentiously, falsifying testimonials, and claiming to do a far better job than he actually did. His charges far exceeded actual expenses, and his costs for labor were twice that of all but the most exclusive contractors who built very expensive houses in gated neighborhoods – places that his usual customers could never even visit. Individuals who signed contracts based on his verbal promises of prices he advertised, promoted, and promised to those gullible enough to believe him, were shocked when the bills arrived.

The contractor was always full of glib excuses: Materials were not readily available, and prices had gone up; on removing old construction material was needed, since he'd found shoddy workmanship by others that absolutely had to be redone and thus drove up costs, etcetera, etcetera, etcetera. Meanwhile, he cut corners to save costs, used inferior materials while charging for the best, and his work was slipshod. He profited at the cost of his customers - some of whom sustained serious and even crippling injuries, as a result of poor construction. When scrutinized, none of his work held up to code. He would work on three to four houses at a time and bang the work out, finishing more rapidly than could have been expected. Everything looked marvelous, but he had usually bribed inspectors; and once he'd pocketed the money from his victims, would then leave town in the middle of the night. Too late, his customers checked out those glowing testimonials and found them to be pure fiction, or totally unverifiable. Better business bureaus across a string of states had open complaints on him and the unscrupulous contractor had a trail of lawsuits pending in several states. To avoid blame, the contractor worked with a dirty lawyer who, in turn, would bribe small claims court arbitrators, corrupt civil court judges, or circuit court clerks who would willingly "lose" filings for a few hundred dollars under the table.

The contractors' usual victims were young newlyweds unfamiliar with construction standards and buying "fixer-uppers" to start their married lives in, taking out loans to buy a home they hoped was a place where they could fix a few things and then build equity, or remodel to make it suitable for raising their children. His other victims of choice were the elderly of modest retirement income. Those who were unable to keep up repairs were often the kind of individuals whom the contractor found, from experience, were gullible and trusting marks, easily fleeced.

While Erik was not quite sure they had the right volunteers to handle this one petition, it caught his eye. He found the prospect interesting, and was sure the Bodhi would find this situation of superior merit, so he set that one aside, intent on looking for terminals ("justice effectors" was the term the Bodhi preferred him to use) who could handle what might be needed as he developed a preliminary proposal for the Bodhi to review.

There were other jobs of course, but the ones that Erik didn't find immediately interesting got filed away for later consideration, perhaps to be taken up on some rainy day when they were actually low on interesting petitions. Erik hummed and set the files to the side, then he sat back in his chair and finished the last swallow of his now-cold coffee.

He still needed a third case, but a current one that was being carried out was taking up a great deal of Tracey's investigative time and was behind schedule for a variety of reasons - including the fact that Plan 'A' had run smack dab into entirely unanticipated complications that Tracey was still sorting out.

At a minimum, the original plans would require modification – or a quick switch to Plan 'B' – Tracey was studying both options, so there was opportunity at some point in the future to find a third case to fulfill the usual trio of justice efforts. And there was always the case of the unscrupulous insurance tycoon.

The afternoon was advancing toward quitting time, and Erik still needed to go through the new files on those patients from University Hospital that Ms. Brooks had brought him. He buzzed for another cup of coffee to fuel his effort.

Ahh, Miss Felicity Brooks.

He relished the sound of her name, but did not allow himself to be distracted by delicious thoughts about the woman.

All her applicant files had signed Consent and Non-disclosure forms, of course, Ms. Brooks had been advised by her referring acquaintance from City Central Hospital to get those signed before she spoke to them about the Kriya Project, so that whatever she might let slip about what they might be getting themselves into, they were sworn to secrecy, under civil penalty.

He sighed as he read. Quite a few were either too far gone, or in constant pain and on medication that might cognitively impair them, or – although capable when in remission, had unstable conditions that quite unpredictably kept them bouncing in and out of hospital. He set those files aside, to be returned to her keeping.

Well, he'd warned her, Erik thought, not everyone could be selected.

If they continued to work together, things would likely improve. She would soon learn what he was looking for, what he needed, and their relationship would become more . . . productive. A sly smile crossed his lips when he realized, then fully appreciated, his unintended double entendre. As he pushed on, Erik found his mind wandering to Ms. Brooks' bared arms, her clipped but polished nails, and those long legs ending in a pair of quite sensible shoes. His mind wandered further, to imagine the possibilities that might present themselves over a long-term acquaintance with Ms. Felicity Brooks . . . but he had to snap himself out of his daydream. He was to meet the prospective contributor for drinks at 6:30.

His prospect was an older woman who had just settled her considerable inheritance, so he needed to get busy making some decisions on assigning the right people to these petitions. Erik was to meet with the Bodhi by midweek and had to have something to present for their consideration. He forced himself to focus his attention once again.

There were files on two men and one woman in the pile before him that appeared as possibilities. The woman, in her early 60s, thought she might be developing dementia or Alzheimer's – but her test results were not yet back. Her symptoms were negligible, just the same slight forgetfulness often experienced by older individuals who were otherwise still fully capable. The woman had sought early testing, it seemed, because of family history. She'd served in the military as a young woman, spending ten years in a Military Police unit, then joined the N.Y.P.D. upon leaving the Army and rose to the rank of detective before retiring from the police force. She had been teaching Criminal Justice courses at the Junior College level for the past few years. She was active, and still in good physical condition.

"This lady's a winner," Erik thought, using his favorite Sharpie to leave a bright red check mark in the corner of her file and setting it atop the two petitioner files which he had decided to make a priority and examine for further development and presentation to the Bodhi.

Two men stood out from the other applications in the University Hospital files, and merited consideration. One man's file revealed he was slowly going into heart failure due to emphysema, but he had qualified for an experimental program to test a new medication that carried the promise of being able to repair damaged air sacs, improve breathing, and delay progression of his emphysema, which would reduce cardiac effects. This individual, an accountant by profession, had conscientiously adopted the recommended dietary changes and had been maintaining a program of regular exercise and mild aerobics which, combined with light weight training, promised to improve his heart condition. He wore a cannula and still carried oxygen, but he was moderately physically active, on doctor's advice. He walked daily and did pool exercises. He was highly intelligent and very interested in the Kriya Project, as it had been generally described to him by Felicity.

The other man worthy of consideration had had a successful career in sales, and was an avowed optimist, now dealing successfully with what doctors had determined was a terminal cancer. But the man was a fighter. He was trying a number of non- traditional medical regimens that seemed to be effective, having kept the cancer in remission. He golfed and swam, and had a keen mind and good sense of humor. Another keeper! Since all three individuals were intelligent achievers, computer literate, and had an array of seemingly useful hobbies and skills, Erik deemed them highly competent prospects. However, he wasn't immediately sure which person would be best assigned to which job, or if they were capable of handling more than one project for Kriya. Volunteers who were not only competent for a single job, but had multiple talents and the willingness to continue with the Kriya Project, long term, were rare jewels to be treasured.

He sincerely hoped the three would be intrigued by the work and would turn into three of those exceptional jewels that he could rely on for some time into the future. The training was intense, demanding, and costly. Once trained, those select individuals would be adaptable, highly competent, and dedicated to their missions.

Erik leaned back, stretched his shoulder muscles and thought that perhaps he would invite these terminals to the Foundation, describe the program, and interview them both together and individually, noting their interactions. He would have plenty of time over a full day's exposure to the Kriya Project to get to know them. Then he and Tracey could go over the petitioner cases and the Project's expectations with them, and perhaps have the terminals pick for themselves the one or ones that most interested them, then sign them up – after testing, of course.

They would use the large conference room, and set up areas for the Kriya Project's introduction and for testing, and another section for interviewing the candidates. They would need a Continental breakfast, catered lunch, and – perhaps - an early dinner. April could take care of the details.

Erik was protective of his space. He didn't like the terminals to visit his office, since it often made things a bit more complicated than he liked. Sometimes it just couldn't be helped, but really, this would be the best way to make this decision – using the main conference room. Interviewing them under pressure. Handling everything in one day.

Pushing away from his desk, Erik checked his appearance in the mirror of his private bathroom, brushed his teeth, ran his fingers through his hair to disturb it just enough to add to his still-boyish appearance, then donned his jacket and set out on foot to meet his appointment in the bar/lounge of the Ritz, just two city blocks from his office. The sky was blue, a breeze was blowing, and he saw no reason to drive to the appointment.

He spent the walk reviewing his day, taking into account what a marvelous day it had been and still was: He'd met an intriguing woman he would soon be seeing again, as she herself had promised. He'd attacked the piled files and documents cluttering his desk, and managed to weed out a considerable number of unsatisfactory petitions from applicants for the Kriya Project's unique services. He'd had had a great lunch with his normally recalcitrant daughter – who was working out wonderfully in the job the Bodhi had encouraged him to offer and hire her to fill, and he had found three possibly superb terminals to be new "justice effectors," selected with care from the otherwise sad stack of files Felicity Brooks had brought him. And now, he would have good news to relay to her, which would surely warm the cockles of her heart. The news might help her look a little more kindly upon him.

The Bodhi were sure to be pleased with his selections, and now he was going to get a large (he hoped) financial commitment to contribute to the Truvenge Foundation, and gain a permanent contributor to the Truvenge Foundation – and newly wealthy addition to his loyal flock...

Indeed, what a stellar day!

Later that night, after a successful meeting at the Ritz with a very attractive older widow still wearing black, Erik spent his time crafting perfect letters to the trio he had picked, vague enough to be read by others without leaving a clue as to the true nature of what was being proposed, but sharing enough details and assurances to give his newly volunteered applicants just enough information from which they could gauge their interest, and from which they could make a preliminary commitment to attend the gathering with an open mind. Enclosed in each letter, the recipient would receive a copy of the contract for each to sign and bring with them to the interview appointment.

Each letter was tailored to the specific individual based on information included in their file. Each envelope contained a signed copy of their original Consent and Non- Disclosure Agreement. Erik then carefully signed each letter, though not with his name but rather, a pseudonym. It was always a temporary ruse. Once fully committed and thoroughly vetted, the applicants would know his name, but in the meantime they will only know him as. . .

"Asura," he whispered to himself, smiling wide. "Mark Asura. I'll tell April in the morning, and she'll advise Felicity how she is to address me in front of the terminals when she first walks in with them."

He addressed the three envelopes to each individual, using complete names and full addresses, although each would be delivered personally by Ms. Brooks. The return address on the manila envelope was a private post office box.

Then, Erik carefully added the organization's unique closure to the envelope – an oval wax seal of purple, stamped with what appeared to be a karmic knot.

"April will call Ms. Brooks in the morning," he mumbled to himself, aloud, "and ask her to stop by to pick up the letters. I know she'll advise Felicity of the Mark Asura alias and how it's necessary to protect me, and to protect The Foundation in the event any of the selected "justice effectors" should decide not to come aboard and sign the agreement."

Immensely satisfied with himself, Erik readied himself for sleep and climbed into his plush bed. Arms crossed beneath his head, Erik stared up at the ceiling of his bedroom, ornamented with the luminescent stick-on stars he'd attached to the ceiling of every bedroom he'd slept in since he was six years old. He always founds great comfort under those stars, clinging to an artificial sky of painted blue on a ceiling that turned midnight blue and would be dotted with glowing stars as soon as the lights were out.

"I dare say, this is actually going to be fun," he chuckled.

Chapter 3 – Tracey

The lunch had gone surprisingly well, Tracey thought, as she climbed into her lemon- yellow Volkswagen "Bug" after leaving her dad in the restaurant waiting to pay the no doubt exorbitant bill for their delicious repast. She was happy she'd taken him up on it.

Of course, it had only worked out because she was dressed nicely today, and was not wearing her usual outfit of ripped jeans and a favorite faded hoodie – of which she had several. This morning, she'd had to appear at the courthouse early to fight an expensive traffic ticket she'd felt was entirely unmerited.

Of course, her dad knew nothing of the ticket. She told him she'd been at the courthouse researching tax records for one of the Truvenge cases she was working on for Kriya Project - which was true, but only after she had managed to be the first case on the traffic docket that morning to contest the ticket, and the policeman who'd ticketed her for going just 3 miles over the speed limit had failed to show. Case dismissed!

Tracey had been thrilled. She'd had lots to think about lately, and she had too many things she needed to follow up on today. The last thing she wanted to do was cool her heels at the Courthouse, waiting hours for her case to be called, or pay a ticket she strongly felt was unwarranted, and unmerited. *Three miles over the speed limit!!* Who'd ever heard of such a thing?

Several weeks earlier, in a meeting she'd had with the Bodhi, she'd asked them the meaning behind the name of the foundation for which she and her father now worked. Their encounter was unusual in that it was the first time her father was neither present, nor planning to join her later. His appearances were generally somewhat delayed, and that increasingly seemed to be the case, of late. Erik tended to join them after Tracey had already been speaking alone with them for quite some time. He would always appear eventually, however.

But not that day.

There were details about what she was doing that were so sensitive that she'd gone directly to the Bodhi to ask for time to discuss her concerns and get their advice. She'd left a message with April to tell Erik she needed to meet with the Bodhi as soon as possible, but he'd never responded. That struck her as odd, since Erik always seemed so anxious for their approval, and attention. Searching to excuse his absence once she understood he would not be attending, she had verbalized those thoughts. And, because Tracey refused to acknowledge Erik publicly as her father, she referred to him by name. That detail did not escape the Bodhi's notice.

Whenever she'd spoken alone with the Bodhi during the time that elapsed on her visits before Erik appeared for the scheduled meeting, they were always very curious about her, asking her opinions, interested in her ideas. And Tracey had gathered from one previous conversation in her father's absence that the Bodhi thought he was intimidated in their presence. They found it amusing.

She had never considered that aspect. Their words somehow instilled within her a new confidence in dealing with the man she'd detested for as long as she could remember. She'd always been convinced, however, that her father was such a bully he could never be intimidated by anyone, under any circumstance; and she said so.

At that, the Bodhi advised her in unison, in their treble-voice, "The angrier the bully, the bigger the coward hiding beneath all that thunder." She had laughed, and felt immediately that they understood her situation.

When Erik failed to appear promptly for their next meeting a few weeks later, Tracey conversationally voiced her opinion that Truvenge was actually in the *revenge* business, and *that* was the unique service she worked so hard to deliver with every case she investigated or researched. Again, the Bodhi had laughed, their three voices tinkling together in sounds akin to the melodic noise a wind chime makes in a stiff breeze. She loved to hear their laughter, and found herself more at ease in their presence then ever once she understood that she could make them laugh. The Bodhi did love to laugh! They had a marvelous, shared sense of humor, and an appreciation of irony.

But she wanted answers. She pursued her line of questioning about the actual purpose of the organization.

It was then that the Bodhi explained about karma and its function in the world. As a charitable foundation, they explained, Truvenge provided justice in generalized sense through compassionate aid – material and mental assistance in an individual's or a family's darkest hour. The Foundation's duty was, however, not to provide a permanent crutch, but to heal the "injured bird" and set it free, stronger and more able to face the world and tackle their own problems. "For that is how the spirit grows," they told her, "through tackling adversity and conquering it."

The Foundation's name, Truvenge, was an all-encompassing term for creating the kind karma that would support their fellow human beings and teach them the virtue of kindness to others. The Kriya Project, however, was their special earthly mission. It was the core of Truvenge. The Bodhi went on to explain everything about the Kriya Project and its origins. The details they offered encompassed Indian belief and folklore and religious practice, and entranced Tracey. She eagerly absorbed every word. On her own, she began reading about India and the beliefs of its Hindu and Buddhist believers.

She had tried to tell her father of what she had learned, only to be met with disinterest and skepticism whenever she'd spoken to him about her conversations with the Bodhi. To Erik, they were just his current employers.

The Bodhi, however, were teaching her a lot. And she was teaching them, as well, about – well, about the world of regular people. And about the West, and Western beliefs – such as they were. In fact, she could not wait to tell them of her courthouse victory that morning, and where and how she had been given the advice to fight the ticket: on a blind date with a fairly young, newly divorced judge she'd met on an online dating site!

As she drove she imagined their conversation:

Once she'd explained to the Bodhi the Western idea of meeting someone online, and then going out somewhere with that person on a 'date' to determine if the two of you might get along together romantically, she would no doubt have to answer a dozen questions from the Bodhi.

Their questions answered, Tracey then planned to launch into her tale, and went over the story in her mind. She doubted any of the Bodhi drove – she had often seen a limousine arrive at the Foundation, and had once witnessed their beaming faces smiling at her as they waved from a lowered window in the passenger section of the vehicle.

"The fellow's profile photo was rather better looking than he *actually* appeared when he showed up to meet for our dinner date," she would explain. "And I'm certain that if being *dreadfully* boring was grounds for divorce, that was more than likely the reason his wife divorced him. The fellow was soooo dull - soooo very BORING!!! However, while making small talk to pass the time as we waited for our food, I lamented the unfair traffic ticket. He promptly brightened up, and was immediately sympathetic. That was his bailiwick: the law, the courts. Once in his area of expertise, he suddenly felt comfortable conversing. And the advice he then gave me made that boring night totally worthwhile!

"As soon as I paused to catch my breath after telling him about the unfair ticket, my date shot questions at me, one after the other: 'Who gave you the ticket? Was the officer from city police? A county sheriff? A state trooper?'"

Tracey would then tell the Bodhi she'd simply shrugged her shoulders, and answered her date's rapid-fire questions by describing the officer's uniform to him as she pulled the day-old ticket from her handbag.

"'You're in luck,' he'd replied, as soon as he heard the uniform description, and glanced at the ticket. 'With a State Trooper, you'd never get off on appeal; traffic tickets are their *raison d'etre* – their very reason for being - and speeding tickets are the bulk of citations they issue, and the penalties the state collects. Judges mostly honor their tickets, regardless the circumstance of issue. County sheriff? That might give you a 50/50 chance of getting off if you appeal the ticket, depending on what else might be going on in the county at the moment. But city police? A cop is torn in 15 different directions daily, with lots of court appearances demanding his time to testify for a variety of crimes for which he's arrested people – crimes that are far more serious than your speeding violation. It was daytime, you were sober, and you only barely broke the speed limit. He probably had a quota to fill, or spotted you speeding downtown and could not ignore the offense. My advice to you would be to contest the ticket. You'll raise your odds of beating the ticket to around 80/20 – 80% odds you'd win. If you fight the citation, the ticketing officer has to make an appearance to defend issuing the ticket. With something so insignificant, chances are, he won't show. And if you contest and he is not there to defend his action, the judge will have no choice but to dismiss the case. . .'

"The rest of the date was downhill from there," She would laugh. "But I filed an appeal the next day, had it set for a hearing, and showed up early."

She couldn't wait to relate that story to the Bodhi. She wanted to hear their wind- chime laughter again. The sound made her happy.

Traffic was terrible, but it improved as she drove out of the city center and took a less crowded route.

Headed back to her apartment, Tracey Alison Walker was still "on the clock" as far as work went, but she couldn't stand wearing a dress and stockings for one more minute, and since her next task was to hang around a certain commercial garage - asking questions and surreptitiously picking up information - she didn't want to stand out like a sore thumb. In torn jeans and her hoodie, no one would think twice about talking with her and answering casual questions.

She knew enough about car mechanics to pull it off, and Tracey was proud that her interviewing skills were top-notch. She was polishing those skills with each passing day. She'd actually garnered complements from 'real' detectives - professionals who'd been present when she was digging around for information that professionals had failed to unearth. She'd gotten the answers she was after, much to their surprise.

Tracey turned on her car radio as soon as she hit the freeway, and was shocked when the song came on.

Which song? THAT song. The one that was the inspiration for her middle name – along with her 'Aunt' Alison, of course – her mother's best **friend.**

Elvis Costello was Tracy's favorite pop singer, even though his heyday as a pop icon had come and gone, years before her birth. He had been her mother's favorite musical artist, too.

Costello's rendition of 'Alison,' a heart-rending ballad he had written, was one with which Tracy deeply identified on a personal level, and not just for those two reasons. She felt the song also mirrored her mother's life. So, as the music played, she sang the familiar lyrics in a throaty whisper, trying to hold back the tears while driving:

"Oh, it's so funny to be seeing you after so long, girl
And with the way you look, I understand that you were not impressed
But I heard you let that little friend of mine
Take off your party dress
"I'm not gonna get too sentimental
Like those other sticky valentines

'Cause I don't know if you are loving somebody
I only know it isn't mine
"Allison, I know this world is killing you
Oh, Allison, my aim is true
"Well, I see you've got a husband now
Did he leave your pretty fingers lying in the wedding
cake?
You used to hold him right in your hand
But it took all that he could take
"Sometimes I wish that I could stop you from
talking
When I hear the silly things that you say
I think somebody better put out the big light
'Cause I can't stand to see you this way
"Allison, I know this world is killing you
Oh, Allison, my aim is true
"My aim is true
My aim is true
My aim is true
My aim is true
My aim is true
My aim is true
My aim is true
My aim is true
My aim is true
My aim is true . . ."

Marilyn Walker was her mother's name. Tracey
adored her mother. In her loneliness within her loveless
marriage, Marilyn had often turned to her young
daughter to voice her disappointments, her frustrations;
and to confess the poor decisions she had made in her
youth.

At a young age Tracey was her mother's confidante,
her friend, and her daughter, in that order. Tracy always

felt as though her mother carried the weight of the world on her shoulders, worn-down by life, by her sorrow. And Tracey had grown up, as a result, feeling very protective toward her mom. Their roles had reversed.

She hated it when Erik's ugly words made her mother cry, which was often. And she grew to hate him.

Her mother's best friend was also Tracey's godmother, her beloved 'Aunt' Alison.

Alison Johnston had been her mother's roommate for a time, but then married and moved to live out of state. She visited them often, however, had aways been Tracey's 'other mother' when she was growing up. The woman whose name Tracey carried was the one individual to whom she always turned for strength, advice, and support - until Alison McGraw died of cancer five days after Tracey's 19th birthday.

But Tracey wasn't going to think about that now.

She was NOT going to think of the history behind the song. She WAS NOT!!

Tracey blinked to hold back tears while promising herself again and again she wasn't going to let it get to her now. She *couldn't* let it get to her now. She had work to do – important work. And she could not show up at that damned garage, sniffling and wiping her eyes, now could she?

Nope. No way, no how…

Chapter 4 – Felicity

Felicity Brooks was an interesting woman, and not someone you would think was characteristic of most social workers.

Felicity had spent many years of her youth in Germany, the oldest child in a family of four. Her father was a good man, but was in the military and was often away for extended periods. Her mother moved with him from state to state after they married, and they had lived in Europe as a family for many years with Felicity and then her younger brother, who was born in Heidelberg. Two tours of duty were separated by a move back to the U. S., where another sibling was born in Tennessee, and then a return to Europe again, to a different post in Germany. When Felicity's mother became pregnant with her fourth child while they were in Germany on her husband's second tour of duty, it was a difficult pregnancy.

It started with severe morning sickness, and then her mother developed potential complications. The family was awaiting her husband's next posting, hoping they could move and get settled before the pregnancy was too far along. When his orders arrived, the news was not good. War had broken out in the Middle East and Felicity's dad, a helicopter pilot who had enlisted at 19 and served three tours in Vietnam, was to go to Kuwait. The family could not follow. At that time, under the circumstances, the decision was made for the family to move to Bonners Ferry, Idaho, where her mother's family lived, and where she would have support throughout the pregnancy, and after the birth. The situation was supposed to be temporary.

However, they never left.

Bonners Ferry, like many of the small waterfront towns in the Idaho panhandle near the Canadian border was stunningly beautiful. The town was idyllically set on a lake in a broad valley surrounded by mesmerizing ranges of mountains. It stood apart, however, in that it over the years it continued to escape notice of both summer tourists and retirement residents; the population continued to hover around 3,000 residents for many decades.

Felicity's mother had felt suffocated in that small town, where everyone knew everyone so intimately. And as a high school graduate from a family where money was always tight, her prospects were limited. Her mom's escape was to join the Women's Army Corps on graduation from high school in 1966, and become a proud WAC.

Her mom had been a superior student, but focused on learning secretarial skills in high school, thinking that with little prospect of furthering her education, she needed a skill. Deciding, as well, that her 'great escape' from Bonners Ferry would require funding, Felicity's mother saved every penny of her baby-sitting money from tenth grade forward. When she saw an advertisement for the Evelyn Wood 7- Day Speed Reading and Learning Program offered by the local Adult Education Institute (in reality, just a group of civic-minded women dedicated to bringing speakers and instructors to the rural community to speak or teach evening courses, and charging attendance fees) her mother proudly informed her miserly parents that she had the wherewithal to take the course without asking a penny from them.

An intelligent young woman, she'd decided that if she could learn to read faster than she could type – and by the end of her junior year of high school, she already typed 100 words a minute – she would be able to find work anywhere.

And she was absolutely correct. Felicity's mom scored top of the class in secretarial skills, and in January 1967 she was offered a position as one of the original 90 enlisted women assigned to the WAC detachment at HQ, US Army, Vietnam, in Long Binh, Vietnam, approximately 20 miles from Saigon, and away from the fighting. Furthermore, based on her superior skills, she was told she would have the opportunity to potentially serve at General Westmoreland's headquarters in Saigon.

This was a magical offer, and she accepted.

True to the Army's promise, Felicity's mother spent only two weeks in Long Binh before she was recruited to work at headquarters in Saigon. And it was there that she met Felicity's dad.

They'd fallen deeply in love, and he and Felicity's mother managed to marry in Vietnam and still see each other. Whenever he could manage a break for R&R, her dad headed to Saigon. When her mother spoke of those years, or their six years spent in Germany, or even moving from state to state as a family, Felicity's mom came alive. But her necessary return to Bonner's Ferry after two decades of adventure and romance took a heavy toll, emotionally.

When her dad came 'home' on leave the first time, and at long last spent more than a few social hours with his in-laws, it was like fire meeting oil. As soon as her dad arrived and saw his family again after many months' absence, he immediately noticed the change in his wife and children, and remarked on it. That started a heated argument with her stern grandfather that ended up with her dad stomping out of the house and renting a room in the Kootenai Valley Motel. From that day forward, that was where he stayed whenever he came to visit his wife and children at Bonners Ferry.

Felicity's mom followed her husband to the motel for his two weeks of leave, taking the littlest child – still a toddler - with her, for the duration of his visit. Felicity's grandparents then proceeded to disavow any responsibility for the remaining three kids throughout their mother's absence, and shut themselves in their bedroom whenever the children were home. Her grandmother came out twice a day to prepare a breakfast of toast and eggs or a heat TV dinner for herself and Felicity's grandfather. The couple ate from TV tables they set up in their bedroom, in front of the only television set in the house.

All responsibility for the children fell to Felicity, who was in tenth grade at the time: cooking for them, cleaning the house - all but her grandparents' room, of course - and looking after her younger siblings during the week. She got them ready for school and to the school bus, picked them up after school and got them bathed and ready for bed, making sure homework was done for the next day. Felicity was also responsible for minding her siblings on weekends, which included driving them all to spend time with their parents at the motel. They often prepared picnic lunches to eat with their parents in the nearby National Park.

That was a lot of responsibility for a tenth grader, driving on a learner's permit.

It repeated the following year when her dad got time off once again. This time, he'd earned a few days longer time away from his duties, because his unit had so many helicopters down for maintenance. But then he was gone again. Now he was needed in a place called Afghanistan.

Then it was Iraq, and a promotion. Then back to Afghanistan. A country in constant, non-productive battle in foreign countries demanded much of its military. And so, again and again, her father went to serve his nation. And provide for his family.

Bonners Ferry was a far cry from the castles of Europe that Felicity had visited as a youngster, and the rural setting was less exciting than sights she had seen growing up in Germany. Throughout her years in Bonners Ferry she wistfully recalled the beautiful things they had seen on vacation trips through various countries. It had taken only a month or two for Bonners Ferry to lose its charm for Felicity.

Her grandparents, as it turned out, were a taciturn older couple, uniformly unaffectionate but bound by a sense of "duty" to provide a home for their only child "now that her husband has abandoned her." That was her grandfather's constant litany to Felicity and her mother. He never let them forget what a burden the family was to the older couple, but how, as "dutiful Christian" (who never attended church, Felicity wryly observed) they had a duty to their only child, a worthless daughter who couldn't keep her husband around.

The longer she was around her grandparents, the more Felicity disliked them, and the more she understood her mother's reluctance to ever visit when she was younger. Her heart went out to her mom as she understood more about the logic that had brought them to live with his unpleasant couple who seemed no closer to them than strangers might be if they were merely roomers, grudgingly taken in due to financial need.

Her father came to visit once again when Felicity was a senior, specifically to see her graduate. It was during that visit that he took her fly fishing on the wild Salmon River. Her Dad had taught her how to fish, applauded her successful efforts – small as her catch was – and cheerfully talked to her about how the Salmon River had played a significant historic role in the exploration by the Lewis and Clark Expedition, and how an Indian encampment close to where Bonners Ferry was located was the birthplace of Sacajawea. He'd asked Felicity about her plans for the future, and she'd told him she intended to follow in her parents' footsteps and join the military "to see the world." He was proud to hear her declaration.

But she'd also voiced her worries about her mother in that cold and unloving household once she left. He promised Felicity that it would not be for much longer. He then explained that war, unfortunately, was profitable for him. For them. Hazard pay and low expenses were allowing him to set money aside so he could retire early. He planned to stay in the Reserves for a while, gaining rank and pay, and to finish a graduate degree he'd been working on, then try his luck owning a small but essential business somewhere – anywhere but Bonners Ferry. Anywhere Felicity's mom wanted to go. The money was what kept him going back.

Felicity was worried for his safety. Her dad was still flying, but very occasionally. Primarily, he'd explained to his daughter, he was responsible for keeping the unit flying. And that kept him safely on the ground more often than not, tending to crucial equipment. He was now involved in managing helicopter maintenance for his unit, organizing crew support, and the like. Because the position made it possible for him to save money for that eventual retirement, he'd begged Felicity and his entire family, to be patient. Then he watched as Felicity graduated, and once again, he was gone.

Felicity enlisted that next week. She had just turned 18.

Athletic and enthusiastic, she actually enjoyed Basic Training, and joked that once completed, she had the best figure of her life. Her no-nonsense attitude and sense of humor served her well, and she was well-liked.

When offered an opportunity to choose an area of specialization, Felicity quickly chose to become an Explosive Ordnance Disposal Specialist. Once she had read through the specialization description that she had been handed on graduation from Basic, she looked no further than the sheet of paper in her hand, which read:

EXPLOSIVE ORDNANCE DISPOSAL (EOD) SPECIALIST (89D)

- ✓ Enlisted
- ✗ Officer
- ✓ Active Duty
- ✗ Army Reserve
- ✓ National Guard
- ✓ Entry Level

OVERVIEW

Explosive ordnance disposal specialist Soldiers are the Army's preeminent tactical and technical explosives experts. They are warriors who are properly trained, equipped and integrated to attack, defeat and exploit unexploded ordnance, improvised explosive devices and weapons of mass destruction.

Explosive ordnance disposal specialists are the culmination of the best tactical and technical training the Army and civilian academia can provide. They are prepared to perform missions in support of Army units worldwide, across all operational environments.

JOB DUTIES
- Research and identify ordnance
- Assist in the preparation and use of advance robotics
- Explosively disposing of hazardous ordnance
- Prepare and maintain tools, equipment and vehicles

REQUIREMENTS
Those who want to serve must first take the Armed Services Vocational Aptitude Battery, a series of tests that helps you better understand your strengths and identify which Army jobs are best for you.

TRAINING
Job training for an explosive ordnance disposal specialist requires 10 weeks Basic Combat Training and 37 weeks of Advanced Individual training split between Fort Lee, VA (8 weeks) and Eglin Air Force Base, FL (28 weeks).

Some of the skills you'll learn are:
- Basic electronics/electricity fundamentals
- Hazards and identification of United States and foreign munitions

- Demolition materials, procedures and operations
- Chemical and biological ordnance and operations

HELPFUL SKILLS
- Interest in algebra, chemistry, physics, geometry and trigonometry
- Ability to communicate effectively
- Aptitude for planning and organizing
- Work calmly under stress
- Effectively use computers

REQUIRED ASVAB SCORE(S)
General Maintenance (GM): 105

Learn more about the ASVAB and see what jobs you could qualify for.

COMPENSATION
Total compensation includes housing, medical, food, special pay, and vacation time. Learn more about total compensation. EOD Soldiers additionally receive monthly Demolition pay of $150 and Special Duty Assignment Pay of $375.

EARN CASH FOR IN DEMAND JOBS
You could earn up to $40,000 in cash bonuses just for enlisting under certain Military Occupational Specialties. Visit Jobs in Demand to see if this job qualifies for an enlistment bonus.

EDUCATION BENEFITS

In the Army, qualified students can earn full-tuition, merit-based scholarships, allowances for books and fees, plus an annual stipend for living expenses. Learn more about education benefits.

FUTURE CIVILIAN CAREERS

The skills you learn will help prepare you for a career with government agencies, civil law enforcement and private industries performing ordnance research and development. You might also consider a future as a Public Safety Bomb Technician (Bomb Squad), bomb-disposal expert, gunsmith or munitions handler.

PARTNERSHIP FOR YOUTH SUCCESS (PAYS) PROGRAM

Those interested in this job may be eligible for civilian employment, after the Army, by enrolling in the Army PaYS program. The PaYS program is a recruitment option that guarantees a job interview with military friendly employers that are looking for experienced and trained Veterans to join their organization. Find out more about the Army PaYS Program at http://www.armypays.com.

- EOD Technology, Inc.
- URS
- Oshkosh Corporation
- Raytheon Company

Her jaw had dropped. Right there, the entire career path of her dreams was laid out, in black and white.

In high school, Felicity absolutely stood out from her classmates in science and mathematics. She knew that her education would be guaranteed through military service, and she understood that an EOD Specialist pulled down one of the highest basic salaries in the military. As an enlisted soldier she'd be earning almost 15% above the average U.S. salary, plus Demolition pay, and Special Duty pay. There was, as well, the potential for a large cash bonus of thousands of dollars, which would go a long way to establish the investment portfolio she'd dreamed of starting. She was young, and, once she'd put in her time, she understood from later research that she could command a six-figure civilian salary as an experienced bomb disposal expert. Lastly, it was a position that would bestow both status and respect – very necessary for an attractive female in a predominantly male environment.

She breezed through her examinations and psychological evaluation. And that was it – she was "*IN IT TO WIN IT!*" – her dad's favorite phrase.

When she called him to tell him the news, his grin could be read across the secured phone line from Afghanistan. He was so very proud of her.

She earned a B.A. Then when two years later she completed a master's degree in Criminal Justice while on active duty, she immediately became a First Lieutenant. She was repeatedly promoted during her 25 years with the Army, and, at what was considered a very young age, achieved the rank of "Full Bird Colonel" - a grade just below that of Brigadier General – a remarkable achievement based on her exemplary work in war zones in Afghanistan, Africa, and across the Middle East. She considered it a blessing that she attained that rank before her father passed away shortly after his 80th birthday.

Her mother was several years younger, however, and she continued on for many more years. Felicity's mom had a form of dementia, and did not even know enough about her surroundings at the time to attend her husband's funeral, which Felicity thought was truly tragic. Her parents had been so in love, and so happy when they could be together!

But her mother was suffering, and had suffered for years, from what was later diagnosed as Alzheimer's Disease. It had been half a decade since she could reliably recognize her husband, or other family members. But her dad had visited regularly, and often. Her mom's caretakers feared how attending his funeral might affect her mother, should she have a moment of clarity and suddenly realize that it was her beloved spouse who had died.

At the ripe old age of 43, and a new retiree, Felicity Brooks entered the civilian world and was once again an instant superstar. Based on her unique experience, education and skills, she was sought after to give expert testimony in a number of high-profile trials. She consulted with the military, and with police departments, nationally and internationally. She spoke publicly; she wrote; she was on the boards of two think tanks. For one reason or another, the several long-term romantic relationships she had tried to maintain over the years never succeeded, although she remained close friends with several ex-beaus, for lack of a better word. Her job was too stressful – and too dangerous. And she loved it too much. She travelled constantly, and often at the last minute, with little or no warning. As one lover had lamented, Felicity was "married to the military."

One by one, the men in her life reached that same conclusion, and moved on to marry and raise families. She did not marry, however. She knew from her mother's experience what it was like to be married to a military officer. However, when she finally left the

Army and could command her own time, and travel, she still responded to every request in the same way, and kept a bag packed for instant travel. There was never time to even wonder what kind of wife or mother she might have been. She was still very attractive, and never lacked for interesting male companionship – or the occasional love affair. But not many men held her interest for any length of time, and those who did frequently decided, as others had, that marriage with Felicity was most likely a losing proposition.

By the time she'd reached her late fifties her mother's Alzheimer's Disease began to prey on her mind. She was convinced her maternal grandmother had shown evidence of what she'd interpreted as the onset of senile dementia – which was what they called all geriatric loss of mental capacity at the time.

Felicity read voraciously, and wondered if there was evidence that Alzheimer's was genetic, or familial. She started watching for her every pause whenever she caught herself searching for the right word in a conversation. Every lapse of memory – no matter how insignificant – became cause for fear. As age 61 loomed, and without a shred of hard evidence, Felicity began to withdraw from many of the commitments she had previously fulfilled without blinking an eye, and started rejecting invitations she would otherwise never have hesitated to accept. She became more selective about her public appearances, and withdrew from the think tank she felt was more the more challenging of the two, and which was rapidly adding younger members. However, she continued as an expert witness – explosive ordnance disposal was a topic she continued to feel confidant discussing and where she was truly unruffled under questioning, regardless the circumstances. And she continued both writing and consulting in her area of specialization.

But she also continued reading extensively, and consulted with specialists on the topic of Alzheimer's. Her fear of mental failure became all consuming, to the point where she figured it was time to set aside other interests and involvements and face her fears head on, answering her questions once and for all. Then, and only then, could she plan for the future.

University Hospital was known to have some of the best geriatric and Alzheimer's experts on staff. She volunteered for a study that was engrossing and required a great deal of time, demanding nearly daily involvement on her part. Dedication to the important study made it difficult for Felicity to accept invitations to speak, or attend meetings, so she deferred everything temporarily, citing health reasons. But idleness was not in her nature, and when the position as Head of Social Services at University Hospital opened up, Felicity applied, so that she could remain active and mentally challenged, while still remaining completely available for the study. It had become crucial to her wellbeing to ascertain whether or not she had anything to fear from the disease that had afflicted her mother and, she suspected, her maternal grandmother.

Of course, Felicity often comforted herself, the old woman could simply have been as ornery and stubborn as her obnoxious and taciturn grandfather, and was therefore intentionally non-communicative and hostile. After, all, consider the man she'd been married to all those years, and the terrible familial relationships those two angry people had fostered.

It was her position with University Hospital that had led her to Truvenge, and it was Felicity's personal background and her experience with and search for answers about a possible genetic susceptibility to Alzheimer's that bonded her to one of Kriya Project's prospects, Agnes Marie Walford. They had become close friends.

Felicity was well-schooled in the criminal justice system, knowledgeable about police work, and highly dubious of any court system's ability to right the wrong inflicted upon or experienced by certain victims. When she'd first spoken with Sarah Knight about the Truvenge Foundation and the Kriya Project, and the potential that it offered their terminal patients – potential to feel worthwhile, appreciated, and active, while contributing to society and the future wellbeing of those they were leaving behind - Sarah had been informative but circumspect.

They had gotten on well at the conference, however, and soon found they had a number of similar interests. They worked together on a panel discussion on the second day and by the third day of the conference, considered themselves good friends. Dinner on that third day, before leaving the next morning, was when Sarah had brought up things she'd perceived about the Kriya Project that left her questioning information she had been given during interactions with the organization, In follow-up encounters with her terminal patients, they responded to her questioning by uniformly telling her they were sworn to secrecy, and there were things they could not discuss with her.

While none of them seemed troubled or distressed about the need for secrecy, she could not help but speculate what might be going on that would suddenly erect such a wall between her and several of her patients whom she'd come to know well, and who had previously confided their most intimate problems and concerns.

Then Sarah had entertained her with speculations – all the while treating them as just that – and inventing wild scenarios and suppositions about the activities of the Kriya Project that had them both laughing hysterically at their improbability. By the next day, when they said farewells, all the chit-chat of the night before had been forgotten.

But Felicity could not help but wonder ...

Chapter 5 - The Interview

Erik had been delighted with the happiness in Felicity Brooks' voice when he told her that a trio of potential applicants from the files she'd brought him had been accepted for consideration to work with Kriya Project, *if* they passed their essential evaluations and agreed to the contract terms.

He explained there would be a new Non-disclosure Agreement they would have to sign that extended to their relationships with her, along with family members and friends, their physicians and – in the future – with eventual caretakers. They had been sworn to silence regarding the work they would be considering at their interviews, and which they would voluntarily undertake. He explained that the work they were being evaluated to do would entail very personal information about the families and individuals to whom Truvenge and Kriya Project provided services that were of an often sensitive and very personal nature. Their privacy was important. Surely Felicity ("May I call you Felicity?") could understand, since she was not even permitted to speak with him about her terminal patients without their written consent.

He set the date and time of the interviews, and told her that the information and evaluation program would take several hours' time, would involve interviews and testing, and that snacks, a catered lunch, and an early dinner would be provided.

Interview day soon arrived. The prospective hires were due to appear at the Truvenge building at 8:30 a.m.

April made sure everything was ready, and greeted Felicity and the three prospects on their arrival. She had informed Felicity of the need for discretion and told her that the trio would be meeting with the President, but would know him only as Mr. Mark Asura until each of them had made a commitment to the organization.

The three prospects were comfortably ensconced in the conference room. April gave each of them name tags to help familiarize themselves with their companions, and easily chatted with them after they'd been invited to partake of a delicious Continental breakfast, complete with toast and bagels, cream cheese and lox, an array of pastries, fruit, coffee, tea, juices and hot cocoa.

She assured them that the breakfast spread would be available until 10:30 a.m. to assuage any hunger they might feel later, if they were not prepared to eat now, adding, "My stomach does not wake up to food until long after I've had my second cup of coffee or tea, usually after I've been up for an hour or so. If any of you has sugar lows, we have candies, fruit juice and sugar sodas. A catered hot and cold lunch will be served at 12:30 or 1:00 p.m., depending on how the day is going. We don't want you to be hungry, but we don't want to interrupt productive interviews or significant tests. Snacks will be available at 3:30 this afternoon, and a light dinner will be served at 6:30, during which time you will be invited to discuss the day, ask questions of Mr. Asura, and make your decision to move forward in working with us and tackle the specific jobs you'll learn about later in the day.

"Before leaving, you will sign the necessary releases to come on board. If that is your decision, you will receive an encrypted cell phone to be used exclusively for our work together, and you'll receive a moderate sum of cash to manage unexpected expenses. We will stay on top of any expense allowance so you will not have to reach into your own pockets for needs like transportation, cell phone costs, miscellaneous costs related to the job, and so forth."

After a half hour of conversation, April slipped away, informing them as she drew the double doors together that they had another quarter hour before Mr. Asura would arrive to conduct the day's program of information, discussion and testing, and suggesting that they use the time to get comfortable. She pointed out the restroom facilities, then smiled and closed the doors.

Seating was informal, and only Mr. Asura's name was at the chair at the head of the highly polished conference table. Beside each place was a small carafe of water and a crystal glass, along with a small bowl of wrapped hard candies, both sugared and sugar-free. A white board with markers stood beside an enormous video screen which had been streaming a variety of live underwater scenes of a scuba diver exploring a reef.

"They've thought of everything," Agnes Marie Walford remarked to the two gentlemen finishing their pastries. She was a tall, slender woman who appeared to be a decade younger than her 62 years. "I used to scuba dive," she remarked rather wistfully, as she pulled out the chair on Mr. Asura's right. Joe Belton refilled his cup of coffee and silently sat to her right, while Victor DiMarco chose hot cocoa, and sat to Mr. Asura's left.

"I can never get enough of this stuff," Victor commented, nodding toward his steaming cup. "I have been addicted to hot chocolate since I was old enough to sip from a cup." He laughed. "Not good for the waistline, but my wife used to keep me in check. Before I married her, I insisted for her to learn my Mamma's terrific recipe for cocoa, plus a few other dishes. Italian dishes, from the old country, you know? She was American – my wife. From the South. Had this sweet Southern drawl that used to infuriate me whenever we argued. Which was not often - believe me. I loved that woman! Made great fried chicken, too." His wide grin revealed gleaming white teeth beneath his dapper mustache. "My wife thanked me later, for Mamma's cooking lessons. She said that she never had to wonder what I might like, or how to make it. But she was like a general, that woman, always watching my calories!" He laughed again, "She would be so mad at me now! She always wanted a movie star for a husband, but look at me now!"

Agnes glanced at his waistline, as he patted his stomach, but failed to see the wide girth Victor was referencing – he appeared in good health and was actually rather well built for his age, which she guessed was somewhere in his early to mid-70s.

She had noted when they first met that the quiet and studious-looking gentleman to her right wore a cannula that extended into what appeared to be a black fabric "man-bag" that hung from a strap over his shoulder. When he entered the conference room, he had been pulling a wheeled travel cart that held what appeared to be a camera bag. He was obviously in need of regular oxygen supplementation, but was he also a photographer? Was he here to take pictures?

He had introduced himself to her as Joe Belton, but had scarcely uttered another word since, except to Victor, although she observed that his eyes were constantly roaming around, probing, taking in the room, watching his comrades in this experience, and eyeing April. He was reserved, and appeared almost professorial. She wondered why he chose to sit beside her. Timidity? Shy attraction? The bulky bag that hung at his right side that precluded a close neighbor at the table? Or, was his motive, perhaps, simply to have a better view of Mr. Asura?

He watched people keenly, Agnes observed. And it was apparent that he took in everything he saw. "Still waters run deep," she thought.

Not at all shy, Agnes promptly introduced herself to the two gentlemen with her customary firm handshake. Much of the initial opinion she formed of others was dependent on their handshake. Victor's huge hand engulfed hers, and his hand movement was vigorous, enthusiastic, and lasted just long enough to indicate sincerity. Joe's smaller hand was slightly clammy; however, there was no hesitation or limpness in his very normal handshake. Agnes attributed his moist hand to nerves, and decided that his quiet attentiveness revealed intellect.

In her estimation, Joe Belton was a listener. Victor DiMarco was a salesman – a persuader. A charmer. Both held Felicity Brooks in the highest regard. They'd related during one conversation between the three of them, which had included April, that when Felicity mentioned she knew of a paying project they might be interested in participating with, both men jumped at the chance to check it out.

And Agnes?

Agnes thought of herself as very ordinary, although few "ordinary" women were trained to arrest lawbreakers, quell riots, parachute from perfectly good airplanes, were Deep-Diving-certified to depths of 140 feet using SCUBA gear, and had led soldiers into battle, or snatched a Kalashnikov from the hand of a dying Talabani to protect herself and her unit. She had married a soldier while serving as a soldier, gave birth to two children, lost her husband at a young age to medical malfeasance, joined the NYPD to support her two youngsters, saw to her children's education and good marriages, watched as they both moved across country with their families to take advantage of career opportunities, retired from the Department, and now found herself alone and looking for purpose – a challenge. She felt she needed a new direction in her life.

Agnes found adventure intoxicating, and was dedicated to service. The only thing she feared, and had in common with Felicity Brooks, along with their military and law enforcement backgrounds, was loss of her mental faculties. She had witnessed that happen, as a teenager, with two relatives on her father's side and had always questioned whether she might be genetically susceptible to either dementia or Alzheimer's Disease. At the time of those relatives' deaths, no real distinction was made between the two kinds of mental failure – everything was called senile dementia. She had contacts at the university, and had met Felicity in one of her many visits to work with a research program she'd volunteered for that was trying to determine if there was a genetic causation for Alzheimer's. Though their personalities were quite different, and they might not otherwise be likely to be drawn to each other socially, Agnes and Felicity had struck up a respectful acquaintance and a supportive relationship.

The group chattered idly upon initially seating themselves, but had grown silent as the moment approached for Mr. Asura to enter the conference room. Joe Belton kept looking around, then down at his watch; Victor stared at the ceiling, arms crossed over his chest. Agnes Marie examined her nails and pushed back her cuticles. Suddenly, the double door was flung open, and Erik entered the room.

He seated himself with a flourish, looked around at the three people before him, and as he did so, took a few moments to look directly into the eyes of each person and hold their gaze without saying a word. Victor was the only one to break the gaze before Asura did. He maintained direct eye contact until he cleared his throat and looked down to grasp the glass of water and bring it to his lips. Joe Belton sat up straighter, and his earnest gaze grew hopeful, almost beseeching Asura as he waited for the man to notice him.

Erik, a/k/a Mr. Asura, turned to look at Agnes, and their eyes met. Agnes looked into Asura's eyes frankly, openly, intently – and without blinking. Erik sensed that she was carefully scrutinizing him. Her gaze was confidant but not aggressive; sure, but not forced. He suddenly felt like a bug under a microscope, and quickly looked away from her to press the intercom on the table beside him and summon April into the room.

April entered, as if on cue, bearing papers in her arms which she immediately distributed as identical packets of information, then vanished.

Asura addressed his small audience, urging them to take a few minutes to glance through the materials, which included the day's agenda, a brief introduction to the Truvenge Foundation and, in particular, the Kriya Project, plus three stapled booklets with blank covers, and a series of Consent and Release forms, plus other Non-Disclosure Agreements specific to the Kriya Project and to the Truvenge Foundation.

Mr. Asura watched them carefully as they quickly perused the materials they'd been given. He was looking for a change in expression that would reveal the initial impact of what they were reading.

He was not disappointed. Joe Belton's mouth dropped open, then snapped closed as his spine stiffened, and - determined – he plowed on through the paperwork, reaching into his pocket to retrieve a pen and a small spiral notebook that he flipped open at his side.

Ahh, Erik thought. Belton is the sensitive one. The thorough one.

Victor took a little time to glance through the materials first, but then read the papers without expression.

Agnes Marie had been done reading for several minutes. With a smile, she'd flipped rapidly through the papers, her smile growing broader with each page she turned over. Her eyes skimmed through the three booklets, and by this time she was grinning. The NDAs, Releases and Consent forms each merited a single glance. When she was done, Asura looked at her inquisitively, and she replied to his unuttered question, "Speed-reading. I learned at a very early age. I can also read upside down, and decipher mirrored writing – even in cursive."

Erik nodded approvingly. Agnes Walford would be a definite asset to the Project. As if reading his mind, the woman informed him, "Agnes Marie. The nametag's wrong. I am Agnes Marie Walford. I answer to both names." Without taking his eye off of Agnes Marie, Erik flipped the intercom on and told his assistant, "April – we need a new nametag. One that reads Agnes Marie Walford. Is that Agnes-Marie, with a hyphen?," he asked, looking directly at Agnes. She shook her head.

"No hyphen," he barked into the intercom. Still not done with their reading, Victor and Joe looked up to watch the interchange, then applied themselves once again to their reading, pressured by the fact that Agnes Marie had finished before they had.

April sailed into the room, amended nametag in hand and the exchange took place. As she exited, Agnes Marie donned her corrected nametag, caught Asura's eye and said to him, "But you can call me Agnes."

The other two men had been following the interaction, and when they heard that, looked at each other quizzically. Victor shrugged and smiled, mouthing to Belton, "Women." But Erik understood what they had not. He had just lost a power struggle. Agnes Marie Walford was to be respected, whether friend or foe.

Then and there, Erik resolved to make her a friend, if not an ally.

The two men indicated at last that they were done reading. Victor had finished first, set the papers aside, and rested his folded arms on the table as he watch Asura. Joe Belton scribbled a few more notes into his spiral notebook, then neatly stacked the papers together, adjusting the edges so they were precisely in line. Then he looked up at the man he knew as Asura.

Mr. Asura – Erik - cleared his throat and began the speech he felt he'd already delivered a good dozen times over the two and a half months he'd been in his position.

He cleared his throat and began:

"During the next few hours, I will get to know each of you very well; and you will get to know me, the Truvenge Foundation, the Kriya Project, *and* Kriya Project's Chief Detective and Planner, Tracey Walker. She is eminently qualified for her position by both education and aptitude, as you will learn. You will meet her this afternoon, and over time you'll grow to know her very well, because she will be the individual who coordinates all your activities. You will each report directly to her every single day, without fail, for as long as you are on the particular job to which you will have been assigned. Assignments are based on your skills and talents, and the nature of what is required, matched with your affinity for the particular case. In other words, when push comes to shove, the individual who has stronger feelings of the need for justice in a particular petitioner's case will be chosen over someone who is just lukewarm about the case that an aggrieved has against a particular person, group of persons, business, or institution. Without a passion for justice, and an inherent sense of right and wrong, you cannot satisfactorily work these cases.

"What do we do at Truvenge Foundation? Essentially, we do the same things that all other truly charitable foundations do. We seek to help the needy, the downtrodden. We assist adults and children, individuals and families, with a variety of injuries and illnesses or circumstances that diminish their quality of life, plus those in financial straits who simply need a temporary "leg up" to get back on their feet. To accomplish good deeds and operate the charity effectively requires a constant stream of cold, hard cash. Keeping a job, meeting extraordinary expenses, paying medical bills, and dealing with sudden homelessness or rapidly increasing expenses for transportation and relocation are the bane of everyone's existence in a world where self-sufficiency is becoming ever more difficult to maintain.

"Our organization is what they call 'lean and mean.' There is little waste. All salaries, commissions, benefits and other compensation are earned, and everything revolves around merit.

"The organization is a charitable mission that is operated by a trio of benevolent spirits. The Foundation is important to them. But even more important to them than continuing operation of the Truvenge Foundation, with all the good it does in the world, is the very special karmic work done by the Kriya Project. It is the heart and soul of the Foundation.

"You are preparing to embark upon a karmic mission.

"I was sought out specifically to head this organization, and to lead the Kriya Project by the eminent and somewhat mystical individuals who founded Truvenge Foundation as the crucible in which to house both a charitable arm and this special organization, so dear to their hearts.

"The world is full of individuals who cruise through life thinking only of themselves, and harming others with impunity. They seem to squirm from the grasp of the law, and often go unpunished, even if brought to trial. They are frequently quite wealthy, well-connected, and somehow manage to hire just the right legal counsel with the right 'relationships' that will enable their clients to be tried by a carefully hand-picked jury – or a before a particularly lenient judge. And somehow, it seems, they always get off the hook or serve the lightest sentence possible, and are right at it again as soon as they are released.

"These individuals or groups of individuals prey on the weak, the weary, the unaware. And they never change their stripes.

"You read in the newspapers and hear announcers tell tragic stories about this sort of malevolent person or enterprise each evening, when you settle down in front of your television set to watch the nightly news. You, yourself, may personally know one or more of their victims. You may have been a victim yourself of one of these self-serving types. Or you simply may have read enough infuriating headlines over your lifetimes to desire doing something to right these many wrongs.

"Well, that, in a nutshell, is the stance of the three kind spirits who first conceived of the Kriya Project: to bring retribution for the harm inflicted upon the injured and aggrieved, achieving what the courts – as they are constituted and operate throughout the world - only rarely achieve and deliver: impartial equity; true justice.

"Laws are like fishnets: while the nets scoop up many who are unable to escape their entanglements, there are far too many other fish – the wily ones - too crafty, too cunning, too slick and slippery to hold to account. They always seem to escape the net. The Truvenge Foundation's Kriya Project is a means to justice, where possible, created specifically to assure that does *not* happen, where we can intervene. We effectively bring karma to bear on the unbearably cruel and unthinking types of humans who victimize and take advantage of others for their own pleasure, or their own gain. It's karma, brought home to roost. Put very simply, the Kriya Project actualizes that old saw we are all so familiar with: 'What goes around comes around.'

"Consider what you will be engaged in as nothing more than that 'coming around' of a force for good that is greater than that of the criminal perpetrator.

"We are a non-profit organization. Our intentions are pure. We have righted many wrongs, restoring faith and hope of a new life free of the anguish left by the unjust. We right the unpunished wrongs of that vile element that causes most of the ills of this world through perpetration of one or more of those seven deadly sins – the capital vices spoken of in the Bible, the New Testament, the holy books of Mohammed and the treatises and credos of other world religions. 'Justice is mine' sayeth the Lord. But who is to say He cannot use us as his instruments?

"The Kriya Project employs righteous men and women, whose compassion leads them – with the assistance and guidance of out karmic consortium, to take action to preserve the faith in justice the underpins every civilized society, and which must continue to underpin an ordered society.

"Now, I have used this word a lot in the past few minutes. But I need to know that you thoroughly understand the concept of karma. Can anyone define it for me?"

Mr. Asura - Erik – paused to lean forward, reach for his glass and take a slow sip of water. He looked earnestly into the three faces at the table, who were looking just as earnestly into his.

To the surprise of all, it was Joe Belton who chose to respond to Asura's query. "Karma is a bitch," Belton stated solemnly. That was not what anyone expected to hear from the small, reserved man with the canula. They all appeared stunned, and for a moment the only sound in the room was the soft hum of his portable oxygen concentrator.

The moment of shock passed quickly, and everyone at the table burst into laughter.

Cascading laughter shattered the dramatic tension that Erik/Asura had intentionally and carefully built to a crescendo. Joe's unexpected statement was the pin that popped the balloon and sent it whizzing about the room, figuratively speaking, resulting in peals of laughter. Agnes actually had tears in her eyes. Joe wheezed with laughter at his own wit, and the astonishing effect he'd created with his single remark. Vince guffawed loudly, his belly laughs booming out into the large room.

The spell was broken – the mood robbed of its intensity.

But this, too, was intentional; and if Joe Belton had not come out with that line, Mr. Asura - aka Erik Walker - surely would have.

Erik was a master at emotional manipulation, and as he knew all too well, people are more strongly driven to take action on the basis of emotion, than logic. Victor, ever the salesman, took note of the clever tactic, and appreciated the verbal device Mr. Asura had used.

As Victor knew, persuasion is a bull fight, in every sense of the word. To persuade another, one must approach, then withdraw, coming at the prospect from every angle, waving the red cape to infuriate the bull and then withdrawing it; blending passion with drama, then breaking the spell with humor. Erik had found – as Victor no doubt often had, during his long and successful career selling life insurance – that to break down resistance, remove barriers and create a friendly bond between seller and buyer, humor is an invaluable tool. Shattering the intensity of the "sell" allowed a "buyer" to regroup, to breathe, to laugh. It refreshed the mind, cleared the air. And then the skillful persuader would acknowledge the humor in what was actually a very serious situation, and press forward with his serious point, having established - without having to express it verbally- the human similarities that united them in laughter.

They had engaged in a moment of levity that built empathy without diminishing the weight of the topic at hand.

Victor recalled his own use of that technique when closing a major life insurance sale, most useful at the point when his prospective client suddenly balked at the premium he realized he'd have to pay to adequately protect his family. His laugh line was, "What can I say to make that figure more palatable? That's the price of love – divide it by the number of nights of great sex and all the hugs and kisses from your kids, and all of a sudden it's not so expensive. Right?" He would pause just the proper length of time and then pass the pen to the prospect, suggesting, "Just sign right here, and make the check out to . . ."

Ah, but he missed those days, Victor thought. Persuasion was in his blood. He was good – really good. His sales figures routinely helped him reach Top of the Table status in his business - Million Dollar Roundtable every year. He made a terrific income while helping breadwinners assure their family's financial security at their passing. Making money while doing good – what could be better than that, Victor mused. By participating in the Kriya Project, rendering "revenge" to the guilty and offering closure to their victims, wouldn't he be doing pretty much what he'd spent over 45 years doing so successfully? Suddenly the Foundation's name made sense to him, and Victor chuckled softly.

Those in the conference room were settling back into a more somber and attentive mood, ending his reverie.

Joe Belton was still front and center, gathering his thoughts to explain his understanding of karma to the group. He'd been nervous when he first started speaking, but the astounding reaction to his simple words and the bonhomie his unintended humor had engendered in the group made him feel appreciated and supported. Their camaraderie instilled the confidence that make it easier to for him to speak.

A forensic accountant by career choice, he was very good at burrowing down into numbers and had turned that faculty into a satisfying and lucrative, if rather focused and solitary practice. He was well known in his field, and even now was called into some major criminal investigation: white collar crimes mostly, seasoned with the occasional Mafia prosecution or murder for inheritance, and spiced with high-dollar embezzlement cases or multi-million-dollar (even billion-dollar), headline-producing divorce cases. His well-written reports were always submitted ahead of time, however, and court testimony as to the various points and analyses his reports contained was perhaps the closest Joe ever got to public speaking. But those engagements had grown fewer as time passed and his health waned, and Joe had closed his office and shut down his practice two years earlier.

Decades of smoking cigarettes finally caught up with him and he had developed emphysema, which, along with the extra pounds he'd gained during years of a sedentary lifestyle and 'bachelor' diet of fast food and takeout, put his heart in jeopardy.

Joe finally threw in the towel when his breathing difficulties worsened. He took it badly when his physician told him he was slowly going into heart failure due to the emphysema, but his doctor had also heard of an experimental treatment regimen University Hospital specialists were developing, and at Joe's request, Doc Owens referred him to be evaluated for the study. Joe had qualified for the experimental program to test a new medication that carried the promise of being able to repair damaged air sacs, improve breathing, and delay the progression of emphysema. He had faithfully adopted the recommended dietary changes and had been maintaining a program of regular exercise and mild aerobics which, combined with light weight training, promised to improve his heart condition and his breathing, independent of the medication.

He wore a cannula and still carried oxygen, but he was physically active on doctor's advice, highly intelligent, and expressed interested in learning more about the Kriya Project when approached by Felicity Brooks. Having shuttered his practice, Joe was looking for a reason to get out of bed every morning, and face they day. A Kriya Project assignment promised to fill the bill.

While the participants took a needed break on the heels of their hilarity, Joe got a fresh cup of tea and munched a ginger biscuit sprinkled with sugar, musing how odd it was that the British called cookies "biscuits" and looked upon what passed for biscuits in America as something akin to scones. Now that his health was improving, Joe had toyed with the idea of touring the British Isles, and had done some reading that pointed out the language differences. But lack of discretionary funds had kept him close to home.

When they all settled into their seats again, Joe was once more the star. He cleared his throat and began, "I'm glad everyone had a good laugh. I think we needed that. No offense, Mr. Asura, but you were getting rather intense. What we are thinking of undertaking is a serious responsibility, though. And we can't forget that. If you do the reading, karma is serious stuff. It has to with a kind of spiritual cause and effect, where a person's actions and intentions influence the future of the person, and bad intentions and bad deeds cause bad things to happen to them – in this life and the next. Of course, it makes more sense if you believe in reincarnation. Karma is a spiritual principle that's embedded in the Asian religions – Hinduism, Buddhism, Jainism, and what's the other – oh yeah. The Sikhs – Sikhism, I guess you call it. Here in the U.S. the phrase that covers karma is just what Mr. Asura mentioned: 'What goes around, comes around.' With karma, you don't actually have to do a bad deed. Just having the intention to do wrong is enough to affect your future in some way, and not a good way."

Agnes Marie nodded her head and murmured in agreement, "Thoughts have power. You should always guard your thoughts."

Joe was on a roll, growing more confident with every word. He continued, "The law of karma pretty much explains an individual's current situation as the consequence of one or more actions taken in the past."

"Everything has consequences," Victor piped in, not wanting to be left out of the loop.

"Yeah," Joe continued, nodding to acknowledge him. "Actions have like consequences. Eventually. And there are two kinds of effects involved with karma. One deals solely with the visible effects of what happens to you, and the other deals with how you feel inside: your ability to feel happy or fulfilled as a person. In that way, karma affects your character, too. In fact, the lessons of karma are what help you grow spiritually. Karma is a Sanskrit word. And if you believe in reincarnation - that we come back again and again, until we finally get it right and our souls ascend to the next level - it makes sense that they say when you do in this life affects not only your current situation, but your situation and the lessons you must learn in the future. Karma is based on your actions and your thoughts in every moment of your life."

Joe Belton had said his piece, and for emphasis, reached for his now-cold cup of tea and downed it in one gulp.

In his persona as Mr. Asura, Erik issued the requisite words of praise: "Very good, Joe. Very well said. And in an ideal world, every hostile or evil action - every bad intention – will result in the proper punishment- to balance the scales of the universe, so to speak.

"But we live in a flawed world," he continued, "and so the balance of good versus evil must be restored in some way. That is the intention of every society in its court and penal system. Misdeeds are evaluated by courts comprised of citizens and of judges. Agreement of guilt and punishment are arrived at, and then delivered by the penal system. But not always. And remedying that defect was the intention of the Bodhi in establishing the Kriya Project.

"You will get to meet them, Erik/Asura told the three Kriya prospects seated before him, all three watching him intently, not wanting to miss a word.

"The Bodhi are magnificent beings – very wise men. Very wise. I learn something new every time I meet with them. They must approve your recruitment, and they will do it with a final interview of their own, which will be far more philosophical than the interview I will do with you shortly. Any questions I can answer for you?"

Victor was the first to respond. "Just what is the process? How does Kriya Project get its 'jobs,' as you call them, and how do you come up with the names of people like us to carry out the tasks you need done to execute that karmic action to balance the scales?"

Agnes Marie added, "And what do we all have in common that made you choose us?"

"Excellent questions, Victor, Agnes Marie," replied Erik, behind the mask of his alter-ego, Mr. Asura. "It's very simple. Karma must be appropriate, and that may entail taking action under less than optimal conditions. Because the tasks we will require of you can be dangerous and – let's be honest here – possibly life-threatening, we prefer to deal with individuals who are and have been dedicated to service to mankind all their lives, both personally and professionally, and who have often taken risks of one kind or another in the course of their service to other human beings. That describes all three of you, in one way or another.

"You will be vetted as to talents, skills, innate abilities, likes and dislikes, weaknesses and preferences. Our petitions of "jobs" are carefully selected, as well, and they are discussed thoroughly before the decision is made to execute justice in each instance. The petitions are planned and gamed out carefully to develop an appropriate and effective series of actions. We have a strong support crew made up of costumers, makeup artists, mechanical and electrical engineers, carpenters, drivers and stunt men and women, as well as a team of researchers operating under the direction of myself and our Chief Inspector and Planner, Tracey Walker. And all of this is under the ultimate supervision and direction of the Bodhi.

"Furthermore, because the risks are very real, we take care to properly train, coach and supervise your activities as you work on each case to its planned end. However, as much as we try to do so, we cannot control everything that occurs naturally, or arises spontaneously. We adapt our plans; and we may even – though rarely -

shut down an operation if things are going badly, in a way that we cannot modify or control. Lives of a very few of our volunteers *have* been lost, either through accident, or because an activity exacerbated their terminal condition and brought about a premature passing - which is why you will be fully informed of everything before taking on this responsibility, and the same goes for every case you will be involved in. But accidents do happen. We will remain in contact with your primary physician to make sure you are in the proper condition to undertake specific activities, and we will regularly test your strength and reflexes as we work together.

"Because of those very rare negative outcomes, we intentionally look for people on whom others do not directly depend – volunteers with no living spouse or partner and only settled, adult children who are no longer solely dependent on them for emotional or financial support. And here is what you may not want to hear. Each of you is facing a potentially terminal illness. Two of you are already in studies reserved for evaluating effects of specific treatment on those who have been diagnosed as terminally ill. Others fear a terminal health development that may have familial roots."

"You look for people who have nothing to lose, in other words," Agnes said softly.

"Yes, Agnes Marie," Mr. Asura/Erik replied. "For that, and for people, like yourself, whose lives are suddenly empty of purpose. Everyone needs a reason to get going in the morning," he went on, "a reason for being - raison d'être, I think the French call it. And a challenge - something to get the blood flowing, the heart beating faster. People who have led lives of adventure and excitement miss it, I am told. As in your case, Ms. Walford. Am I correct?"

She nodded.

"So," Mr. Asura continued speak, directing his attention to the others. "The unifying reason the three of you were selected is precisely due to all that just mentioned: You are all in search of a reason to keep rising every morning and eagerly dress to face the day. You are each living on borrowed time – as we all are, of course. You have heard the worst from your doctor, or fear hearing the worst – and you want to still find purpose and contribute to others, because it makes you feel *alive.* As every soldier knows – that decision having made the moment the enlisted – to serve effectively you must be willing to put your life on the line, and to die in the service of others – that, the Bible tells us, is the highest purpose of all. *Should it come to that.* But it is my job, and that of April, Tracey, all of our great technicians and researchers and security people – and it is certainly the intention of the three Bodhi –that we all work closely together to ensure that the worst does not happen.

"Lastly, while you have all built wonderful lives - not lives of affluence, perhaps, but of plenty – that plenty is dwindling rapidly as you pay for increasing medical needs. Without insurance, there must be funds available to your families or friends to pay your final expenses, however modest or extravagant they may be, and to pay whatever bills are owed - lest you invoke bad karma!"

They laughed.

"Because our unique charitable purpose is known to a very limited number of first responders and healing professionals like police and fire units, pastors and social workers, hospitals and clinics, we rely on those individuals to discretely refer cases to us in the form of petitions for redress, which must be signed by, but not necessarily initiated by the aggrieved individual or victim of the wrongdoing. But we do also have many direct petitioners for karmic retribution, and these require even greater scrutiny, before undertaking their cause.

"I read every petition submitted, then consult with the Bodhi about those that appear in greatest need of being addressed expeditiously. Petitions that are rejected are returned regretfully to the petitioner. For each petition we accept, we develop a plan of action, then scour the files of our referrals for employment – people like yourselves whom we call 'justice effectors' – and specifically match the plan for redress with the skills and attributes necessary to carry it off and then search for those who display the characteristics required. Unfortunately, we seem always to need either more 'justice effectors' or more suitable petitions to work with, so some petitions may have an extensive wait time before we can act on them to produce the requisite justice.

"And now, if that answers your basic questions, let us proceed with the interviews and testing, to see how the Kriya Project can best utilize your services."

Chapter 6 – To commit? Or not...

Decision time was rapidly approaching, as each of them was well aware.

How had they done? What were their test results – physical and mental? Would they ultimately be deemed capable enough? Up to the task? In what role might they be cast, or would they be required to wear many hats? Would they make the cut?

Did they even want to go through with this?

Really. Did they?

Were they certain enough to sign on the dotted line and not immediately regret it? There could be no backing down.

Would they suddenly feel overwhelmed, and chicken out just before the Consent and Releases, balking at signing – putting pen to paper at the very last moment? Mr. Asura told them that *had* happened, once or twice in the past, and it set the particular petitions back for two whole years, in one instance – and six months in the other.

But it was such an enormous commitment!

What to do; what to do . . .

By 3:30 that afternoon, right at the time Tracey Walker was to appear to talk to the group, these were the thoughts whipping through each of their minds.

Tracey walked in abruptly, and with no fanfare. She was wearing a tailored pantsuit, with her hair tied back severely in in a short braid at the neck. She introduced herself briefly and launched into her usual monologue.

"When I spoke with Eri . . . uh, Mr. Asura in the hall just now, on my way in, he was highly complementary about the three of you. 'Real winners – very bright,' he said. And the good news is that you all tested very well on your physical abilities. You don't know how much that pleases all of us. You have to consider that the Kriya Project, to serve its purpose, needs a constant flow of referrals, as not all applicants, will qualify, and many will be hesitant to take on such responsibility, and back out at the last minute. Others may be unsure of their ability to make smart decisions, or question how they might react under pressure.

"Believe me, if you waver at all before signing on the dotted line, follow your instinct. Once we embark on a plan, we cannot tolerate quitters. As much as we would like you to join our ranks, we will not push you into making a decision you may later question, or regret. Changes in your health are a valid reason to back out after making your commitment to Kriya. Nothing else is, however.

"So if you have any doubts, let me thank you for attending. Please gather your things and stop by April's desk on the way out. She will write you a generous check for joining us today and giving us your time and attention. Then she will smile nicely as she calls you a cab to take you wherever you need to go.

"Do I have anyone who is not ready to commit?"

Tracey stopped speaking and met the eyes of each person seated before her. No one moved. Each of them met her eyes and held her gaze.

"Terrific!" Tracey declared. "I will be your best friend, your taskmaster, your confidante, our resource, your inspiration and the one who finds a solution to all your problems. I am going to become the first person you speak to every morning and the last person you speak to at night.

"My job is to make this plan work as it is supposed to, and to help you create a gratifying and successful experience as a justice effector. I will check in with you throughout the day to learn what you are working to accomplish and how it is going, or what your next step is that you have to prepare for in order to position yourself to act or observe and fulfill your assignment.

"I maintain communication with the entire team throughout every day, and into the night. I work insane hours, but my number will be on speed dial on the encrypted cell phone you will receive. Do not – I repeat – DO NOT ever hesitate to call with any question or need, at any hour of the day or night. It is my task to coordinate everything, and I cannot do my work if you do not share your concerns in time for me to handle an impending issue.

"Understand that not every petition will develop into a major case, involving an ultimate justice. Some cases will just involve embarrassing the perpetrator of an injustice, or somehow coercing them into making amends, or doing the right thing. You are to follow direction to the letter. Improvisation will occasionally be necessary, but you are never to deviate from the plan you are told to follow unless the reason is something that has been cleared with me.

"Everyone is strictly on a need to know basis, and everyone signs the strict NDA. It is airtight, and violations will be severely dealt with. Don't ask me how. Compartmentalizing knowledge on a need-to-know basis is very effective in keeping secrets. It is how all intelligence agencies and the military function - along with many scientific organizations. Some people can work a lifetime in a position and yet know nothing about any other part of the organization or what anyone else actually does or is responsible for doing.

"Discretion is essential, and loose lips may get you killed or injured. Justice is a serious business, and if the people we will be dealing with were nice people, we would not need to be involved with them at all.

"Those who have referred you to us know only that these are confidential jobs for The Truvenge Foundation that will provide the qualifying hire with adequate funds to help handle medical and other bills, plus pay final expenses, and leave a little something for their heirs. They are told each of you has signed our NDA and is unable to discuss your work for the project with them, or anyone else. Those who refer petitions or cases to Kriya are also told nothing further once a job is referred except that, while all jobs or missions will be considered, not all can be accepted. Only the named petitioner receives notice of acceptance or denial.

"Complicated jobs will require a team to be assigned, with larger teams assigned for large jobs, while as few as one person may be able to handle others.

"We will be immediately working on two out of a possible three petitions. Usually we introduce and work three petitions, or cases, at a time. Mr. Asura introduced you to the two higher priority cases we will tackle. A petition case has been postponed because a case in the last set of petitions we've recently worked on has run into some logistical complications that I am currently working out, and the third case in this set of petitions will require intensive research, as it is a commercial case.

"I want you to think about and discuss the petitions you were introduced to today by Mr. Asura. Imagine how your skills might best be utilized, and what you could bring to the table, so to speak, to provide an effective contribution. I understand you know nothing about the kind of plan that has been or is being devised to achieve a form of justice in each case, but I want you to start thinking along those lines because your input is always welcome, and your ideas could possibly be incorporated into the plan under development, or in need of modification

"Since it is late in the day, and because I will soon grow closer to you than your own skin, there will be plenty of time for you to ask me questions. Victor, Joe and Agnes Marie - I know your tummies are probably begging for attention, so snacks, coffee, tea, bubble water and soda are being provided. You will be left alone to chat with one another for the next half hour. Avail yourselves of the restroom facilities, discuss your experiences, enjoy your snacks and take a break.

"Mr. Asura will be back in about a half hour to answer any questions and get your feedback, while the company doctor will administer a physical exam to each of you and interview you to see how you've held up through a rather stressful and busy day. Those not in with the doctor will be given aptitude and preference tests. When everyone is done with the physicals and the testing, Mr. Asura will conduct a group interview, sort of like a round table discussion - and then it's decision time.

"Once you've signed your contracts, you'll be issued your personal encrypted cell phone and a set of portable chargers. That phone is to be kept with you, and charged, at all times. It is to be used exclusively for Kriya Project communications, You will also be issued a money belt with a moderate amount of cash for Kriya- related expenses. After that, our superb caterer will provide a five-star dinner, at which April, Mr. Asura and I will join you. We can spend some time over dinner getting to know one another on a more relaxed basis.

"So, until later . . . unwind a bit and enjoy your snacks."

With that, Tracy was gone, and the three applicants were left to their own conversation, and the delicious array of snack foods and beverages that had been wheeled out behind their backs as Tracey was speaking to them.

Chapter 7 – The Bodhi

While the Colonial period of the British Empire was far from perfect, colonialism contribute both good and ill to the countries the Crown dominated for over three centuries.

The British established an initial presence in India through the *England East India Company* – a stock-ownership trading company founded in London in 1600, as *The Company of Merchants of London Trading into the East Indies*, an organization that maintained a government-sanctioned monopoly in trade for another 150 years as it gradually encroached on the subcontinental territories of South Asia. Its purpose was to trade in tea, spices, opium, silks and Indian cloth, and other exotic products. From the edge of the East Indies and into the surrounding Punjab and surrounding countries, then into the subcontinent itself, British traders and merchants competed with Dutch, French, and Portuguese traders who were likewise attempting to expand their territory.

In 1611, the company's first toehold on the subcontinent was established on the Eastern coast of what is now India, when permission was granted to build the first 'factory' – a combination of warehouses and office buildings - in Masulipatnam. A few years later, the Mughal emperor permitted the company to construct and operate another factory in Surat. There was but a thin force of soldiers and civil servants It was a rough and tumble period in the century before India was India, when hard-drinking and sometimes wild British young men risked their health, their futures, and sometimes their fortunes in the lottery that was precolonial India – hoping to avoid death or debilitating incident, accident or some 'gawd awful' tropical disease long enough to generate a great deal of money with which to return to England, marry, and settle into the life of a well-to-do country gentleman, or build a business in London and enjoy the glittering lifestyle of the city.

Many never lived long enough, however, to realize dreams of a windfall from trading, or increased status and advancement in the civil service. "Smallpox, cholera and plague" were described as the trinity that laid low many aspiring traders and civil servants. Parasites could also ravage one's health. Fevers ranked as the primary cause of death. Life expectancy in the hot, humid and culturally unfamiliar land was short – age 28 was the standard for men, and age 24 for women brave enough to follow their husbands in the 1700s, when women began following their spouses into the tropics. While many of the women had less exposure to certain elements, complications in childbirth claimed many. Short stays of no more than two years were recommended.

Over that first century of British presence, what later became known as India evolved into a quasi-confederation of provinces and presidencies directly governed by the British, through the Viceroy and the Governor-General of India, plus a collection of scattered principalities – actually a type of vassal state – was governed by Indian rulers, but under the authority of the Crown. From 1757 to 1858 the East India Company began forging agreements and alliances with the various Indian principalities, constructing warehouses and offices and establishing an army of natives to provide security for British properties and personnel. As the army grew, so did the British incursion into the subcontinent that they had name India. To support the army, and a growing civil service, taxes were implemented in areas the British had taken over. The centuries-old Indian system of castes was employed by the British as a means to select and utilize the native workforce. Caste was seen as a means of determining intellectual ability, occupational aptitude and social status among the native population.

Friction with the natives in service to the British grew, however, particularly in the army, and cultural differences the British were unable to understand and bridge led to the first Indian rebellion in 1857. The mutiny was put down with great difficulty, and increased the distrust between the native populations and the British. As a result of the revolt, and increasing anger in England over the exclusive monopoly the East India Company retained in conducting all trade between India and England, the British Parliament stepped in and began to limit the authority of the company in the regions that had fallen under its control over the 150 years of its dominance. In 1858, following the rebellion, the East India Company was ultimately abolished.

The British Raj – rule by the Crown of the subcontinent of India was a more formalized period of governance that began after the rebellion and encompassed the period from 1858 until 1947, when India gained its independence from the Crown and became the only democratic country in Asia.

While British rule of the subcontinent brought with it both benefits and burdens to the native population. It primarily aided the population by establishing a single legal tender and uniting the country with a common language, English. The Crown's many social reforms made life better for the Indian population, the foremost of which was outlawing the horrendous practice of *Sati Pratha* – a form of self-immolation urged upon widows who were faced with a future of abuse, poverty and shame. British education reforms included building schools throughout the subcontinent, and universities in the major cities of Bombay, Calcutta, and Madras. The British introduced many public health advances and instituted the Indian Civil Service, which provided a variety of important and prestigious official government posts for educated and talented Indians, regardless of caste, and laid the groundwork for an administrative underpinning that supported the later self-governance of India. The Imperial Civil Service continued to operate as the Indian Administrative Service long after the British left India following its independence in 1947.

British engineers structured a series of canals and dams that greatly improved agriculture and the availability of water throughout the subcontinent and developed the infrastructure of India. British engineers also directed the laying of heavy railroad tracks that linked the provinces and major cities of the subcontinent, employing thousands of workers to build what became the world's fourth largest modern railway system. Backed by investors in England, the two initial and largest railroad companies, the East Indian Railway Company (EIR) and the Great Indian Peninsular Railroad (GIPR), commenced construction in 1853-1854, starting their lines near Bombay, and, on the opposite side of the subcontinent, Calcutta. Initially, the railroads were privately owned, and were built and operated by British craftsmen, engineers and administrators, with Indians being the only unskilled workers.

The plan was to construct trunk lines that would connect India's principal geographic regions, and the first passenger rail line was opened in 1859 to connect Allahabad and Kanpur. As investments flowed in from England and the continent of Europe, greatly encouraged by British government backing, smaller companies added their efforts and India's new railway system was rapidly built. Large principalities began to construct their own internal railways, and by the end of the 19th century the subcontinent of India boasted a rail network that united the country at long last, and contributed to its efficient rule by the British Crown.

Eventually, responsibility for the railway system was taken over by the British Colonial government, which nationalized the system in 1923, after the end of WWI, while the companies continued to run their particular rail lines. In those later years, much of the railroad construction was completed by Indian companies. However, until the 1930s the two Raj railroad lines, and many smaller companies continued to hire civil engineers, supervisors, administrators, operating personnel, and even locomotive engineers from England, and from Europe.

India was still a British Colony in 1930, the year a set of identical triplets was born to an older Hindu couple in the crowded city of Calcutta. The couple was educated, of upper caste, and worked in the service of a senior official of the East Indian Railway Company, Sir Bruce Hambleton, and his family.

The couple had married young, and had lost their only two children, born many years after their marriage, and only after the wife had suffered several miscarriages. There had been much difficulty conceiving the children, and both pregnancies were fraught with problems. Their first child, born prematurely, did not live for longer than an hour after birth. It was a boy. The other, a girl, was born with severe disabilities, and only lived to age 4, dying of whooping cough. After losing another pregnancy at five months gestation, the couple had given up on ever having children, and so the young British children of the household in which the wife served as the ayah – the children's nursemaid - became substitutes for the little ones they had lost.

As *ayah*, and governess to the children until they reached school age, the wife, whose name was Caitri, had a position of limited authority, but of great respect. And the children adored her. As the children reached school age, a young British woman, wife of a military officer and educated as a teacher, was brought in to give the children their lessons, but Caitri, their ayah, retained her responsibilities for the children's wellbeing and instruction in all other matters. They were attached to her, and she to them.

Sir Hambleton and his wife, Beth, whom all the servants addressed as *Sahib* and *Memsahib* – the customary term Indians used to address white men of authority and white women, usually their wives – were the parents of three children. The oldest, a girl, was named Mary Beth, and was about four years old when Caitri began caring for her. The Hambletons had just moved to Calcutta, where Sir Hambleton, from London, England, had just been named Senior Administrator of the EIR. Sir Hambleton had spent two years in India as a young man and was acquainted with the customs, sights and sounds of Calcutta. For his wife, Beth, culture shock set in the instant she stepped off the dock where their ship had landed, and she was having a difficult time adjusting to India. The ayah the family had inherited from the previous British family that lived in the home they now occupied, which was furnished by the railroad to whomever was Senior Administrator of the EIR, was a plump country woman whose English was quite poor. Beth felt awkward around the woman and could barely understand a word she said. Furthermore, Mary Beth did not take to the woman at all, leaving Sir Hambleton with a dilemma.

Sir Hambleton was impressed with his young secretary at the railroad, an Indian man who had also worked for the previous Administrator, an unfortunate man who had suffered a stroke and was forced to returned home to England with his wife and younger brother, who had traveled to Calcutta specifically to accompany the family on their voyage home. Sir Hambleton had been appointed to replace him. His Indian secretary was exceptionally intelligent, presented himself very well, and spoke impeccable English; he was an efficient and educated man whose name was Davaram. After a month in his new position, Sir Bruce felt fortunate to have someone so capable to help him understand what would be expected of him in his new role with the railroad. Davaram was able to explain everything succinctly and accurately, and often with a subtle touch of humor. There seemed to be no question for which Davaram did not have the precise answer.

Sir Bruce was at his wits end upon learning what had transpired between Beth and the ayah. Beth, who was newly pregnant, and hormonal as any young mother might be in her first months, had lost patience with the women and impulsively sacked her, on the spot, without having a replacement, or even a clue as to how they might go about hiring someone new. Beth had then apparently realized, too late, that she would need help communicating with the other household servants, who spoke barely a word of English, but had been working in that house so long that they moved about silently and efficiently, and required little direction. Still . . . Beth would require someone to help her with Mary Beth, her young daughter, as her pregnancy advanced.

Sir Bruce entered his office, the morning after Beth told him about the impulsive sacking, wearing a gloomy expression, which prompted his man, Davaram, to become concerned and ask if there was something he could help with, or if, perhaps, *Sahib* was displeased with him for some reason? Sir Bruce denied any displeasure with his secretary and proceeded to explain the problem. Davaram brightened immediately.

"My wife, Caitri," he explained to Sir Bruce, "is a very bright and refined woman who loves children. She is very good with our nieces and nephews and gets great pleasure in looking after them, to help her sister. We have no children, and she is always looking for some way to occupy her days. I am certain that she would be happy to meet *Memsahib,* if that is acceptable, and learn if she could be of service. May I bring her to meet. . .?"

"Absolutely," declared Hambleton, slapping the desk with his hand. Relief flooded his countenance as he beamed at Davaram. "I will tell her tonight, and let you know on the morrow when would be appropriate!"

The meeting went even better than could have been expected. Mary Beth took an instant liking to Caitri, and there just happened to be a cottage on the grounds of the large villa, which was located on a leafy street in the suburbs of Calcutta, that would be suitable for the couple, so that Caitri could be available to care for Mary Beth, and for the baby. Davaram could ride to work in the limousine with Sir Hambleton each morning, and they could schedule their day on the way to the railroad office.

Caitri's salary was agreed to, and all was settled.

The couple was Hindu, and followed their religion faithfully even though, on the whole, British colonialists were inclined to think less of those who "clung to old ways and ridiculous superstitions." Davaram and Caitri were, therefore, entirely circumspect when performing their duties and never brought notice to themselves for their religious beliefs. In fact, after the baby was born – a little boy - and Davaram and Caitri had spent a little over a year in their respective positions with Sir Bruce and Beth Hambleton, the Indian couple consented for a minister friend of the Hambletons to give them the barest of Christian instruction, and to baptize them both.

This pleased the Hambletons to no end - particularly Beth, who was newly pregnant with her third child, and the little boy was barely a toddler. Although Beth had hesitated to voice her concern, as the children's ayah, Caitri's Hindu creed had suddenly become of concern to Beth, as soon as her oldest had begun to speak and understand the language that was still so foreign to Beth. The Englishwoman had chanced upon Mary Beth and Caitri chattering away happily in a tongue her mother had yet to learn to any degree, and while she understood the usefulness, that familiarity with Caitri's native language worried her, in that the girl might also pick up elements of a heathen religion.

Beth had been the daughter of missionaries. When a child, she had spent time with her parents in Africa. So, while the color of the native population gave her no pause, and she was more accepting of cultural and physical differences than most of the British wives of military officers, or the merchants, railroad men and civil servants, she had spent many years in England in late adolescence and as an adult, and now had the management of a full household and responsibility for a small child weighing on her as she assessed her surroundings and struggled to adapt to a country whose customs, religions and language were truly foreign to her.

However, as the daughter of missionaries, she fervently wanted her children to be raised in a Christian home, with Christian influences. That was what was most important to her.

Davaram and Caitri were fascinated by Christian beliefs. When one has been raised in a certain culture and belief system, however, change is difficult. And so, while on the surface the ayah and her husband learned the hymns and studied the Bible, they still secretly followed the traditions they had known all their lives – including a healthy respect for the many superstitions that have abounded in India for centuries.

Superstitions surrounding the bearing of children circulated in the villages and cities alike. Early child mortality, and the demands of physical labor in the countryside that required many hands made the birth of a large number of children necessary. City life made large families difficult, but childbirth and a child's earliest years remained subject to superstition because of the cultural requirement for children to care for their parents in old age and make their funerary arrangements. Only a son, for example, would light a parent's funeral pyre. While superstitions were most strongly held by villagers, even educated Indians like Caitri and Davaram were not immune to their influence.

In the early years of their marriage, Caitri attempted to adhere to every rule governing impending maternity and with each child lost, she rigorously recollected her every decision, examined her very movement before, during and after pregnancy to understand where she might have failed. For one thing, Davaram loved Caitri's long, black tresses, and loved the fragrance of her hair after it was washed and oiled. He refused to go along with the old wives' tale that warned expectant mothers not to wash or cut their hair for the duration of their pregnancy, or at least from the time of the traditional baby shower in the seventh month to the actual delivery. Neither child had been named before their birth, but with the children she had miscarried, she had sat on the floor with her legs bent to one side – a favorite position – before realizing she was with child. Again not realizing she was pregnant, she had repeatedly eaten spicy foods, which she loved, before all of her miscarriages, and before delivering the tiny, premature son she had lost within an hour after he had emerged into the world.

With her daughter, who had been born with severely clubbed feet, Caitri had been in her seventh month of pregnancy and at her baby shower when a cousin who was crippled from birth, with one leg shorter than another and curvature of the spine, had appeared at the party. Caitri had forgotten about the girl and had not invited her, but the misshapen cousin had accompanied an invited friend of Caitri's, from the same village. She was certain her baby girl had been cursed as a result. An expectant mother was never to permit herself to be around a crippled individual, but when her cousin limped across the room to greet her after years apart, with arms outstretch to greet her, Caitri had been frozen in place, and tried to return the greeting as warmly as possible. But her child had been cursed, she was sure of it.

Life in the Hambleton household was pleasant enough. Caitri adored Mary Beth, and the child loved her. The little boy, Robert, was still being nursed daily by the dhaye, or wet nurse, that Caitri had found to spare *Memsahib* Beth the rigors of nursing one child while carrying another to term. He was a clever, roly-poly child with pink cheeks, a ready smile, and pudgy little arms and legs he used to grip his ayah's body as Caitri carried him around the house, and when he grew tired after walking for a bit.

Following their baptism, Davaram and Caitri were continuing to study the Christian Bible with the Reverend McMeacham. They had reached the Biblical passages where Abraham's wife, Sarah, who had been infertile into old age, and had yearned for a child, found herself expecting a baby. Caitri had studied the story with the Reverend, asking him many questions, to fully understand. And then she had reread it twice with Davaram. She accepted that with the Christian God it had happened because Sarah had prayed, and Abraham had 'beseeched.' She did not know what "beseeched' meant, but the Reverend had taught them both how to pray. So, one night before bedtime, Caitri persuaded Davaram to pray with her, making up the words from her heart, and at the end saying, "Amen!" – loudly, and with a flourish. Then, like Sarah, she waited. And waited.

Beth Hambleton was in her sixth month when Caitri felt the quickening in her belly. She had just finished a spicy meal in the kitchen, and dismissed the feeling in her gut as a reaction to the peppers. But it persisted overnight and the next day, and so she told *Memsahib* Beth about it. Beth knew Caitri's sad story, and Caitri had recently told her about the story of Sarah and the prayer she and Davaram "had sent to Almighty God," as Caitri describe it. Intrigued, it was Beth who suggested that the next time Doctor Owens came to the house to examine her, perhaps he should examine Caitri, as well.

A week later, Dr. Owens paid a house call. He told Beth Hambleton she was progressing nicely, and then examined Caitri, who shared her story about Abraham, Sarah, and her prayer. Dr. Owens confirmed that, indeed, Caitri was about three months along, at which point the ayah fainted. Mrs. Hambleton was equally shocked, but her concern focused more on the position that the ayah's pregnancy left her in. Once revived, Caitri read the concern on Beth's face and divined the reason. "Do not worry, *Memsahib*, Caitri assured her employer. "I have a favorite aunt and cousin in Calcutta who can come each day to help us both, and I will be certain to care for Mary Beth and Robert as well as I always do, with them to do the lifting and carrying of the children, and tending to their room. And my sister will also come to help."

And that is how Caitri's younger sister, Cuksani, came into the Hambleton household, to act as wet nurse for the *memsahib's* new baby, and as a maid or *matranee* to help both *memsahib* Hambleton, and her own pregnant sister, Caitri.

Cuksani was ten year younger than Caitri. She was the widowed young mother of a year-old little girl to whom she'd given birth during the very week that her husband was killed in a freak accident that took place during repair of an EIC railroad mainline track. He was struck in the head by a length of railroad track that was being lifted into place by crane, and died instantly when the crane collapsed. Because her husband had spoken ill of his Irish foreman the week before her baby was born,

Cuksani named the child Karma, a Sanskrit word that stood for an accomplished 'act' or 'deed' – yet it also referred to the ancient Indian spiritual principle that teaches one brings upon oneself the consequences of every act or deed. Cuksani could not be dissuaded from her belief that she was left a single mother as the result of her husband voicing hostility toward his foreman.

And so it went. Sir Hambleton and his wife generously saw that Dr. Owen examined Caitri on each of his visits to Beth. But Caitri insisted she would use their own family midwife, who had delivered the many babies born into her extended family, to help her deliver her child in the cottage. However, it was when Dr. Owen listened for the baby's heartbeat on his third visit after he'd ascertained Caitri was indeed expecting a baby that he stepped away after listening, readjusted his stethoscope, and listened again, then stepped back once more, took out his clean handkerchief from his suit pocket, polished the disk-shaped resonator intently, and listened once again. He shook his head. "It's no mistake," he told both Caitri and Beth, who was standing nearby, anxiously watching.

"There are three heartbeats," he intoned, solemnly. "Three."

At that, Caitri passed out from shock, and had to be revived once Mrs. Hambleton had retrieved a vial of smelling salts from her room, and handed it to Dr. Owen. Caitri came to with a start, and asked, "Three, Doctor?" She grimaced, as old Indian lore viewed multiple births as unlucky. But the Christian God of the Bible had demonstrated a miracle.

Like Sarah, she was an older mother who had been blessed with child at an older age. Not just one child, but two more to replace the two children she had lost through miscarriage! That sincere belief restored her confidence. And she told Beth, "*Memsahib*? I will have to see Reverend McMeacham to tell him of this miracle." Beth nodded.

Doctor Owen went on, "I believe delivering triplets may be beyond the skills of your family midwife, Caitri. At least, to handle the delivery alone. I would like to be there." She nodded.

He turned to Beth. "We will have to arrange something in the house, Mrs. Hambleton" he said. "I fear the cottage is too small."

She nodded assent and said to Caitri and the doctor, "This villa is large enough. We can create a delivery area, and a temporary nursery. Then we will have to think how we can enlarge the cottage, adding a nursery, and a bedroom for Cuksani and her child." She sighed. "I will have to speak with Sir Hambleton this evening."

Memsahib Beth leaned over Caitri. "You are only to worry about taking care of yourself, now that Cuksani is here to help us as both *dhaye* and *matranee*. You can work with the children until you feel tired, then let Cuksani take over, and rest with your feet up. My ankles swell with one child. I cannot even begin to imagine carrying three!"

Davaram, too, was shocked by the news. But he hastened to warn Sir Hambleton not to congratulate him for his impending fatherhood. Sir Bruce had been in India long enough to understand that to do so would likely cross the line and trigger some fear of misfortune, so he merely grunted and began to talk of plans to expand the cottage.

When *Memsahib* Beth's child was born, Cuksani was ready to wean her own child and so was able to nurse little Peter, the Hambleton's third child.

To everyone's surprise but Caitri herself, her pregnancy proceeded without a hitch. She was able to participate in the usual household routines and care for the children until the beginning of her eight month, with Cuksani and one of the housemen, a bearer by the name of Burit, helping to carry the children, and their toys, outdoors to play and back inside again. When Caitri suddenly felt like a large blimp and found movement difficult, she knew that her time was near. Davaram, as was traditional, had indulged her every craving, for that was said to prevent birthmarks. But when Caitri saw a bowl of strawberries in the kitchen one day, she simply could not resist her favorite fruit, and gobbled three in quick succession before the *mussalchee* – the dishwasher - entered the kitchen and observed her with strawberry juice running down her chin. He wagged his finger at Caitri, who was by then visibly pregnant, and put the strawberries in the cool chest, out of her sight and reach, warning her that strawberries would leave her children with unsightly birthmarks. Strawberries were the only thing forbidden to her. She pouted, but immediately feared this impulsiveness could bring about the consequence that the *mussalchee* had warned about.

She had been so careful, despite her overriding belief this multiple pregnancy was a gift from the Christian God, and therefore protected by Him. Unlike her prior, unhappy forays into motherhood, Caitri had felt good throughout the eight and a half months. Now that the birth was but days away, she was glad that she had two faiths to guide her. And she had done everything right – except for eating those three strawberries. She and Davaram had agreed to follow custom, with regard to her hair. She had not cut it, and washed it less frequently than usual. She avoided sharp objects, spicy foods – which she missed terribly - and avoided the funeral preparations and funeral of a *buriah*, a very gentle older servant who had died in her sleep. The deceased was a woman whom Caitri had like very much, and to stay away from the funeral ceremony was a form of insult for which she prayed to the dear woman to ask forgiveness.

She listened to religious music on the gramophone and read to the children in her belly from the Hindu texts Davaram had brought her. She did these things to fill the three infants, who would soon emerge into the light of the world, with holiness and wisdom. Caitri was careful of the ways in which she sat and walked, and avoided anyone with a visible defect.

At the end of the first trimester, her sisters joined her in the cottage for a ritual called *punsavana*, where prayers were said to ensure the birth of a male child. The *seemantham*, held in her seventh month, was a baby shower, attended by *memsahib*, and the wife and daughter of the Reverend McMeacham, her sisters, and many friends. Her disabled cousin had died some years earlier, so Caitri did not fear her sudden appearance. She received many lovely gifts.

As a gift to the new mother and father, and to accommodate Cuksani and her child in their own quarters, with a separate room for the triplets to grow up in, the Hambletons had spent a modest sum to add two bedrooms and a modern bathroom to the cottage. Their generosity was much appreciated.

When Caitri woke in the middle of the night, with the silver beams of an auspicious full moon sliding through windowpanes and into the bedroom, the midwife was called, along with Dr. Owen. A messenger was sent to fetch Mrs. McMeacham and her daughter, who both insisted on waiting in the parlor with Beth Hambleton, Sir Bruce, and many of the household servants, for the announcement of the momentous event – the birth of triplets. Reverend McMeacham joined the household in the parlor as they waited for the event. Praying for a good outcome was his job, which he undertook immediately, and did not cease, except to eat a homemade scone and have a cup of tea.

Cuksani was with the doctor and midwife, helping as she was asked, and comforting Caitri when she was not otherwise assisting. The expectant father, Davaram, continued to pace the parlor floor, too nervous to eat. He would then walk outside, wring his hands as he listened for the sounds from the back of the house, where the event was taking place in a room prepared for the multiple delivery, wince at hearing his wife's screams of pain, then rush back in to join the others, only to repeat the exercise a half hour later. Because the night promised to be a long one, tea and sandwiches were served all night long while everyone chatted, gossiped, and waited nervously to hear the wailing of a newborn. Hours passed. The sun rose, breakfast was served, then a late lunch, and at dusk the group went out to watch a spectacular sunset before returning to sit properly at the long dining table for the evening meal, and return to sit once again in the parlor after the light evening repast had been consumed. At last, just as the stars winked on in the cobalt blue sky, the first wailing was heard. Everyone sat up sharply, simultaneously holding their breaths as they listened for the second cry.

They heard it, loud and clear, and after a few tense minutes of silence a third wail broke the stillness, and the entire gathering broke out into applause, laughter, and chatters of relief. Sir Hambleton had the servants bring out his best sherry and glasses for everyone, including the gathered servants, and a huge tray with two dozen tiny glasses and a bottle of Sir Hambleton's best sherry was carried into the dining room and placed on the table just as Doc Owen entered after washing up, to announce the birth of three healthy boys of good weight, and all in excellent condition. "They are identical," he announced, beaming. "Identical. I never imagined I would have the privilege of bringing three identical infants into the world, from one mother – who is doing just fine, by the way, and sends her greetings. I swan, this is the highlight of my career!" Toasts were declared and the doctor was praised again and again for his great skill.

Meanwhile, Cuksani was bathing and oiling the little ones, dressing them in identical little gowns for their introduction to their father and debut to the waiting gathering. To be certain to ward off the evil eye, the midwife was in the garden with the bearer, digging a hole far away from the house and the cottage, to bury the placenta and thus protect the infants from the wrath of jealous Hindu gods. Davaram rushed to see his wife, bursting with pride. Caitri held her little ones, nursed them, and once they were fed and Cuksani had bathed and dressed the new mother, the celebrating crowd would be allowed to stream through the cottage to see the newborns and congratulate their proud parents.

The children would be named on their sixth day of life, Davaram and Caitri informed their employers and their friends. And on the seventh day, the parents would reveal their names.

What they did not mention was that Caitri and her sisters would perform a hallowed Hindu ritual to choose the named for the three little boys. The *Chaathi* ceremony was traditionally performed by the women, late at night – usually around 10 o'clock. A lamp, a red pen, and paper would be laid out on a wood plank for Vidhaati, the Hindu goddess of destiny, to write the future of the newborns. The mother would kneel before the lamp, which symbolized the goddess, and would hold each child while the child's destiny was written.

Six days passed, and on the morning of the seventh day, Caitri announced her sons' destinies, and the Sanskrit names they had been given, to reflect those destinies.

The first infant to issue from his mother's womb was *Alivesh Abrer*, whose destiny was to be an investigator; a truthful person, naturally curious, and habitually thorough. The second born of the triplets was also the smallest of the three. He was to stand for Forgiveness, and the King of Wisdom: *Asif Ariv* was his name. The final son to be born was also the largest of the three in height and weight, and he was named *Aadil Adish*; his destiny was to carry the message of Justice, and he was to be noble, knowledgeable, intelligent, and full of wisdom. Caitri revealed that she had been told the boys were to grow strong and wise, and that together they would be known as the Bodhi, for their perfect knowledge.

Thus were the triplets to grow up in the company of their cousin, Cuksani's daughter, Karma, and the two Hambleton boys – Robert and Peter – who were to become as brothers to the triplets. Mary Beth would always be the older sister the younger children looked up to, and whose praise they sought to earn.

Happily, this merry little group spent days playing in the sunny gardens of the Company villa, and splashed in the shaded water of a shallow pool next to the deeper adult pool, when the weather became so hot it was unbearable, whether indoors or out. Naps were a welcome respite after a morning in the sun, and fans in the house kept the air moving as the children and adults napped in the early afternoon. Tutors hired by the Hambletons taught the children and provided the same quality education equally, to all of the children. While Mary Beth had special lessons appropriate to her age and grade, the younger children were all within a year or two apart in age, and so could be taught together as a small class. Morning classes in calligraphy, mathematics, geography and history were followed by playtime, lunch, a nap, and then in the late afternoon, they read, learned science lessons, and then applied themselves to memorizing poetry and famous speeches by important men. Lessons took up a total of five and a half hours split between morning and afternoon, five days a week.

When all but Mary Beth were still toddlers, the world was faced with the great Depression. However, for residents in India under the Raj, and for the native population of India, the Depression had little impact. Trade was affected, to some small degree, but military and civil service salaries remained stable, and costs remained low. What did have a severe impact on Colonial life in India was World War I and its aftermath, the still larger military buildup to WWII, and the hard years of the Second World War, itself.

During both world wars, India's supply chains were diverted to the war effort. Staples from Britain were in short supply, and were rationed. Many items were simply unavailable, and substitutions had to be sought on the local market.

The war years subsequent to the Great Depression were tough times for the railroads; even worse than WW

I had been. Indian railroads had been used during World War I for troop transport and to move grain to the major ports of Bombay and Karachi. Trade and troop transport to the Middle East, Africa and Britain took precedence over interior India rail traffic. Maintenance was increasingly difficult; manufacture of artillery occupied the rail workshops across India. Skilled railway workers enlisted, or were drafted into the military.

Britain had poured a great deal of money into its railroad system, and like so many things the British made, the railways were over-engineered and overbuilt. Constructed to a standard that far exceeded need, its heavy tracks had been laid primarily for military purposes on the heels of the 1857 Indian Mutiny, although the anticipated use never materialized.

A networked railway system was born from the hope that implementation of a rail system linking the entire subcontinent would stimulate the growth of industry. It never did. Constructed in "fits and starts," its cost was never justified by the small amount of freight that was actually transported throughout India by rail. Furthermore, its nationalization under the British Crown subjected the railroad system to state mandates, and made the rail system dependent on the state largesse to meet its budgetary need.

On the basis of the Empire's Stores Policy, instituted by the British Parliament, bids on all railway contracts had to be submitted to the India Office, in London. Indian companies were thus closed out of the bidding process, for all intents and purposes. Railway companies in India were forced to purchase all parts and hardware in Britain. Although highly competent railway maintenance companies operated in India, only rarely were they given permission to repair or manufacture locomotives.

During the Second World War emergency, Indian railroads were severely handicapped as Indian railways' rolling stock was diverted by the British to their Middle East operations. That rolling stock had already been depleted and was in serious disrepair after World War I. The railroads had never actually supported themselves with freight and passenger fares alone. When, under the severe shortages of the second World War, railroad workshops were converted to produced munitions, the increasing problems with existing rolling stock became apparent Rail costs were already high, but raising the inadequate fares simply wasn't practical.

At the end of WWII, forty-two individual railway systems – including thirty-two private lines which had continued to be owned by former principalities - were operating cooperatively at the end of the war, without centralized control and budgeting. After India's independence in 1947, these systems were brought together in 1951 in a single, nationalized amalgamation that was called Indian Railways.

Meanwhile, the children had been growing up together, oblivious of the state of the world and relating to one another as brothers and sisters might – and not as members of different families with different ethnicities, cultures, and customs. Mary Beth had married a young British officer who administered important colonial offices, and was no longer a member of the household, but she visited regularly with her husband and their infant son.

In 1946, in preparation for major changes that Sir Hambleton anticipated would be necessary upon India's attaining its independence from the British Crown the following year, he dispatched Davaram on a journey into the Northern reaches of India – up into the Punjab and to Allahabada and Byram Ghat in Oude. The boys begged Sir Hambleton to allow them to accompany Davaram, who was to be away for two or three months. Robert, who had turned 18 the previous year, his brother Peter, and the triplets, Alivesh Abrer, Asif Ariv, and Aadil Adish – the Bodhi, as they were already being called, for sake of simplicity and memory - all begged for permission to go with him, citing their limited knowledge of India, north of Calcutta, or of Nepal, which was, ultimately, their intended destination.

The unbearable heat of summer would be upon Calcutta during the months they would be gone, and respite from the heat in cooler climates at the higher altitudes was a big selling point for Sir Hambleton, who declared aloud that he wished he were going with them.

A trusted household servant and companion to Sir Hambleton, the man who had accompanied his master on many similar trips to the Punjab and was considered very wise and trustworthy, was named Atiksh. When Sir Hambleton spoke with this stalwart manservant and bearer about the idea of letting the five young men spread their wings on a supervised journey of discovery, Atiksh agreed to accompany the boys, and travel with Davaram and another manservant who was to assist Sir Hambleton's secretary for the duration of his journey. Atiksh promised to never leave the boys' side, and vowed to keep them out of trouble. While the triplets' father, Davaram, did his work visiting various points along the railway network of the region, it was agreed that he could work more effectively if he were not also the ward of five rambunctious adolescent males. When Robert and the boys were told that Sir Hambleton had approved their travel with Davaram and Atiksh, and that Atiksh had agreed to be their guide, translator, companion and guardian as they toured Nepal for two months, the boys whooped in joy, jumping up and down on the broad veranda of the villa.

The younger boys and Robert - who now insisted he was nearly an adult and no longer a child – were thrilled, and stayed up late into the night sitting on the veranda of the main house, drinking sweet tea and planning their great adventure.

Beth Hambleton visited the railroad library, with her husband's permission, and brought home many illustrated books that showed the areas they would be visiting. Reverend McMeacham owned several books personally that had photographs of Nepal and the Himalayas, with illustrations of Tibetan dress and pictures of Buddhist monks praying and ringing huge, ornamented brass bells of religious significance, in one of the many monasteries they would see, and perhaps visit. He also lent them books about Buddhism, the monasteries perched on mountainsides, and even photographs of the last two Dalai Lama. With months to plan ahead, Robert and the young boys would have plenty of time to read aloud in the evenings and discuss an itinerary, each one choosing his top three choice of sights or experiences, for debate, and to arrive at a consensus with the others to on the three best sites.

Beth Hambleton wrote to relatives in Britain and ordered Davaram and the young men, as well as the two bearers, a quantity of heavy winter clothing: Thick wool jackets and pants, long underwear, highlander socks, hiker boots and mountaineering shoes, and Scottish sweaters, lined leather gloves, wool knit caps and long Shetland wool scarves as well as salves to keep their lips from cracking in the cold which, while summer, was an ever present danger at high altitudes. She also packed lighter clothing for lower altitudes. Packages were shipped and arrived over the next few months as their gear was assembled. Robert, the other boys – who were now 16-year-olds, and Atiksh would travel with Davaram and his manservant as far as Byrum Ghat in the Oude where they would disembark, hire guides, buy mules, and employ native men who were used to the high altitude to carry their gear. They planned to set off into the heart of Nepal the week following their arrival, and embark on their travels.

Memsahib Beth, Caitri and her sister, Cuksani were sad to see their children leave for such a long time. The huge villa would be barren without them. Karma – the one child remaining at home – would no doubt be spoiled by the women and the servants, now that she could command the full attention of her elders, so she gleefully anticipated the departure of her "brothers." Sir Hambleton would be in constant contact with Davaram by telegraph and telephone, and so would keep the women, the McMeacham family and Dr. Owen apprised of their wellbeing and progress.

The day of their departure finally arrived in mid-June of 1946. Friends and family gathered to drive to the East India train station, help them aboard the carriage in which the large party would be traveling, and wave them off, in joyful celebration.

Little did anyone know that the travelers would not return home for five months, and that Robert, the oldest, would not return at all.

Furthermore, no one realized at that happy moment of departure how profoundly this journey would alter the hearts and minds of those young men.

Chapter 8 – Forging The Plan

The newly hired trio spent the weekend in isolation, reading and re-reading the particulars of their agreement to better understand what would be required of them in their new roles as justice effectors, and as new employees under a commitment to the Kriya Project. They also planned to commit to memory the details of the two petitions they would be taking on to resolve, in their first assignment enforcing justice.

Tracey had suggested that they each spend the weekend alone, with no distractions, and read every detail of the two petitions until they were committed to memory. She further instructed them to meditate each morning and evening for at least 20 minutes each session, contemplating the awesome responsibility they were about to undertake and dealing with any feelings that might arise when carrying out what was to be asked of them.

Monday morning they would be at Truvenge early to enjoy breakfast with Tracey and Mr. Asura, chat about their weekend, and ask any questions they needed answered before proceeding. Then they would have the great honor of meeting the Bodhi, who were looking forward to interviewing each of them privately.

When Monday arrived, Tracey greeted each of the new hires warmly as they entered the boardroom at Truvenge and invited them to serve themselves from the bountiful array of breakfast foods spread out for them, including hot omelets prepared to their liking by an Asian chef.

"I wonder if we'll get sushi for lunch?" Agnes Marie whispered to Victor, who stood next to her waiting for his omelet. "I love sushi," she added.

"Not exactly my preference," Victor whispered back. "Anything uncooked is never on my plate."

"You can request cooked sushi rolls. Spider rolls, for instance, have fried soft shell crab in them. Other sushi rolls have shrimp tempura, or if you are vegetarian, there's always cream cheese and avocado, with chopped vegetables."

"Why are we whispering?" Victor cleared his throat and repeated his question, aloud.

"I have no idea," Anne Marie laughed. "It's just so quiet in here."

Across the room, Joe Belton was studiously unpacking his larger breathing apparatus. Tracey had vanished.

"Good morning, Joe," Agnes and Victor called to him.

Boardroom furnishings had been rearranged and sound-absorbing privacy dividers that had been set up for their interview and testing sessions of the previous week had been removed. The room did, indeed, appear rather empty, and much larger, compared to the way they'd seen it previously.

"Huh? Oh, good morning you two. Victor, is it? And Agnes Marie?" Joe greeted them. The two of them nodded.

"Come order an omelet – any way you like it," Agnes Marie urged, watching Joe meticulously set up his seating area with pens and notepad to his right. Joe had made a beeline to his seat from the previous week, unaware that Agnes, the first to arrive, had chosen to sit next to the place name for an Eric Walker. Odd, they observed, since no marked place for Mr. Asura was visible. Agnes Marie set her handbag in her chair and wandered over to view the breakfast spread after talking a bit with Tracey. She spotted Victor entering, greeted by Tracey.

Joe Belton joined them, and longingly looked at their two plates with several slices of crisp bacon already on them. Joe sighed. "Of all my dietary restrictions, I miss bacon the most. But it's definitely not what my doctor would permit me. Not even for an occasional indulgence." He then proceeded to order an omelet with lean chopped ham, mushrooms and spinach.

"No cheese on the omelet, either?," Agnes Marie asked, empathetically. "You're a good man. I couldn't handle those sacrifices. Bacon, egg and cheese just go together, in my mind."

"It was hard for me at first," Joe admitted. "But I'm used to it now. Giving up those things seems to be working. I feel better; and I can breathe much better. So ... here I am."

"Where did Tracey go?," Victor asked, looking around for the detective.

Agnes Marie shrugged and held out her plate for the steaming omelet. "See you guys over at the table. The humongous conference table."

And indeed, the conference table could seat twenty-two, ten seated on each side, with a chair at each end. Agnes had counted the seats that were now arranged around it.

As the two men watched Agnes Marie take her chosen seat, they noticed Eric Walker's bronze name plate. "Looks like we are going to meet somebody new," Victor intoned solemnly to Belton, who pushed up the glasses on his nose and squinted at the name plate. "Somebody new? I can't read the name from here."

"Erik Walker," Victor said helpfully. "Walker. Hey, that's Tracey's last name. Wonder if there's a connection?"

Joe shrugged. "Guess we'll find out." He was slightly miffed to see that Tracey would be sitting elsewhere, and that Victor would be sitting next to him, instead.

Just as the two men were seating themselves, plates in hand, Eric Walker entered the room.

"Mr. Asura!," the trio exclaimed. All were glad to see him, but Agnes was the first to point out that there was no place setting for him, and asked, "Aren't you going to be joining us today?"

"Of course I am," he responded, as he drew out the chair at Eric Walker's place. "And this is my seat." Erik took a moment to enjoy the bewildered look on their faces, then launched into his explanation of the privacy and security needs for the ruse.

"And yes. Yes, I am related to Tracey Walker. She is my daughter. After today, you will be dealing primarily with Tracey and the Bodhi, who are anxious to meet the three of you."

Victor was curious. "How did the two of you end up working together like this, Mr. Walker? Isn't that nepotism?"

"Well, some may view it like that. But private foundations operate under different rules, and many are family endeavors. The Truvenge Foundation is a private charitable foundation operated by three wonderfully mystical Asian gentlemen, born in British India and raised in a British household by Hindu parents who converted to Christianity, and their Hindu aunt. The

British family had an older daughter, and two sons of the same age as the Indian triplets, who were great friends with the three Bodhi – who were known in the Indian community of Calcutta by that collective name, from the moment of their birth – which was considered miraculous, for many reasons."

"What does 'Bodhi' mean, exactly?," Joe asked curiously, pushing his glasses to the bridge of his nose while leaning forward in his seat to better peer around Victor – a much larger man than Joe was – to meet Erik's eyes.

"In Sanskrit," Erik explained, "the word 'Bodhi' means 'perfect knowledge.' And to simplify their names, which In India are bestowed on the sixth day of life and reveal a child's destiny, friends and relatives all simply referred to them as a single entity, the Bodhi."

"What are their actual names?," Agnes asked. "This is helpful to know, since we will each be spending a good amount of time with them today."

"The names of the three Bodhi are *Alivesh Abrer* – who was the first infant to be born; his Sanskrit name means 'truthful person – an investigator.' The second-born was named *Asif Ariv*, who was the smallest boy. His destiny was to be Forgiveness, and he carries the Sanskrit meaning for the King of Wisdom. The last born was the largest of the three infants, and he was called *Aadil Adish*; his destiny was Justice, and to be a King of Wisdom, for he was to be knowledgeable, wise and just. Their mother was told that they would grow up strong and would be very wise. Together, they would be known as 'The Bodhi' and would do great things."

"But Tracey said they were Buddhist," Victor blurted. "I'm confused."

"To be frank, I do not know much about that," Eric confessed. "The Bodhi have not divulged anything about their conversion to Buddhism – at least not to me. While they told me that they had specifically recruited me to run the Truvenge Foundation and the Kriya Project, none of our conversations have been particularly personal. All that I know about their conversion is that they traveled to Nepal and Tibet as teenagers, and the older British boy never returned with them, but became a Buddhist monk. I think he is also still alive. Most of the personal information that I just told you about the Bodhi actually came from Tracey, who has had far more direct interaction with them on a very different level than I have.

"Which brings us back to where this conversation first started. I commenced by answering Victor's question about nepotism and unexpectedly wandered into the history of the Bodhi.

"When I accepted this position and we came to the city a few months ago, I was immediately busy, but Tracey felt lost. I started bringing her to the office to do simple tasks to help April, my assistant. But she had just completed a two-year A.A. – Associate of Art degree in Criminal Justice, and was bored and unhappy doing odd jobs. She'd intended to go on to a 4-year university for a degree, but the cost of non-resident tuition in a New York state threw a kink into her education plans. Some of her tasks included bringing papers and documents to the Bodhi, and, unbeknownst to me, she started to stay and spend increasing amounts of time with them on these visits. They were curious about her, and she was intrigued by them. They acknowledged the value of her education to the organization and recognized skills Tracey has that as her father, I had missed. It happens.

"As part of your training for the Kriya Project you will be taking psychology courses and reading as directed to enhance your native skills. But just from life experience I believe you likely understand that sometimes family members interact in a routine manner that blinds them to talents and characteristics of other family members. People are often not very transparent. And they often reveal different facets of their nature to different audiences."

Victor nodded. "I absolutely agree. The more I think I know about human beings, the more they surprise me. People – some people, at least, are able to compartmentalize. And they are the ones who can be particularly deceptive. Just when you think you know them, they can show an entirely different character; one you never suspected. They make the best con men."

Erik nodded wisely, and complimented Victor on his discernment.

Then Victor added, "But there is always a 'tell' – and I am pretty good at picking up on little clues that tell me when I am listening to bullshit – oops, pardon me, Agnes Marie!"

She laughed, distracting Victor from his rather intense focus on Erik Walker. "You forget I've been in the military," she laughed. "And I have heard far worse."

Victor smiled, then turned his attention back to Erik. "I was in sales. Time is money, and a 'no' is as good as a 'yes.' I had to get good at reading people, picking up on motivation, objections, attitudes. Some people try to appear more important or financially solid than they actually are. Others have something to hide. With me, they are rarely successful."

Victor turned his attention to buttering a biscuit, but Agnes was conscious of the fact that Erik suddenly looked very uncomfortable. Joe was intent on his omelet and oatmeal, and Agnes Marie wondered if he'd even noted a change in the conversational atmosphere.

Because he had been focused on his food, Belton was the most startled when Erik Walker slapped both hands on the table and announced loudly, "Well, Tracey will be here shortly to give you some reading assignments. What you will be given are introductory psychology textbooks to begin reading, today. One by one, each of you will be called in to speak with the Bodhi. You can expect the interview to last at least an hour, perhaps longer. When you return from your interview, April will show you to Tracey's office, where you will be debriefed, and where you will discuss possible roles you will play in effecting justice in each of the petitions we will be addressing over the next one to two months.

"The rest of you will be concentrating on your reading. Feel free to discuss the material you read with your reading companion. It is important that you acquaint yourselves with the psychology of both normal and aberrant behaviors. You will be attending psychology classes each day as the plans to address the petitions are developed by our team. Remember that you are a crucial part of the team. Do not hesitate to share ideas and observations, or even criticisms. It is vital that each plan succeed. And we have but one opportunity to achieve success.

"Most plans are carried out over two months, so you will be totally involved in these two petition projects for the next two months, after which we will spend two weeks in a debrief of your experience and performance, then give you six weeks off – and you will receive compensation during that time off – then you may choose to take on another round of petitions. At all times, we will be in contact with the primary physician overseeing your treatment program and health maintenance, and respect their advice.

"Are there any questions?"

The trio occupied the next half hour asking Erik a variety of questions, until Tracey entered the conference room, followed by April, who was pushing a trolley loaded with psychology textbooks and the course syllabus that would govern their reading. An instructor – actually a practicing psychologist – would hold morning classes on Mondays, Wednesdays, and Fridays for the next two weeks, Tracey informed them. Afternoons would be reserved for physical strength and coordination exercises with a physical therapist, and group discussions on how each plan was to be implemented. It was important to spend time in conversation and bonding with one another, and there would be time to destress and do some fun activities together.

Then Tracey asked, "Who wants to be first to meet with the Bodhi?"

Simultaneously, hands shot up on either side of Erik, who had been diligently writing something down in a notebook while Tracey spoke. Now, he looked up and laughed. Both Agnes Marie and Victor held their hands aloft. Eric then said, "Ladies first, Victor!" And it was settled. Agnes would go first.

Tracey escorted Agnes Marie into the lobby and pressed the elevator button. "The Bodhi's domain is two floors up, past the gymnasium and the classrooms."

"Classrooms?" Agnes was curious. "You have lessons going for more than one group at a time, or different lessons for different people?"

"Yes. And yes," Tracey answered. There are several groups – teams, as we call them - involved with different petitions at any one time. Some participants work on small roles they may have in several petition plans at the same time. Others – those more experienced in working with the Kriya Project - are involved with complex scenarios that require particular expertise or knowledge. Our professional actors often require training in specialized topics, as well. You'll have the opportunity to meet and interact with them, too. They will have parts to play in the two petitions your team will start with. Your trio is quite talented, each in his or her own way. And, overall, your team's health and stamina are very good. Erik and I are hoping the three of you will be with us for a very long time. My job is to make sure your experience with the Kriya Project is continuously interesting, intellectually challenging and spiritually rewarding."

The elevator doors opened, and the exotic odor of incense wafted into their nostrils. "Patchouli?" Agnes asked as she breathed the air.

"Nag champa," Tracey replied. "Tibetan temple incense."

Tracey opened the double doors to the Bodhi's softly lit chamber and led Tracey to the dais where the three Bodhi were seated in the lotus position, eyes closed.

Agnes Marie looked at Tracey quizzically. Tracey silently mouthed, "They are meditating." She reached to pick up a crystal bell on a small table beside the dais, and rang it gently, in three sets of three rings. Then she folded her hands at chest level and waited, head bowed. Agnes followed Tracey's example, and stood with head bowed until she heard three soft voices speaking in unison;

"Ah, Tracey. We are so pleased to see you!" the trio brought their hands together and bowed their heads to Tracey, in greeting. "Namaste, dear friend."

"*Namaste*, my esteemed Bodhi," Tracey said in reply. "I bring you Agnes Marie Walford. She has newly joined the Kriya Project, and volunteered to be the first to meet you."

Agnes looked up and smiled at the three Buddha-like figures before her. She stood straight.

"Agnes Marie, this is the eldest of the Bodhi – but only by a few minutes." Agnes heard the tinkling laughter of the triplets. "This is *Alivesh Abrer*, whose destiny from birth was to be an investigator; a truthful person."

Alivesh nodded at Agnes in greeting.

"And this is *Asif Ariv*, his names stand for Forgiveness, and the King of Wisdom"

Asif piped up, humorously, "I was the second born of three identical brothers. When I issued from my mother's womb, I was also the smallest of the three of us. But I obviously caught up to my brothers, at least in size, "for look at me now." Asif beamed and patted his belly. The brother's tinkly laughter brought smiles all around.

"And lastly," Tracy said, continuing the introductions, "this is *Aadil Adish*, the final son to be born to their mother, Caitri, who believed their birth to be a miracle – the result of prayer to the Christian God. Like Abraham's wife, Sarah, children were absent in her life for many years. Aadil*'s* first name destined him to be a force for Justice.. His second name, Adish, reflects that he was to grow noble, knowledgeable, intelligent, and full of wisdom. Their mother, Caitri, revealed when they were named that she had been informed by the goddess, Vidhaati - the Hindu goddess of destiny - that the boys were to grow strong and wise, and that together they would be forever known as The Bodhi, for their perfect knowledge, which is the meaning of Bodhi."

The Bodhi sat beaming beatifically at Agnes, then together asked, in one voice, "Would you like some jasmine tea?"

Agnes nodded, enthusiastically. She suddenly was parched. "That sounds lovely."

Tracey rang the crystal bell once again, and a server appeared out of nowhere with a pot of tea, a delicate porcelain cup, and a small plate of English biscuits on a silver tray that was set on the small round table to the right of the comfortable- looking leather armchair set before the dais.

"Now I must leave your august company," Tracey told the Bodhi, and turned to Agnes to say, "I'll see you later."

With that, Tracey was gone, and Agnes faced the Bodhi alone.

"Please, be seated," they told her, in unison. "pour some tea. And do not be afraid."

"We do not bite," Asif – Forgiveness - told her, gently; he then grinned, as if delighted with his joke. He may have been the smallest at birth, Agnes thought, but he was certainly the most outgoing.

Asif could have been reading her mind, for he said, "Forgive my humble attempt at American humor. I am often told I am very forward; how do you say? Outgoing. Perhaps too much so for my own good."

She could see that Aadil Adish – Justice – seemed the most dignified and reserved. Alivesh Abrer was the observant one. The investigator – and a truthful person. She could see that his attention was focused on her every move. She imagined he would be more brusque and to the point in his communications.

The room was silent. It appeared it was up to her to initiate the conversation. She needed a safe topic.

After a moment of thought she began, "I am unfamiliar with your ways, but they fascinate me, and I would like to know more. Could you kindly explain to me the meaning of '*Namaste*'? Is it a greeting?"

That should work as an icebreaker, Agnes thought, sweetening her tea and taking a sip. The flavor was divine.

"*Namaste* is both a greeting, and a farewell. It is an ancient Sanskrit word that means "the divine in me recognizes and bows to the divine in you." It is a formal, courteous and respectful greeting to acknowledge a stranger, acquaintance or relative. It is a greeting expressing hospitality and welcome to a guest or to express thanks or gratitude for assistance, or for a favor or a kindness given. The way you are expected to place your hands is called *anjali mudra*, holding your hands fingertip to fingertip and palm to palm, hands pressed together, as if in prayer."

Agnes pressed her hands together as the Bodhi described, and as she had seen Tracy do.

Together the triplets intoned, "Excellent. Very good. Firmly press your open hands together, and point your fingertips to the heavens. And rest your thumbs right at your heart chakra, in the center of your chest, with the thumbs at rest on your sternum. Exactly that way, yes. This is called *anjali mudra*. And when you say, *namaste* to others, you must always say it in the most positive manner, and make a small bow of your head. With your eyes closed. Just so."

The Bodhi clapped their hands together in delight, and Aadil Adish – another Justice - and the most somber of the three brothers, said. "You are a very apt pupil, Miss Agnes Marie Walford. Remember always, that when you say "*namaste*" you are creating a spiritual connection to the person you are greeting. Your positive energy will then create spiritual power in what is known as an auric field - a ring of positive connection, as it were."

The tea was lovely. Agnes poured cup. The Bodhi answered a few questions that she had about India and its history, and then the Bodhi's interview began in earnest. It lasted an hour and a half.

Then they wish Agnes a happy afternoon, and bade her "*namaste*" once again. A servant appeared at her elbow, to escort her to Tracey's office, while another cleared away her tea tray. The Bodhi's murmured conversation was muted by the gossamer curtains that had been silently drawn by a third.

Tracey looked up from her laptop, on which she had been typing away rapidly before Agnes walked in to see her. "Have a seat," Tracey instructed, looking at Agnes intently. "How did it go?"

Agnes flopped into the chair and declared, "The Bodhi very gently put me through the ringer. I have never been through that kind of questioning. It was certainly not what I would call a standard employment interview!"

"Oh?," Tracy asked, casually.

"Yes! No. Not at all." Agnes leaned back in her chair, and locked her fingers together over her waist. She met Tracey's eyes, then glanced around the office and out the window, and watched the boats moving slowly, languorously floating on the glittering surface of the Hudson River. "I like them. I liked them a lot. They taught me about their religions –" she laughed, adding, "at least Hinduism and Buddhism. I think I have a pretty good handle on Christianity! And they told me about India, and Nepal, and Tibet. I mentioned that a trip to Nepal has been on my bucket list for ages! They like that.

"I learned all about the traditional *namaste* greeting, and farewell – how do it properly, and what it means. But most of all . . ." Here, Agnes leaned forward conspiratorially, and lowered her voice to almost a whisper, as she confided in Tracey, "They know more about me than I do myself!"

Tracey chuckled.

"What's so funny?," Agnes Marie asked.

"That was precisely my thought when I walked out of their haven – because you cannot call their work area an office! That they really knew more about me than I could ever have imagined. Perfect knowledge – what their name, Bodhi means. The Bodhi attribute it to their almost constant meditation. When I first started, and the very first time I was introduced to the Bodhi, I did not know what to expect. Eric failed to warn me. I walked into a dimly lit room to see three mysterious figures clad in hooded white robes, heads bowed, and sitting in the cross-legged Lotus position on a woven floor mat on a raised dais, behind a sheer curtain. The hoods obscured their faces in shadow.

"Their 'office' – if you could call it that – was sparsely decorated, with a small sofa, just a few leather armchairs, a small tea table that held a tea tray and a few small trinkets, and a soporific waterfall feature along a side wall covered in stone. Listening to the waterfall has an immediately calming effect."

"I noticed that as soon as I walked in," Agnes noted. "And I must admit, despite all my life experience meeting important people, I was very nervous walking into that interview. The waterfall was much appreciated."

"As soon as we walked in, an assistant promptly rang a small bell at the door, and escorted us past the chairs and onto the dais, where we were motioned to seat ourselves on the mats in front of them. Fortunately, I was wearing jeans that day – something my father hates me to do." Tracey laughed. "But I still do it from time to time. Luckily, my position now allows me to dress casually, on occasion. In fact, it is sometimes necessary to blend in, rather than stand out. I recall that my father rolled his eyes before taking a seat on the floor." She chuckled. "He hates to be inconvenienced like that. It messes up his suit. All in all, it seemed as though we were consulting oracles."

"Were you in a different position at the Foundation at the time?," Agnes asked.

Tracey responded. "I was. And that is part of my experience that relates to yours today. When Erik took the position, he did not consult me. I has just finished coursework in criminology at the local junior college and just received my A.A. degree. My plans were to go on to a four-year state institution. It was all we could afford at the time. The deal was, I could remain at home, but had to pay my own books and tuition."

"A paid education was why I joined the service," Agnes remarked.

"I – we – had just lost my mother, and a move to New York City was the last thing I wanted. To keep me occupied until I figured out what to do with myself after the move, my father had brought me on as an assistant, and his 'go-fer.' It was my duty to screen prospective short-term employees brought on to work with us in the Kriya Project, and the Bodhi asked me to be there for this specific meeting, for some reason. I was nothing special to the organization at the time. My job was pretty clerical. It was purely to eliminate those whose illness had progressed to the point that there was nothing they could possibly offer the program. It was very routine, although I did get to know Felicity quite well when validating the medical status and progress. I talked to her a lot by phone.

"I had only met the Bodhi a handful of times, usually escorting them to or from their limousine when they left the building, or arrived, and I did not know what to make of them. The way they dressed, and talked – it was difficult to discern much about them. All I knew for certain was that they lead the Truvenge Foundation, and that the organization is wholly theirs.

"The Bodhi spoke quietly, in unison "We have been made aware that Miss Felicity has brought us some prospective terminal applicants." It startled me when I first heard them speak in unison. It is so unique. I am still unsure how they manage that. They tell me that the three of them vibrate on the same frequency, and are capable of telepathy."

Throwing her head back in laughter, Tracey added, "They assured me telepathy is a learned skill, and that meditation opens our way to such powers. They keep urging me to meditate. As if I could still my monkey mind long enough to commune with my inner self!

"What is their status currently?" they asked me. "The new applicants, what is their medical status?" I recall being very uncomfortable. I felt as though I was being scrutinized. As if reading my mind, they lowered their hoods, and I was looking at three immensely kind faces. I began my report, going through the files on my lap. Erik excused himself, and left the room, ostensibly for a bathroom break, and the Bodhi kindly asked, "Is something amiss?"

"Well," I started, shifting on the floor, "It's just that none of the new ones really have the capability to perform the tasks we need them to do." I tried not to mumble, but the end of my sentence trailed off. "I have sent out some letters to the employees we already have on file, as Erik requested, but none to the new prospects. There are too many unknown variables for me to feel confident that they are able to work with us. But I have not gotten a call back from Felicity, so I'll need some time to gather more data. Only she can tell me if they are well enough – if they can be counted on to do the work assigned to them."

"Enough about the applicants. We would like to hear of about you." Bodhi responded in their treble voices, hands clasped in their laps. I shifted uncomfortably again. "We know you are terribly unhappy, dear child. You have been quiet this entire time. Perhaps you would like to speak your mind while your father is away?" they murmured, coaxing. I could not help but shake my head, wondering, how could they have determined that?

"And then my father returned.

"The rest of the meeting was mostly a blur. I stayed busy taking down notes as my father and the Bodhi discussed what would be needed for them to bring on more capable applicants to work with the petitions and fulfill jobs. Head down, I almost didn't notice when Erik left the room once again to take a call, until a pale skinned hand reached out towards to me, making me flinch, and lovingly stroked my hair. But when I looked, the three of them were regarding me quietly, their hands folded - palms up - in their laps. None of them had moved. I was immediately flummoxed Who had stroked my hair the way my mother used to, whenever we had heart-to- heart talks?

"Tracey, dear, what is wrong? You are so pale; what is wrong? How may we help?," the Bodhi asked me, to which I replied, "It's nothing."

"It certainly does not seem like merely nothing." The white robed figures watched me, and jointly released a soft sigh. "There is a deep seated fear in your eyes, dear Tracey. What has you so afraid?" they whispered, gently, as though they knew the answer. "Have you been hurt?"

"I gave a quick, curt nod, and cast my gaze to the doorway again, afraid my father would walk in. With a disapproving click of the tongue, and the Bodhi we know as Aadil Adish – Justice - stood up and walked over to the waterfall, watching the water spill musically over the rocks. "There is only one true cure for the pain in one's heart, and that is karma," he told me. The other two Bodhi, watching him, nodded. Aadil turned to look at me. And I watched as his pale pink lips curled into a grin. He then told me, "Karma cleanses the spirit of those who have been harmed."

"I blurted out, "But isn't Karma revenge?" And that is when I learned the true meaning of Karma. I could explain my understanding of karma to you, but I want you to ask them yourself."

"I did ask," Agnes said. "And the answer that I received was beautiful and full of meaning. I have so many questions that I would like to ask the Bodhi, but did not think it was the time. They have long interviews today. Forgiveness – Asif Ariv, did the explaining. We Americans are so crude in our description, but in shorthand, what goes around does come around – often to bite you when least expected. If they weren't such gentle beings, I might have been terrified by the extent of their knowledge. I have been vetted twice for confidential clearances, but never to the depth of what they knew about me. They knew things that I have never discussed with anyone! Things I am not even comfortable discussing here, with you. Do the Bodhi tell you what is discussed in our individual interviews?"

"No reason to fear, Agnes. All I hear from the Bodhi after your interview is restricted to the strengths, weaknesses, talents and aptitudes that they have discerned from your conversation, and from being near your energy. They read your aura – the energy field that surrounds one's body; and they sense from your vibrations much that you may not even recognize in yourself. In my situation, they knew some personal dissatisfactions – and even the reasons for them, which is more than I had known or figured out for myself. They also knew of my terrible boredom at work, of my father's inability to see and utilize my natural talents, of my training and aptitudes – everything. Better than a job counselor! In fact, this position I occupy in the Kriya Project was specifically designed for me, on the basis of that first encounter. I have since become very close to the Bodhi, whom I collectively adore. And they have come to know me as a sister."

"I figured as much – that whatever they figured out about me, and whatever we'd discussed would remain with them. If anything, it would be used to help me become a better and more effective person. We talked a lot about the two petitions, which I preferred and wanted to work with, and how I saw my skills and experience being used. They really wanted to know my ideas for handling each situation to achieve some element of justice. You will hear all of that from them, probably."

"Yes," Tracey replied. "The Bodhi will dictate a full report of your preferences and how they see you fitting into roles in the two petitions we have before us. Our post- interview debrief, as I like to call it, is purely to get your feedback and impressions, and to quiet any fears from dealing with such truly mystical beings. And to address any cultural questions. You have had experience in foreign lands. That makes this much easier for me. But I expect that the two gentlemen will be full of questions.

"In fact, Victor should be about done with his interview and will appear shortly. We will be doing a lot of talking over the next two months, so do not hesitate to ask me anything that will smooth the way for you. You have lots of challenges ahead of you."

Agnes actually encountered Victor on the way out. As she told Tracey later, "I could see the steam rising from Victor's ears as he tore past me, and I immediately sympathized with you!"

Victor was, indeed, furious with Tracey.

"You ambushed me! What the hell kind of organization is this, anyway?," Agnes heard Victor demand, as she left the anteroom to Tracey's office.

"Please have a seat, Victor," Tracey said.

"I'd rather say what I have to say standing up," Victor roared. He paced back and forth in from of her desk, cracking his knuckles. He was obviously stressed, and Tracey figured that was a habit resulting from his distraction and anger. What did the psychology textbooks call it? A 'compensating mechanism to relieve emotions.' Tracey instinctively knew what he needed.

"Can I get you a drink?, she asked.

"What! Tea?," he fired back.

"No," Tracey replied. "You look like you need a real drink. Rum and Coke? Vodka Tonic?"

Victor stopped mid-stride. She was serious.

"Gin and tonic?"

"Gin and tonic, it is. And a few snacks. I'll join you." Tracey buzzed for April and put in the order. By the time Victor had stopped pacing and settled into the chair in front of Tracey's desk a young man had appeared, tray in hand, with two drinks and a bowl of nuts alongside a bowl of salted taco chips. Tracey reached for a drink, raised it to Victor, and toasted, "Cheers! It's five o'clock somewhere!" – then took a sip and addressed Victor. "So, tell me your impressions of the Bodhi."

"They know too damned much. And I don't know how. Did you feed them that information? Did Felicity?"

Tracey shook her head.

"Who did you talk to?"

"No one. You have seen the information we had on you before making the selection. The only information we received about you from others related to Felicity's referral and comments about your interest in the Kriya Project, and willingness to participate, plus your medical records and doctor's prognosis. Everything else came from you, in one way or another."

"Exactly what do you mean by "one way or another?" Victor was now curious. He took a gulp of his gin and tonic.

"Hey, slow down champ," Tracey cautioned. "You only get one of those. Doctor's orders. Now, I don't know how much you know about Indian mysticism . . . "

"Absolutely nothing."

"Well, you will be learning. Fast. The gentlemen who run Truvenge Foundation are Indian mystics. They are triplets, if you remember. And they are deeply involved in their cultural beliefs – all of them Hinduism, Christianity, and Buddhism.

"As you get to know them, if you chose to learn, you will be told about vibrations, and auras, and the energy that each of us emits. Fingerprints of a sort, actually. We in the West have limited our understanding of the earth, our galaxy, and the universe, on the basis of logic, and our five senses. That is actually a very limited way to observe and understand our environment and the individuals who inhabit it. Plus, we have a very limited understanding of ourselves. But even we rely on things which we refer to as 'instinct' and 'gut feelings'- of experiencing chills and goosebumps when facing the unknown, or 'the hair standing up of the backs of our necks' when sensing danger. In all we do, day in and day out, we are emitting clues – 'tells' if you are a poker player.

"We are all born with psychic abilities, according to the Bodhi. Meditation, they tell me, is a means of enhancing those innate abilities that the West does its best to stamp out by the time we enter school. We stifle the insights and observations of children, telling them to 'stop imagining things' and laughing at their 'imaginary friends', while other cultures we see as 'backward' treasure the information obtained from dreams and keep their senses open to sights and sounds that we ignore, laugh at, or explain away.

"I want you to give some thought to your behavior with the Bodhi; the manner in which you spoke, and the things you emphasized. In my experience, they can read people better than anyone I have ever seen."

As they talked, Victor's blustering faded. She told him her story, and watched as understanding sank in.

"Whatever you do," Tracey cautioned, "don't ever, ever lie to the Bodhi, or try to fool them. They will see right through that shit – er, baloney. They value honesty and sincerity above all. They know your intentions before you do. Nothing escapes them."

"I'm gathering that. Now I wish I could go back and redo the interview. I am afraid I was a bit of a jerk. I do have a downside to my charming personality," Victor joked.

"Then I recommend that you attempt to make amends when you next meet. I do not know what you said or how you acted with the Bodhi. But they value honest communication, and will take you in hand to teach you whatever you need or want to know. I expect I will have their recap of your meeting by tomorrow. They provide me with their observation of your strengths and weaknesses, intentions and aptitudes, as they relate to the petition you have chosen to part in, and they assess where and how those can be best applied to achieve the desired end."

Victor had finished his drink and was munching nuts with a studious look on his face. He understood, and from his furrowed brow and he comments he'd made, Tracey was certain he would make good on his promise to speak with the Bodhi to correct the impression he had made.

"I'd better go," he said suddenly. Tracey nodded assent. "Belton should be on his way out of his interview with the Bodhi any minute now," she remarked, looking at her watch.

"Thanks for the drink," Victor said. "Sorry about bursting in like that. I do feel a lot better about things now. Except the impression I left with the Bodhi. But I'll fix that. They do know a lot I'd like to learn. Until later. . ." On that note, Victor left.

Tracey sat for several minutes, eyes closed, and tried to meditate. Even a few minutes to begin with was a start, according to her mystical friends. She had been trying to still her mind for a few minutes every now and then, and she was getting better at it.

As usual, her undisciplined mind wandered. She wondered how Joe was doing with the Bodhi. Tracey anticipated that his reaction would be the most difficult to deal with. As the minutes ticked away, she wondered what was going on, and why he was not yet out of the interview.

Returning not long after these thoughts crossed her mind, Joe knocked hesitantly on the door frame to her office. Tracey had been meditating, eyes closed. She opened her eyes when he tapped on the metal frame. He stood with a frown on his face, and she motioned him toward the chair by her desk.

"Sorry to interrupt your nap," Joe said. "But I believe we should start our meeting promptly now. I have some calls to make in a little bit, and I have work that needs attention now, with all the reading. I have a few things I need to stay on top of yet."

Tracey slowly opened her eyes and told him, "I was meditating while I waited for you to show up, Joe. She invited him to take a seat and asked, "How did it go?"

"I'm not into that voodoo stuff. Those guys are strange. I don't think I want to deal with them again."

Joe cleared his throat, and looked away as his face reddened, and his hands shook while adjusting the canula in his nostrils.

"Voodoo is an African religion, practiced predominately in the Caribbean. As has been explained in our meetings, Joe, the Bodhi are mystics from India."

"Yeah – that mystic shit – uh, sorry. Mystic stuff. Meditation and that kind of thing. It just gives me the creeps. And they talk together, like they are programmed. Definitely creepy.

"Oh? What was the problem, Joe? That the Bodhi knew things about you that you've never told anyone?"

Tracey was smiling at him, chuckling - which totally disconcerted the poor man. "Now you're laughing at me!," he accused Tracey.

"No, Joe," she explained, "It's that you are just the third person to tell me that in the last four hours. I felt that way at first, also. The Bodhi are very spiritual. They have spent their lifetimes studying the secrets of the soul, and the abilities that all humans possess, but are unaware of and do not cultivate."

"Huh? How old are they anyway? They have no wrinkles."

"The Bodhi are triplets," Tracey replied. "From what I can tell, based on their childhood history in India, and from my research, they were born around 1930. That would make them around 90 years old. But they spend little time in the sun, and therefore their skin is undamaged by the solar rays that cause wrinkles and dark sunspots.

"I have the opportunity to speak often with them, and they are very open with me. They have taught me much. And they will teach you a great deal, as well, Joe - if you open your mind to new information, and to what they have to offer. The Bodhi have explained to me that everyone has a level of vibration, depending on how dependent they are on what they believe is a solid, material earth. Those of use with lower vibrations trust only things that can be seen, heard, smelled, tasted or touched. But the world, and our universe, are not as we have been taught.

"We are all composed of energy, energy that vibrates, and in vibrating we are emitting information about ourselves with every encounter we have with other human beings. It's like when you walk into a room where there has been an argument, and you can sense the tension in the air. Or you can sense when someone is emitting dark energy, and cannot be trusted, or has a criminal mind. Further, it is common for identical twins, triplets, and even close friends to be – as we call it – 'on the same wavelength.' The Bodhi shared their mother's womb for nine months, and they have never been apart since birth. They grew up together and decided to follow a spiritual life while still in their teens. Their vibrations share the same resonance, and they have perfected a form of telepathy between them, so that at any moment they are fully aware of what each is thinking. That is how they manage to talk in unison. However, they do speak singly as well, and have their own thoughts."

"I know that. They are different, but the same. The one they call Justice is particularly critical."

"Aadil Adish."

"Yeah. He is particularly critical. And the Investigator. . ."

"Alivesh Abrer."

"Man, he's the one who knew *everything* about me. Stuff so private I knew it could not have come from

Felicity – or you, even though I've heard you are an outstanding detective. It kind of worries me . . ."

"Don't worry, Joe. Your interview with the Bodhi is between you and them. They are very discrete. All I get is a dictated report that is their observation of strengths and weaknesses, talents and aptitude, and how they see your potential role or roles in the petitions we are considering. Anything more personal than that are the characteristics and actions that they can help you change, improve, develop, or resolve. In future private meetings, they may use their knowledge of you in their wisdom, only for your benefit. Their mission is to help, not to hurt."

"Except those who might need punishment?"

"Except to assist those who have intentionally harmed others to come face to face with their karma at some point during the lifetimes of those they have harmed. To bring closure to their victims, so they can release the hurt, the anger, or depression caused by the malice of another."

"I have to admit I don't quite understand Karma. But I do understand revenge. Except, having to drag this oxygen around everywhere, I don't know how I can do a great deal."

"Numbers, Joe. You know numbers. And accounting is a very important function. Indispensable, in fact. And in western society, a potent weapon, indeed."

"When I first spoke alone with the Bodhi, I felt much as you do. Frightened that anyone knew so much about me without ever being told - verbally, at least. Set your normal reactions aside, my friend. What you are about to embark upon is a journey that cannot be considered normal at all."

Chapter 9 – Death of a Dream

Quirky Lewis – "Quirk" to his close friends - had a dream. An actual dream. A "while you are asleep" kind of dream.

Now, Quirky was not one to attribute meanings to dreams. But the idea presented in the dream intrigued him. And as the weeks went on, he could not get that dream out of his mind.

That dream was one of candy: a flavored, rainbow drop that one could eat, but that changed flavors as you ate the goodie. He imagined chewing on a gummy and experiencing a burst of flavor the moment it was bitten into. A combination of compatible flavors that then dissolved into a third, unique flavor. A candy that tasted like a rainbow.

But Lewis didn't know a single thing about making candy. He was a banker. He could tell you anything you wanted to know about money, but when it came to the candy industry, he didn't know the first thing. He *did* know how to market, however.

And he realized that he would need to create an actual product - a prototype - before he could do much else. And so he searched, and pitched his idea to contract manufacturers, one after another. But the majority of those with whom he spoke quite frankly thought he was crazy, and told him so. It had never been done before; it would require specialized equipment; it would cost too much; it simply couldn't be done! And it probably would never sell. A gummy candy for adults? That changed flavors? Impossible.

"An idea like this will never make it in the industry! The ultimate product will cost too much. The market only supports certain pricing for the various types of candy. It won't break even on production and distribution expenses, unless you create huge volume," they told him. "And that will never happen with a gummy candy – not even one that elaborate."

Lewis didn't give up though. He knew, *knew,* that it was a good idea; that would make millions. If only he could get someone to believe him!

While Quirky was on the hunt for a company that could make the sweets his imagination had created, he decided that perhaps if he hyped his idea to the public, he could win someone to his side. While he'd been told that a product like his would never become popular, he instinctively knew that it would.

Newspaper ads, commercials, radio interviews, television interviews! He dove into his savings, sparing no expense to hype his imagined confection. He talked to candy store owners and candy cooks to get input and feedback. Colorful, mouth-watering images were created by an artist friend, and he wrote the verbiage - then he went fishing. Lewis published his brief, illustrated articles on various sites, and trusted his fate to the Internet.

He got a bite a little over a week later. Thrilled, he contacted the interested party.

"We've seen your articles and publicity for this crazy candy idea of yours," a man who'd introduce himself as Mr. George Fitz said over the phone, "and we are interested in helping you manufacture it." Lewis couldn't believe his luck. "We are definitely interested. The idea is intriguing, and we want to make it for you.

Or at least attempt it. I believe we have all of the equipment that's needed. Gummy candies are our best sellers. We have extra capacity at the moment, and were looking for another line to manufacture. There's just the little issue of the contract itself."

"I've considered that," Lewis responded, nervously rubbing the back of his neck while he held the phone to his ear. "I want to name the product, control the marketing, and keep the rights to the trademark. But we'll split all profits the candy brings in."

Negotiations on the profit split went easily, and soon candy production was at full speed. Mr. Fitz had assumed that the candy would just be a fad, easy enough to produce and offering a possibility to make a quick buck, until the product failed to take hold and started losing money for the inventor. Fitz knew that candy was a tough, highly competitive business, with big players. An amateur with a wild idea and no backing didn't stand a chance at success.

Multiple attempts were made to materialize the dream in the form of a delightful confection. Each production run was an improvement over the last one, so they persisted, with Quirky's most loyal friends acting as taste testers. Finally, they developed a means of production and a few recipes that filled the bill. The first was a lime-watermelon flavor; the next a pineapple-cherry, and the hunt for unusual flavor combinations continued as the candy went into full production. They named the confection Rainbow Gummy Drops.

Quirky already had marketing plans in place, and started selling Rainbow Gummy Drops in boutique grocery stores, ice cream shops, and the like.

Neither Quirky nor the George Fitz Candy Company, however, truly anticipated just how popular the sweet confection would become in the following weeks and months.

In no time at all, the product started to fly off the shelves. Quirky Lewis built an identity as the "Candy King," an alter-ego complete with Court and Crown, and his quick vignettes and Royal Festivals took hold in the popular imagination. Lewis held kingly pageants with fake jousting tournaments on toy horses that rolled, complete with troubadour bands and regal balloons, plus loads of samples to be distributed. It was a festive, family environment that garnered local media attention and developed loyal followers and participants.

Lewis was endowed with tireless energy, an engaging personality, clever patter and a great idea. Candy magazines reviewed the confection highly. State and local media trumpeted the novel candy, lauding the many flavors. Outlets that carried the confection at the beginning included ice cream and candy shops, mom & pop grocery stores, toy and novelty shops and eventually, high end grocers kept increasing their orders.

Quirky Lewis built a website for the candy, featuring giveaways, games, prizes, and a flavor of the month, and sold it directly to customers via mail order. The masses demanded it, clamored for it, and in less than a year, Rainbow Gummy Drops had become a common name in households across the nation. Both Quirky and the George Fitz Candy Company began to benefit from the increasing sales; but within 18 months, the Fitz contract manufacturing candy company could barely keep up with the volume of orders. New equipment was ordered, and a factory addition was built to house it. One entire section of the candy factory was devoted exclusively to the production of Rainbow Gummy Drops.

A phenomenon in the candy market, nothing could compete with the gummy drops. Imitators tried, but nothing even came close in sales. Or in taste. Kids loved it. Adults loved it. There was no comparison. Rainbow Gummy Drops focused on constantly developing and introducing new flavors, while retaining the most popular ones, and Lewis kept up the public pageants and media appearances. His persona took on a life of its own – and that further increased sales.

Lewis was at a loss for words as he watched the brand blossom, and as serious money began to roll in on a regular basis. He bought a larger house in a better neighborhood, and took lavish vacations, combining marketing efforts with every aspect of his new life.

Had he really been as lucky as this? Had he won the 'idea lottery' that every so often saw a daydream take off in nationwide sales?

Once in a lifetime, one idea – that's all it takes. He had always believed that, but Quirky kept pinching himself to test whether it was all real, or just a fantasy.

He'd left a stable, sedate banking career behind. Promoting his candy invention became everything to him. And with its popularity, he became an affluent man, while having the time of his life. He upgraded his lifestyle again, and bought a huge oceanfront spread near Malibu where he worked from home, when he was not on the road. Distributors came to him, as did the media.

As he relaxed in his lounge chair beside the pool, replying to emails on his laptop, his assistant - hired weeks prior to help him manage this new way of life - seemed to magically appear out of nowhere whenever a new idea stuck, ready to note down his instructions and make the necessary contacts. It was a bit startling how well she managed to do such a thing, Lewis thought. She was pleasant, efficient, and always gave him a cheerful enough smile to brighten his day.

"Mister Lewis, it seems that you have an interview scheduled in fifteen minutes with *Confection* magazine. They're wishing to write an article about you. Did you let it slip your mind?," she would remind him, a manicured nail tapping away at her tablet.

"Mr. Lewis. I was contacted by a reporter for Entrepreneur Magazine an hour ago, and went ahead and checked your schedule. You have an appointment for tomorrow at eleven." Lewis could not help the look of panic that crossed his face, eyes going wide at the announcement.

Struggling to get up from his recliner and stand, he set the laptop aside and shook his head at her. "I can't do that! The company chemist is going to need me to review his new flavor sample tomorrow, and I can't afford to spend time in traffic!"

"I knew you had that meeting in the early afternoon. Luckily for you, this is just a Skype interview. Nothing requiring much preparation, or - heavens forbid - a drive to a studio in traffic! But you *will* have to wear a shirt and pants. And I recommend taking the call indoors."

Lewis couldn't believe his luck. If he remembered correctly, these would be important interviews; one with a top candy magazine, the other with a general business magazine that would likely increase demand for Gummy Rainbow Drops. He could point out what a great business gift the delightful candy would make. It would really bring Rainbow Gummy Drops on center stage in the minds of the public. Who knew his "crazy" concept would take off like it had? Celebrities were actually naming it as their favorite candy treat in 'Q & A' interviews in magazine and on television! Quirky chortled. He was getting top-of-the-line publicity and celebrity testimonials now, without spending a dime!

Of course, the interviews went as smoothly as could be desired. Quirky had charisma, passion, excitement. He loved his creation, and the public did, too. They also loved the character he had created, the "Candy King." His persona was what drew people in. Of course, the delicious candy he promoted had now started to sell itself. But people enjoyed the face he had attached to it, as well. Lewis now had two writers who helped him with publicity ideas, and helped him write and produce the now-televised commercials as well. He was the much-beloved "Candy King." Children and adults called out to him at publicity pageants, and he had to admit he liked the sound of his fictitious name, "Candy King" and delighted in the cheer his events brought to people.

Not even four years into production, just as the "Candy King" was getting comfortable with his newfound fame, and being able to offer his family safety and security, and fulfill some of their dreams at last, Lewis got a call from the President of his contract manufacturing company, Mr. Edward Fitz.

Quirky noted, when the caller was announced by his assistant, that Fitz had gotten a promotion. Wonder what happened to his old man, Quirky thought idly as he took the call. No one had notified him that there had been a change in management.

The old fellow probably retired, Quirky thought.

Lewis held on as the call was connected, and Quirky launched into hearty congratulations, saying, "A call from the new President of my contract manufacturer! Well, I am impressed! Congratulations, Mr. Jason Edward Fitz! What did I do to deserve this?"

"Yes. Well hello, Quirky. What can I say? My father passed away. I'm the oldest son, and was next in line to succeed him. But that is not why I called. I'm afraid it's quite urgent, Quirky."

Those were the words with which Fitz began the call. They would be seared forever in Quirky Lewis' memory.

Fitz claimed urgency, but sounding exceedingly calm. That alone set Quirky on guard.

"How soon can I have you in my office?"

"I'm very sorry to hear about your father, Jason. George Fitz was a really good man. Salt of the earth. I'm really sorry to hear he passed. But about the urgency. Has something gone wrong in production? Is there a problem with the new Rainbow Gummy Drop flavor we're rolling out?"

"It's important," Fitz replied. "But I'd rather discuss it in person. How soon can you get here?"

"I'll be there as soon as I can!," Lewis said, trying to suppress the panicked note he detected in his own voice. "I'll drive up tomorrow."

As he arrived at the manufacturing facility the next day, assistant in tow, there was nervous sweat on Lewis' brow. Something didn't sit well with him. Doubly so, as he walked into Mr. Jason Edward Fitz's office, and was met by a broad smile on the young man's face. That immediately had Quirky concerned. If there was something wrong with the candy, or if there was a serious production issue, he doubted Fitz would be smiling quite so cheerfully.

"Quirky Lewis, my man! Glad you could join me here so promptly," young Mr. Fitz greeted him. He and Quirky shook hands, then Fitz left Quirky standing as he took a seat behind his desk and clasped his hands together as he leaned forward, his elbows on the desk. Lewis shifted awkwardly in the seat directly across from Fitz, sweaty palms rubbing against his nicely pressed slacks. He recalled sitting in that same chair under entirely different circumstances, and saw himself happily shaking hands with Jason's father, George.

"I've called you here today to let you know that I believe we need to review our previous contract. It was executed some years ago, when my father was in this seat, and quite frankly, at the time, neither of us thought your idea had staying power, never mind ever achieving this degree of success."

Eyes wide and jaw slack, Lewis' nervousness was slowly turning to confusion. "I don't understand, Edward. May I still call you Edward? Or do you prefer Jason these days? Edward is a rather old-fashioned name!

"I use Jason nowadays. My father always called me Edward, and I hated the name. You can also address me as Mr. Fitz.

"Well, look, Jason. I offered to discuss changing the profit percentage some time ago, but you and your father both said everything was fine as first negotiated. We agreed the contract we'd been working from had been just great for both of us! Is it the money? We can renegotiate the split of profits if you're worried about that, or increase the production fees if your costs have risen."

Jason Fitz sighed loudly, and shook his head. He rose from behind the desk and moved to the window, forcing Quirky to contort painfully in order to follow his movement. Fitz clasped his hands behind his back as he rocked on his heels and stared out the window. "Well, I suppose it is about money after all . . . You see, Lewis, we've supported your effort completely, buying more equipment and expanding our facilities to accommodate your increased demand for product. While we encouraged your growth, we have had to absorb those costs . . ."

"Yes," Quirky remarked, speaking to Fitz's back and thinking, the man doesn't even have the decency to look me in the eye! What skullduggery is this?

"Yes, you have, Edward – I mean, Jason. But that new equipment, the factory expansion and the recent addition are *your assets*, not mine. They can be used for your other manufacturing purposes, other products. You're benefitting from the depreciation, and if well-maintained, that equipment will still be functioning twenty-five years from now, if not longer. Besides, I was never consulted about any of those expenditures, or even told that they were driven by increased demand for Rainbow Gummy Drops! How can you hold that against me?"

"We aren't. Not at all. Actually, since my father's demise, I've been doing some thinking. Now that I am in charge here, I've decided that I want to buy the trademark from you for Rainbow Gummy Drops." Mr. Fitz turned, a slow smile growing on his face. Lewis felt as though he had been punched in the gut. Rage bubbled up, but he choked it down. Hands balling up into fists in his lap, he stood with enough force to knock his chair over backwards behind him.

"There is no way I'll sell you the trademark! It's registered to ME!" Quirky shouted, slamming both fists down hard on the wood desk. But Mr. Fitz hardly flinched. In fact, the man laughed.

"I'd be careful what you say, Quirky. We are in a negotiation here, in case you hadn't noticed. And you need to listen to my offer. After all, the fate of the Rainbow Gummy Drops rests with my factory. You do not have the recipes. I do. Can you prove you own the recipes, the flavor formulas? You don't have the facility, or the equipment, nor the manufacturing know- how, or the wherewithal to recreate all this, which was built by my family over nearly a century and a half of sweat, toil and sacrifice. And without the flavor formulas – the recipes – how can you even take your candy to another contract manufacturer? You just have a trademark Lewis. And a clever marketing schtick."

Quirky Lewis knew he was right. His heart sank. One wrong move, and it would be all over. His candy dream would become a candy nightmare, and everything would be lost. Without deep pockets, he was on the losing side of this argument. But what an unethical snake Edward Fitz was! Edward. Jason. Whatever the hell he was calling himself these days!

"Your father would be ashamed of you today!," Quirky Lewis declared in his fury.

"My father is no longer here to hold me back, or to criticize my decisions," Fitz retorted, angrily. "Leave him out of this. My father had a penchant for collecting strays – people who needed him. He relished their gratitude. Bathed in it. He thought he was buying his way into heaven with good deeds. You needed him, Lewis. You had no one else. And you were grateful. And now he is gone, and I am making the decisions around here. I'm a businessman to the core. I do not get carried away with sentiment.

"It's quite simple, you know, Lewis. We'll just write up a new contract, giving over the trademark to my company, and we'll continue sharing profits, in a fashion. I will buy the trademark from you for the sum of two million dollars, paid out over fifteen years. That's $100,000 a year, and you can still work somewhere, or use the money to fund another bright idea! It should carry you to retirement. The payment will be governed by contract. I am committing to pay out that amount, come hell or high water. After all, candy fads come and go. So I'm taking a fifteen-year risk that the candy may diminish in popularity over time. At the end of the contract, we go our merry ways. For a time, you can keep up promoting it as the "Candy King," which you've said you enjoy. For the duration of our contract we will continue a homage to the original creator, so that the candy's origin doesn't completely fade into obscurity." Jason Edward Fitz laughed again.

Gritting his teeth, Lewis glared at the man who had moved back behind the desk. The kid was taunting him, and not taking him seriously at all. There was an outstretched hand, waiting for him to shake it, but Quirky Lewis ignored it entirely.

"I'll never sell the trademark to you. You'll never have it, Edward Fitz!" Quirky snarled, and headed for the door.

There was a sneering laugh from Fitz. "They always say that, Lewis. Little people in this business think they can stand up against a smart man building an empire. You're no different. You'll be back in a week. In fact, I think I will give you three days to give me your answer, or the offer is off the table, and I simply stop working for you, and start manufacturing the candy myself, under another name. Remind me again ... You never did keep a copy of the recipes, did you, Quirky?"

"No. I trusted your father, your company! We had an agreement, and it was working for both of us. When I broached increasing payments to your company, both you and he told me not to worry – everything was working out just swell for everyone involved. I TRUSTED HIM. I TRUSTED YOU!"

"Tsk, tsk. And that was your second mistake, Lewis. You had an agreement with my father. I am not my father. You have no recipes. Without them, you cannot even go to another manufacturer. The company is now mine, and so are the recipes. You have three days to give me an answer. Monday morning by noon, I expect to see you return to sign the documents. All in all, I think it's a pretty fair offer, considering you have no product to leverage. All you have is a trademark, which I am willing to purchase from you for two million dollars."

"Yeah, paid out over fifteen years! That's peanuts!"

"Who knows how well Rainbow Gummy Drops will continue sell? The public is so very fickle. And we *are* assuming all costs and risks of distribution and, possibly, advertising."

"But it's Friday afternoon! I need a lawyer! How am I supposed to find a … a lawyer? On a Friday afternoon!! You've given me no time at all, Edward!" "Jason. It's Jason. See you Monday morning, Quirky, ready to sign."

Chapter 10 – Getting Down to the Nitty-Gritty

"Sequestered!!! You mean, like a jury? Stuck in a hotel somewhere?" "What? I have a dog! Who's going to take care of my dog? I can't do that!"

"Well, *you* can kennel your dog at some dog-sitting place, Victor!" Joe retorted. What about me? What am I going to do about my oxygen?? I have to have my oxygen! And medicine!"

"Sequestered – that means we cannot talk to anyone. Really! For how long? And where?" Agnes Marie asked.

Tracey waited calmly for the consternation to die down. This was not unusual. Most Kriya Project participants responded identically. She was used to it. She imagined that those conscripted to serve on juries reacted in the same manner, as well, when learning they would have to be sequestered for the duration of a major trial.

"Sequestering our teams is a normal procedure when we get to the point in handling a petition resolution that the serious work begins. You will find our accommodations, here in the building, are quite pleasant – actually the level of a four- or five-star hotel.

"You will each be assigned a room. A suite, actually. Living and sleeping areas are large, comfortable, nicely appointed and well decorated. They are like studio apartments. Each room has a small kitchenette, but room service is 'on the house'. We will also be meeting for dinners from time to time. You must pay for cocktails or wine, but all else is gratis, including lodging. We have a library. We have a gym and separate spa for exercise and spa services, including grooming, hair styling, massage, all that. In fact, the gym is where my yoga master teaches me kriya yoga, twice a week, and I am certain you can participate, and learn the practice with us, if you choose. It can be arranged. There is a pool, a running track, a rooftop garden with outdoor swings, lounge chairs ... And yes, Victor, you can bring your dog, as long as it is housebroken, and well behaved. You can walk him in the garden on the roof top. There is a sunning area up there, as well, Agnes, so you can keep your tan, and relax outdoors. And Joe, we are constantly checking in with your doctor, who can make house calls either in person or by video conferencing. There's a pharmacy down the block for prescription and oxygen refills or other necessities. And we have a personal shopper should you need items, or to help you create your specific wardrobe for the job. You will want for nothing.

"We will have amusements for you, as well. Movies and sports events to watch in the small movie theater. Puzzles, cards, board games and a pool table in the game room. There is a piano. I understand you play, Victor?"

"I do."

"You'll have to play for us sometime."

"How long is this necessary?" Agnes Marie asked. "And for how long?"

"You have to all complete your general preparation to undertake this work. Each time you work on a petition, together or separately, there will be a period of becoming acquainted with the situation, learning the basic elements of a plan, and studying for your potential or assigned roles. During this time, we will be adjusting the plan, tailoring it specifically to you and accommodating whatever strengths or weaknesses each one of you may have in approaching a particular role. You may stay at home during this period with no difficulty. However, once we get down to the real nitty-gritty, putting the plan together, it is like preparing for a play. A very important play that must be carried out flawlessly. And at Truvenge, the Kriya Project is most successful when the participants on a team can work very closely with one another, at whatever time most closely approximates the times when you will be "onstage" - as that acting term might apply to this line of work. Plus, I stay here during that time, as well, so that I am available to you 24/7.

"The closeness facilitates communication, gives you my complete support, provides access to other factors, people and things necessary to the "production" of the event – the costumers, the actors, the equipment."

"Will our contacts be limited?"

"Yes, but primarily to ensure that you are available and at your best when preparing for, or carrying out the assignments, and that our time is utilized most efficiently and effectively. It also prevents any accidental encounters that might jeopardize the job. Folks you haven't seen in a while, for instance, who may want to grab some lunch on the spur-of-the-moment, or have a follow-up meeting when you are busy, or someone who needs to "catch up" – to learn exactly what you are doing these days. Curiosity has killed many a cat – and it goes both ways. Also problematic are those situations where you may encounter people whom you might run into later, while undertaking the assignment in another guise. Inconvenient encounters at the time of an assignment that involve someone's recognition of you as yourself, in particular, have been problematic in the past.

Hard to explain what you are up to and why you cannot talk with them. This can possibly put you in danger. As well. Cornered people, paranoid people can be unpredictable.

"So, with all those potential difficulties, we devised sequestering as the best solution - a way to avoid such incidents, as well as a variety of lesser problems like others interfering in your routine, accidents or traffic tie-ups while trying to get here early each morning, and conversations that are excessively prying and put you on the spot. All elements of what we are working on are strictly confidential and held close to the vest until executed, and forever thereafter. Discretion is absolutely crucial. As that WWII saying goes, "Loose lips sink ships." If you do encounter someone you know and get into an awkward situation we will debrief you to see if plans will have to be changed as a result. It will be a while before you'll be permitted to speak with anyone outside this tight circle, I'm afraid. At least two months. I hope you understand why."

Tracey looked from face to face, making direct eye contact and holding it to be sure her words had sunk in.

"Any questions?" Tracey asked. "None? Then let's get down to work. I am sure there will be plenty later, but I assure you we ask this of everyone. We are going to start by going over the rough outlines of what we will be doing to respond to the petitions. Joe will have a lot of research to do to begin with, so I will start with his project. You two will be involved in something far more complex, in terms of "moving parts," while Joe's job is going to require him to be desk-bound and use his detective skills with the telephone to track this miscreant down and build on the basics of the plan.

"Because we must all be cognizant of what is going on with every one of the team, Joe, I want Victor and Agnes Marie to sit in on our discussion, even though the plan that's been developed, with your input and the wisdom of the Bodhi, is going to be very specialized - right up your alley, in fact, and will depend a great deal on your professional expertise in forensic accounting - they may have some walk-on parts in the little drama you are going to create for our errant building contractor.

"As both of you probably already know, Agnes, Victor, our mild mannered friend here," Tracey smiled at Joe Belton while gesturing in his direction, "is a highly reputed forensic badass, or was in his day, and is quite used to tracking down malefactors and reading their game from columns of numbers and sequences of transactions. He also knows the U.S. Tax Code inside out, and six ways to Sunday. What Joe told the Bodhi as they were working together to develop the punishment framework within which we intend to trap this Ace Hollander, allegedly a certified building contractor, par excellence – if you believe his advertisements and customer solicitations - is that we can trace his movements in a number of ways that are related to his purchases of building materials, and how he paid for them, as well as how he accounted for them in his tax filings. According to the victims, Ace Hollander is the name he consistently uses as he moves from state to state, ripping off the elderly in need of repairs and young and innocent couples just trying to take a fixer- upper and turn it into the kind of home where they could raise a family. Those seem to be his primary victim groups, right, Joe?"

"Yeah," Joe responded. "Exactly. When I spoke with several of the victims named in the petition, they all recalled his name, after prodding their memories. It's distinctive; not the kind of name you easily forget. It seems apparent that he moves around so often that he doesn't bother to use aliases. Perhaps it's hubris, or perhaps he somehow feels protected from consequences. Right now, I'm still just getting started on my investigation. I'm trying to pinpoint the cities and towns where he's been scamming people, trying to understand how he purchases and pays for his building materials. Build a pattern of his moves.

"When a contractor buys necessary building materials, he has to provide either a Social Security number or an EIN – Employer Identification Number. We need to learn if the number he uses is consistent. I have a friend with Internal Revenue Service tax enforcement, in the business sector. I've worked with him before. Rob may be able to do a few favors for me if I can bring him another scalp. I have helped him nail a few cheats, so he respects what I do, and how I do it. If I can get one of those tax- related numbers from Ace's business receipts, my friend may be able to suggest some ideas to help us locate the fellow's permanent or last filing address and anticipate where he is headed next.

"You may or may not be aware of this, but the IRS has a Whistleblower Office, and a formal policy that rewards informants for turning in tax cheats, if done properly. Based on the value of information they furnish, informants to the IRS can get cash rewards. If the IRS uses information provided by the whistleblower, it can award 15 to 30 percent of the additional tax, penalties and other amounts it collects from those who fail to pay taxes they owe.

"Maximum reward is $100,000. In terms of an IRS tax recovery, that equates to a collection total of approximately $9 million."

Vincent whistled. "Wow! A tidy little sum . . .

Agnes was curious. "You mean, Joe, if I suspected a person or business was a tax scofflaw, I could turn them in anonymously, and collect a reward?

Laughing, Joe replied, "It's not that easy, Agnes Marie! Thank heavens! Could you imagine how swamped the IRS would be if they had to track down every suspected incident of tax fraud or non-payment, whether validly predicated or simply malicious? As it is, the IRS receives about 87,000 reports annually under this provision. Before you make any moves to turn in a tax cheat you must be absolutely certain you know what you're doing.

"First off, a tax whistleblower is not anonymous. To start the process, you need to file a Form 211 – and that cannot be done anonymously, since it must be signed with your legal name, and then filed, although you can ask that your name not be publicized. You also have to provide solid evidence – which means you either must be in a position to specifically know the particulars of any wrongdoing, or have completed an investigation of some sort to acquire the information detailing the crime. The key to a successful referral of any tax cheat is solid evidence, documentation to back your report. It's suggested that you work with an attorney, and file your information through that individual, since scofflaw reports prepared by or professionals are more likely to be given credence, and prompt follow-up.

"But being a tax informant can be mentally, physically and professionally dangerous, if not terminal. Individuals who cheat on their taxes are breaking the law. You can be outed. And vengeance can take many forms, including being blackballed professionally, closing all doors to future work in your industry. Also, you know the world is full of thugs for hire and hitmen who have no compunction in roughing someone up – or worse."

"Humans are creatures of habit. Most contractors have certain preferences in the materials they buy – usually because of cost, or ease of use and results they like. When purchasing, there's usually a good deal of interaction with sales staff. If I can examine some of his work – houses he has worked on - I may be able to pick up information to track down sales of large quantities of these items, tracking vendors in the towns or regions where he has done work. Staff may recall their interactions, have his address at the time. Once I establish a purchasing pattern, I can dig up more information, like determining the specific geographical locations where he has been working, and the time frame when he was there, based on delivery information. I can find that by isolating the brands he uses and the manufacturers and distributors of the particular materials he uses. Once I can discern his movements from his orders, I'll find a progression, find out his most current location, and learn if he's currently building. Then perhaps I can interview folks who have dealt with him and anticipate where he's going next. The Idea is to get there ahead of Ace, and manage my referral to Hollander from an as yet undetermined "local acquaintance" who will sell him on my wizardry and expertise in tax law, and numbers, and with the best ways to effectively utilize the Tax Code to his financial benefit. That individual will promote my accounting services, and me, as being someone who can save him big dough.

"A fair deal of travel and leg work will be required, which I can manage, as long as I know where to get my oxygen refills. This is obviously a work in progress, with lots of digging involved. But you have the right person on the job to nail this guy. I am an excellent researcher, and I can't wait to dig into this, Tracey!"

"Point of inquiry, Joe; Have you turned in a lot of tax evaders? What happened to the money – if you were awarded anything ..." Agnes was honestly curious.

And Joe was forthright in his answer. "Excellent question, Agnes. When I work forensically for individuals and organizations on matters such as this – and it happens often in embezzlement cases and securities cases – I negotiate a contract. As part of the agreement, I specify that I will be filing information with the IRS, if it appears that taxes should have been paid and tax-related laws have been broken. Then we negotiate a fair split of any reward. The potential reward keeps the organization interested and cooperative, and it spurs me to keep working harder to zero in on the miscreant."

"You will have a traveling companion, Joe. Truvenge will give you an assistant to travel with you, help you with luggage, and act as your secretary and go-fer to assist in your investigation," Tracey told him. "It is important that you succeed. After all, Al Capone was brought down by tax evasion – not extortion, or his many murders."

Vincent offered to assist Belton with some of the digging whenever possible, and Agnes Marie followed suit, "since our tasks will likely be a good deal less cerebral. And we may have a good deal of 'down time' between assigned tasks. We can make calls, send emails, gather information. You have a big job to do in a short amount of time.

"Thanks, guys. Tracey – what can I say? You're a peach!"

Joe gathered his belongings and set off in the direction of the office down the hall from Tracey's that she had given him to use as his headquarters for the duration. Tracy then turned her attention to Agnes Marie and Vincent.

"Okay, gang. It's down to business. Let's discuss the plan you two will be carrying out for Kriya Project – at least, as it has been developed so far with the Bodhi, and with your input. We will have to start working on it and adapt our planning as we proceed.

"The plan centers on a carnival that we – the Truvenge Foundation – that we will be sponsoring in town within about two months. It will be here for one week.. The plan must be fully executed by the time the carnival strikes its equipment to leave town. That timeline sets the parameters of our task, which will center on the Ferris wheel."

"Ferris wheel!"

The duo sitting with Tracey was incredulous.

Agnes laughed, "I haven't been on a Ferris wheel since I was 18!"

"What does a carnival have to do with what *we* have to do?" Victor demanded. "What the heck are we supposed to do with a Ferris wheel?"

Tracey was amused. "The Ferris wheel is going to be the tool we use to deliver justice."

"How?" Agnes Marie and Victor asked, in unison, genuinely curious.

"Well, the Bodhi feel that fear is a powerful motivator. The damage done in this situation, the Candy

King's petition, has certainly been devastating to Quirky Lewis, financially. The primary damage, however, has been emotional.

"In the Bodhi's estimation, emotional damage deserves an emotional response. They divined that over their many years on this earth. I am still learning of the many experiences that forged such attention by the Bodhi to the intentional harms done to others, and how they observed that a need to settle scores and find resolution can dominate and ruin lives. Justice is the Bodhi's passion. Justice through karma. They founded the Kriya Project to do just that – help karma along, and speed it up a bit."

"But how are we going to do at a carnival, Tracey, in public. And what the heck are we going to do with a Ferris wheel? Push the fellow off, at the top? We don't even know who he is yet. How are we going to accomplish our task? And exactly what is our task?" Agnes Marie was curious.

"All in good time, Agnes. I will be explaining a great deal of the plan that I and the Bodhi devised to handle this character, Mr. Jason Edward Fitz – a real creep, if you ask me - whom you will get to know very well over the next two months.

"We are going to rent a Ferris wheel – a large one - through one of Truvenge's subsidiary corporations, so that we will have full control the Ferris wheel and all its personnel. And through that subsidiary, a private LLC, we are going to sponsor and participate in a special carnival at the fairgrounds in Queens – At the moment, I'm thinking about Flushing Meadows–Corona Park."

"But how are we going to get Mr. Fitz to show up at a *carnival?"* Vincent asked.

"Easy-peasy," Tracey responded. "We will organize a fundraiser carnival for Fitz's favorite charity, and make him the guest of honor. I just got hold of his donor records, so I can figure out how best to approach him on this. I have an assistant going through the records now, as we speak. And I should know something by this afternoon."

"How in the world did you do that? Get his donor records. . ." Agnes-Marie inquired.

"Joe may seem very reticent, meek and mild," Tracey volunteered, "but he knows people. Extremely helpful people. Lots of them. And he certainly knows his job. That's why, in his heyday, he commanded huge fees for the work he did, and does, so very well: Forensic accounting, which is the equivalent of being a financial detective. Joe Belton will be extremely beneficial to the Kriya Project during his tenure with us. And we will do all we can to accommodate his health needs, and follow his progress on the experimental meds he is taking. As we will do with all of you, in fact. As a team, you have unique talents. It is in our best interests – all of us – to keep you as healthy as possible for as long as is possible. The Bodhi and I are here to help you in every way we can.

"We can discuss Mr. Fitz as we go along, today. However, our primary tasks are to find a location for our carnival, and locate a suitable Ferris wheel that we can rent."

"You can actually rent Ferris wheels? Big ones?" Vincent was dubious.

"Yup. You sure can. There are literally hundreds of companies, nationwide," Tracey explained. "And for the right price, they will truck one to you on a semi-tractor trailer, and set them it for you beforehand, and take it down at the end. Not only that, but they can take care of all the perrmits and inspections. There is an Amusement Ride Safety Division within the Department of Agriculture . . ."

Agnes was curious. "Why the Department of Agriculture?"

"For County Fairs, of course," Tracey replied.

She was reading from the website of rental company, and continued aloud, "Rides must be registered by the owner, and approved to operate by individual states, according to their specific laws. It is the owner's responsibility to submit Affidavits of Inspection for the states where they do business and must provide itineraries detailing scheduled events. Apparently, the New York Department of Labor does the ride inspections on or before the date of the event, but just outside New York City. The city has its own requirements. Thankfully, we do not have to worry about any of that.

"The rental company will also provide necessary staff to set up and operate the ride, and to handle riders inside the ride area. Their personnel are usually trained in operations as well as rider safety and conduct – whether alcohol or simple rowdiness is the problem. Most rental companies have a policy of shutting down the ride if that occurs – any behavior that could jeopardize the safety of any riders. That might be problematic. But rental companies usually don't provide security for large crowds or lines that form outside the immediate ride area. . ."

"So, we'll have to put on out thinking caps as to how this is going to happen, huh? Whatever is supposed to happen." Vincent was frowning.

"When the event is over," Tracey read, "the rental company dismantles and removes all their equipment from the site in about six to eight hours – depending on weather, at the closure time on the last day, of course.

"What about insurance?" Vincent piped up. "That must be our responsibility."

"Actually, it is not," Tracey remarked. "Says here that if we contract with a rental company, they will schedule the required State inspections that are necessary, and provide us with an insurance certificate, adding the Truvenge Foundation as an "additional insured, per our request. In the alternative, we might want to self- insure. Keep things close to home."

Vincent wanted to know more. "Self-insure? How would you accomplish that, Tracey? Truvenge must have very deep pockets."

"Actually Vincent, it does. The Truvenge Foundation is much larger than it might appear to the casual observer. The Foundation is owned by, and is affiliated with a number of subsidiaries owned by Truvenge, Inc., including an independent property-casualty insurance firm, and a life insurance agency that brokers for several carriers. Insurance is not a problem. Nor is out-of-pocket payment beyond our means, in the event of a claim denial under certain instances, should it come to that. The Bodhi may be very spiritual, but they are also exceptional businessmen who made a great deal of money in the import-export business they owned and operated for decades. None of them married, and they live frugally, so their combined fortune grew exponentially over all those years."

"What about other rides? A carnival needs more than just a Ferris wheel," Agnes pointed out.

"We can rent some of the smaller rides, or invite smaller charitable organizations with compatible missions to join us, and sponsor their efforts under the Truvenge Foundation's annual budget for such things. Organizations that could not do this on their own. That will be my father's task. He runs Truvenge Foundation, itself. And one of its missions is to assist smaller service agencies and charities when we can.

"I've done some preliminary research. I've scouted the New York area, and there are two desirable locations for our carnival: Flushing Meadows Corona – that is where the 1964 World's Fair was held. It's a stunning setting. That's where the Queens County Fair is held."

"And the other location?"

"Astoria Park – Astoria, Queens, New York City. From the top of the Ferris wheel, you can see the Manhattan skyline and the Hudson. I looked at Governor's Island, too. It is ferry access only, however which might be a financial and logistical problem for large families and those with few financial resources, since a bus or train ride will also be involved to get them there. But this same rental company I am looking at using has provided their larger Ferris wheels to both Flushing Meadows and Governor's Island."

"Any of the three sounds good to me," Vincent responded.

"I have not seen any of these parks, so I am not the person to ask," Agnes remarked.

"Well, Truvenge Foundation can look into these three spots, figure which locale is the most usable, considering all we want to accomplish. But first we have to consider the type of Ferris wheel that might best serve our purpose. For what the Bodhi have come up with, it cannot be enclosed gondola seating – we need one of those old fashioned, open-seat gondolas with the old iron safety bar. All the major Ferris wheels – the really tall ones – now have fully enclosed gondolas, in part, due to liability fears, but primarily because you can pack 20 to 40 people in one of those, and the vista goes for miles. More money, more money, more money."

Vincent had already been thinking ahead. "Speaking for myself, I have next to zero knowledge of how a Ferris wheel is constructed, and how it operates. I assume that's going to be important for us to know. Will we be going over that, Tracey?"

"There are so many variations of the original concept nowadays, Vincent, that we could spend a great deal of time learning details we do not need to know. "Suffice it to say that a Ferris wheel consists of an upright wheel that rotates, and has multiple spokes, and components to carry passengers. Those components can include tubs, cabins, gondolas, capsules, pods or passenger cars, and the oldest of all – open seating with only the most rudimentary of safety elements. When we find the appropriate Ferris wheel, we will study that specific ride, and how it is constructed, and operates.

"That last kind is what we need to find, in order to pull this off."

Tracy explained Ferris wheel design a little further, "The passenger carriers are attached to the rim of the wheel in a manner that permits them to remain upright as the wheel turns – generally by the force of gravity alone. More modern Ferris wheels, generally called observation wheels, mount the cars, or capsules, or on the outside of the wheel's rim; electric motors rotate each car independently. Those are called observation wheels. Ferris wheels have been around since the 1893 Columbian Exposition at the Chicago World's Fair.

They can go up to 157 feet these days. But we only need one that is about 45 to 60 feet from the ground platform to its highest point, point, or apex. That height was once considered quite high. But we also need to find the most basic kind of open seating, and uncomplicated design."

Agnes had been silent for quite some time, but finally spoke up. "What about the Ferris wheel at Coney Island? The old one? I recall it quite well. I rode it several times during a visit to New York when on vacation, about 20 years ago. It was old then. Is it still around? That is exactly the kind we need. It's precisely what you're describing, Tracey. Is it still in service?"

"Let me Google it, Agnes." Tracey fell silent as the keys clicked in the silence at the table. "Sure is. Built in 1947, the design – Model #5 - was originally created by the Eli Bridge Co. in 1912, with a cable-driven wheel. Cable driven wheels are no longer manufactured since a great deal of skill and experience were required to properly balance the wheel. 'The wheel rim is now driven by tires' – no idea what that means. Have to investigate that further. It was installed at Coney Island in 1925, and seat belts were added in 2007. This model of his invention has 12 cars, with capacity for 36 riders, and the wheel is 45 feet tall; the cars are 55 feet from the ground at its highest point. A kid has to be 36" tall to ride with an adult; 48" tall to ride on their own."

Tracey turned her laptop around so that they could all look at the several photographs together. They studied the photos, and then Tracey enlarged the pictures and printed copies for each of them.

"Do not rock the seats, huh?" Agnes murmured gazing at the sign plastered across the back of a passenger car. "Now, there's an idea."

Then she asked Tracey, "Why create a carnival? Why not just lure this Fitz character to Coney Island?"

"Think about who this is, Agnes. Busy man. Big ego. Self-centered. Little time to spare on 'nonsense.' Under what pretense can we lure him to a crowded, aging beachfront filled with college kids, and families on low-cost vacations, or simply a weekend outing? Think strategically. Would a man like that go to Coney Island for a weekend jaunt with total strangers? We need a venue that affords control."

"I see your point. I went on vacation to Coney Island with a beau. And even so, I thought it was a cheesy weekend." Agnes Marie laughed. "But we were in a relationship and so not into impressing one another superficially. Tell me again, now, what are we to do to this fellow?"

"Young Mr. Fitz is to be terrified into doing the right thing. And we are the ones to make certain that this is carried out. You two will be working as a team with a number of Kriya Projects' actors, gymnasts, drivers, the Bodhi, and with me," Tracey told them. Vincent was busy studying the photos, but raised his head long enough to declare, "I'm with you, boss; we can do this, Agnes," he said reassuringly, then again focused on the photos.

The rest of the day was devoted to finding the right Ferris wheel to bring justice to a man who had abused a pure trust, out of pure greed.

Robbie Zerhusen/Coney Island Central

Tracey assured them that as their plans developed, Erik Walker would be popping in from time to time to check on the plan's progress. After all, this carnival would be sponsored by the Truvenge Foundation and, hopefully, one Jason Edward Fitz. The team would report directly to her as tasks were accomplished, and they would all consult with the Bodhi, with great regularity.

"I know this was a bit of a shock, so I'm going to let you go for the day so you can handle things at home, like getting a neighbor to collect your mail and water your plants. And yes, Agnes, you can bring a few of your favorite orchids to keep with you in your room – I know you wanted to ask about that. And here, this is a standard check list to inform you about how we help you handle issues like bill payment, picking up important mail and the like, and a variety of cover stories you can use to explain your absence. Since the three of you are in experimental programs, it will be simple to explain you will be doing on-site treatments that need to be monitored and will check with the neighbor tending your plants and collecting your mail from time to time. Pick out the clothes and items you will want to have with you, and pack your bags for an extended stay. Be sure to get everything, because there will be no traveling back home until the end of the mission.

"Be here early tomorrow morning, Victor; Agnes. Have a good evening! Class dismissed!"

Chapter 11 – Premonition

Erik hadn't been sleeping well, and he could not figure out why. He'd never had problems with insomnia and usually slept like a log, falling asleep as soon as he hit the bed. He refused to fret over problems at night – rather, mornings were when he took time, while still waking, to organize the day in his mind, setting objectives and going over priorities.

He rarely dreamt, and when he did, could never recall much about the dream. Nightmares had been a childhood problem that vanished as he matured

Erik generally described himself as practical and motivated. His focus was always on seizing opportunity and achieving results – not weighing the merit of how those results were to be achieved. He fancied himself straight-forward and 'no nonsense' in his approach to things. Introspection was not his forte, and he spent little time attempting it.

Now, however, he found himself standing at the floor-to -ceiling window across from his desk, staring out at the moving cars crawling down the Avenue below like ants on a mission, and wondering at the cause of the initially vague dread he had been feeling on waking lately. That sense of dread had inexplicably been growing worse with each passing day. . . why? Erik was not one to put much stock in gut feelings and premonitions, but could not argue with the sense of foreboding that greeted him each morning lately, at the moment he opened his eyes.

Things had been going well at work. His relationship with Tracey had been better than ever before – amazing how her attitude toward him had improved with her satisfaction in her new job; and, of course, without her mother around to stoke the girl's resentment of him that he knew Marilyn had fueled, transferring her own disappointments and unhappiness to her child. Their child. Although in their last years together, Marilyn had inexplicably become certain he was not Tracey's father and had evidently shared that foolish doubt with their daughter. It certainly was not what Marilyn had told him when she was tearfully pushing him to marry her.

He'd never questioned her assertion at the time – perhaps from the strange pride of fatherhood..

And he had been quite fond of Marilyn, in the beginning – fond enough that he believed her deep conviction that laid her pregnancy at his feet. He married her, and thereafter took pride in calling Tracey his own. His relationship with Marilyn, however, deteriorated rapidly, to the point Erik became convinced that marrying her had been the worst mistake of his life.

Tampa police detectives had his address in New York, but he hadn't heard from them in months, and when Erik checked in with them before he and Tracey left Florida, he'd been assured their investigation had failed to link him to his wife's disappearance, and thus absolved him of complicity or guilt.

TPD detectives had concluded that, since their marriage had hit the rocks, she had likely just taken off on her own or with someone else, to make a new start somewhere. The U.S. was a big country, with many states, lots of open spaces and huge cities, isolated communities and foreign possessions. People vanished every day, and were not found for decades – if ever.

If they'd had any news involving Marilyn, Erik had no doubt that they would have contacted him immediately.

Tracey had confirmed to police that her mother had accumulated a fairly large amount of cash – she had seen the money - which Marilyn told her was for one single, and often-expressed purpose: to leave Erik Walker.

Marilyn never used her husband's credit cards and, to his knowledge, had never gotten any of her own. She had no income, and whatever money she had managed to set aside, was derived somehow from skimping on necessities and on clothing for herself, saving whatever she could from the household and clothing budgets, which Erik allowed her to manage. Never a clotheshorse, Marilyn spent most of the clothing budget on Tracey's outfits and shopped for herself at discount stores.

Mother and daughter had a strong bond. After her mother's disappearance Tracey had been distraught, and was adamant that her mother would never would have left her behind. They had talked so often of leaving Erik together. Forever.

Deep in her heart, Tracey was certain about one thing: that her mother would never have left her behind. And if she had left alone of her own volition, Tracey fiercely believed that Marilyn would have never gone without telling her daughter, "farewell."

Something very negative loomed. Erik was certain of it. But had there been any new developments in the investigation of Marilyn's sudden vanishing, Erik had no doubt he would have been contacted immediately.

So from whence did this terrible feeling of gloom arise? That sickening sensation he got on waking, that something terrible loomed over the horizon? Erik realized his sunrise anxieties were starting to permeate his workdays. He noticed it was affecting his concentration. And he couldn't risk his performance suffering. The Bodhi were constantly asking how he felt, how he was coping with his duties, and with adjusting to big city life. When inquiring about requested progress reports on a specific matter they were sharp, inquisitive, and seemingly prescient - usually when he least expected them to be. The trio absolutely unnerved him.

April buzzed him and Erik strode to his desk to respond. "Felicity Brooks is here to see you, Mr. Walker. Did she schedule directly with you? I don't see her on your calendar."

Damn! He had forgotten about Felicity.

"She called the other day and we loosely discussed her dropping by this week, April. Since we didn't finalize anything, I never mentioned it. Give me a minute, and then show her in, please."

Erik sat at his desk, and had pulled two files in front of him and opened them, so he would appear to be reading the contents, when April tapped on the door and let Felicity into his office.

"Hello, Felicity. I see you were serious about dropping by. Welcome! Have a seat. And tell me how I can assist you with the reason for your visit. Whatever it may be. Not that I don't enjoy seeing your lovely face. What do you need? How can I help you? This stuff can wait." He closed the files and pushed them aside.

This was why the growing preoccupation with his morning gloom was dangerous, Erik thought. He had entirely forgotten his phone conversation with Felicity!

He watched her as she took a seat across from him. She looked particularly well put together today. "New dress?" he asked.

"Why yes. How observant you are! As we discussed, I'm here to learn how our new participants are faring with their projects. Are they meeting expectations?"

She watched Erik as he closed his eyes and rubbed his neck, searching for an answer. He had no idea. None at all. He had not seen or heard about Victor DiMarco, Agnes Marie Walford, or Joe Belton since they were brought on board, and realized it had been more than two weeks since he had discussed the three new recruits with Tracey.

He and Tracey had passed one another in the halls of Truvenge on several occasions, but never shared more than a perfunctory wave or a 'thumb up' in response to the query, "All good? Everything going well?"

Felicity was watching him closely.

"Are you okay Erik? You look tired. Problem with your neck?"

"Thanks for asking. Truth is, I have been sleeping poorly. The usual job pressures. And I think I must have strained a neck muscle sleeping in a poor position." He was still rubbing his neck muscles, which he realized actually did feel strained.

"Trained masseuse here," Felicity replied. "let me work on your neck for a minute. I think I can relieve some of that tension."

Before Erik could reply, she was up on her feet and moved swiftly behind his chair. Her strong fingers began working his muscles at the base of his skull. The relief was instant. It felt so good that he decided to let her work her magic. He hadn't been aware that he was so tense. Erik's eyes closed and he began to relax.

"You are good at this," he told Felicity.

"Should be," she responded. "Two years of study, lots of yoga. I am well aware of human musculature, and how tension can affect you both physically and emotionally, and, conversely, how emotions can trigger physical ills."

Her fingers were amazing, Erik thought. Wonder what else they could do to me, for me. . ." The ideas flitting through his mind as she worked on his neck were erotic, and his body responded. Felicity did not fail to notice.

"There, that should do it," she told him, patting his neck and stepping away. As she rounded his seat he turned toward her, grabbed her arm, and pulled her into his lap. His erection could be felt as it pressed against her bottom. He pulled her to him, and he kissed her. It was a long, slow kiss which she did not resist, although she reminded herself repeatedly that she should. When Erik's hand moved toward her breast, the spell was broken, however, and she stood up abruptly and took a deep breath.

"Well," she declared, "I was not expecting *that* – not at all."

Erik grinned at her like a schoolboy. "I have been wanting to do that, Miss Felicity, since the day I met you."

"I see. Mission accomplished, Mr. Walker. Now, let's address the reason for my visit." She realized she was trembling, and pressed both hands together so he could not see they were shaking. Her voice was shaking, as well.

"I startled you. Surprised myself, as well. My apologies. I find neck rubs very, shall we say, stimulating. . . I might have warned you, had you not moved so quickly, before I could say a word."

"Oh! So now, what you just did is *my* fault? Just how many charges of sexual harassment have been leveled at you?"

"None, actually, Ms. Brooks. But I do have a bad habit of allowing my heart to guide my actions."

"Your *HEART?* Yeah, I hear you! Funny place for a heart! You must have a good lawyer."

"Actually, any accusations usually were resolved in a different way." "Oh?"

"Yes. I started dating the ladies in question, and it was no longer a problem."

"I thought you were married for years, Mr. Walker. That's what Tracey said. To her mother."

"Our marriage failed early on, but I stayed for Tracey. And I took her mother's rejection of me as permission to find affection elsewhere. I notice you did not resist the kiss. Turned on, were you?"

"You realize I think you're a beast for what you did!"

"But now I am single, Miss Brooks – for all intents and purposes. . . And admit it, you enjoyed it. Your Beauty and my Beast. Not a bad coupling! What are you doing after work on Friday?"

"I … nothing with you, that's for sure!"

"Let's go see Tracey." He flicked the switch on his intercom. "April, is Tracey in at the moment?"

April's voice over the intercom was tinny: "She is, Mr. Walker." "Please let her know Miss Brooks and I are on our way to see her."

Side by side, the two of them walked down the hall, took an uncomfortably awkward elevator ride, and walked in on Tracey, who was studying some diagrams. She quickly folded the large sheets, tucked them into a drawer, placed her hands flat on the table before her, and greeted them.

"Hey, Felicity! How are you? "Hi, Erik. What's up, guys?"

Erik took the lead. "Felicity here came to see me to ask how her patients were performing in their work for us. I realized I needed an update, as well – it's been a while since we've had a chance to talk, so I figured it was a great opportunity for us all to catch up."

"Have a seat. Can I get you some coffee, a soft drink, water?"

Tracey took their beverage requests and relayed them over the intercom to the service staff.

"Felicity, I have not been in this position long, but I do speak regularly with the Bodhi, who meet regularly with this team we're particularly interested in, and have met with all the teams who've worked for Truvenge over these many years of the Foundation's existence. Let me assure you this particular trio you recommended and that we have employed is absolutely stellar, in our judgment. Skilled, personable. Very sharp and very professional. I cannot say enough good things about my interactions with them.

For their convenience and ours, although you know I cannot address the project they are working on, they will be housed at the Foundation in the Guest suite of rooms that we have prepared for them. They will be sequestered for about two months. It is routine. Sequestration, as you may know, can last up to three months, if a project is complex. In this instance, this trio is undertaking a set of particularly complicated projects. We met early this morning and I have sent them home to prepare for their time away from their residences.

"Felicity, it you can, stay for a bit after our discussion with Erik, I need to go over their medical conditions and make certain we are in sync with their physicians' instructions and that we will be able to keep the doctors apprised of their performance and apparent physical conditions as we progress. Much of what they will be doing is physical, as well as intellectual. Agnes and Victor are agile and strong. Joe's wonderfully useful skillsets are mostly mental. He will be traveling a lot, which he has assured us will not be difficult for him. Much of his job will rely on his accounting and forensic skills. We will have to be certain he is well stocked with oxygen and that all his equipment is in good shape. But I believe he is up to it. "Everything is progressing as planned, Erik. I'll call you later this afternoon to bring you up to speed on the details so that when you meet with the Bodhi tomorrow you'll be on the same page as the rest of us.

"Oh, good. Here come the beverages," she declared, "And some cookies! What a treat!"

Eric requested that Felicity, "Tell us about other prospects you may have lined up for us, and so redirected the tense conversation."

They talked for another twenty minutes before Erik excused himself, and Tracy and Felicity focused on the medical appointments and health details involving Joe Belton, specifically, as well as Victor and Agnes.

"How has your dad's mood been of late, Tracey?" Agnes queried. Has Erik been under a lot of stress?"

"Not more than usual. Why?"

"Not sure. He says he did not sleep well, and he does look tired. But then, he did something very out of character. . ."

"Like what?" Tracey asked, curious.

"Well, it was probably my fault, sort of – he was rubbing his neck and looked as though he was in pain. I have had massage training, so I offered to massage his neck, loosen some of the muscle tension. Then, when I finished and stepped away to go back to my seat at the front of his desk, he swung his chair around, pulled me into his lap, and planted one. A kiss."

Tracey laughed. "Hate to tell you, but that was not out of character. Not for Erik. His admitting to sleep difficulties, however, is. I have obviously known him my entire life, and I can tell you that man has never had a problem sleeping. Waking, maybe. But not sleeping."

"Oh. Okay. I will consider that information a word to the wise. Thanks."

Tracey was amused. It seemed Felicity was somewhat disappointed in what she had said. Had she fancied there was more to his action? Not a good assumption for her to make.

"Look, Felicity. I really like you. You are an asset to this foundation, and in particular, to the Kriya Project. I would hate to see you get hurt. And I would really hate to lose you, as it relates to Kriya Project. Your role is very important. Vital, in fact. As are your incredible skills, and your background."

"I appreciate that, Tracey. Thanks for your openness. I think I've learned my lesson for the day. Erik Walker is one of those men who sees a warm greeting as a license to take things further. I just need to establish firm boundaries. Thanks for letting me know that.

"I think I have all the information I need for my records. Keep me apprised if there are any medical changes. I should be aware of, and I'll take the best possible care of your patients. I very much like these three. They display excellent promise, and an interest in staying with us as long as they can. The Project needs experienced people, still in fairly good health, like Agnes, Joe and Victor. Should I see you out?" "Thanks, but I've been here often enough that I know my way out."

Felicity took the elevator down, and was curious when it stopped on the floor where Erik's office was located. When the doors opened and Erik stepped in, she was nonplussed.

"Look, Felicity. I owe you an apology. I am *very* sorry. I realize I was unexpectedly forward. It was highly inappropriate, and put you in an awkward position. Can you forgive me?"

The elevator doors slid together slowly, and the elevator car began to move

"I don't know, Erik," Felicity began. She was appalled that her voice was shaking. He really is good looking, she thought, and began the little speech she had composed in her mind while standing on Tracey's floor, waiting for the elevator. "What you did has altered the nature of our relationship," she primly informed him. "And ..."

Erik moved quickly to stop the elevator between floors. "I want to see you again, Felicity. Seriously. Outside work. I have thought of you every day since we met, and catch myself daydreaming about you instead of focusing on my job."

He cornered her and leaned forward to kiss her. Heart pounding, she moved her head aside and he kissed her ear, rather than her lips. His lips rested on her ear and he began breathing softly into it. Felicity was paralyzed. She felt his tongue teasing her ear, and melted. How had he known her weak spot?

His lips moved to her neck – another weak spot, and Felicity felt herself melting. It had been a long time since she had been in a relationship, and struggled to keep command of her emotions.

"Friday," he whispered into her ear. Let me take you to dinner this Friday."

Felicity quickly decided that agreeing seemed the best way to escape from this situation. Surely, someone would need the elevator, and she did not want it to be Tracey. She was confused, both willing yet unwilling for this to continue. That would give her time to think.

"Alright, alright," she told Erik. "Friday it is. We can meet after work. But I need to get going now. Can you please start the elevator? We can set the details by phone. You have my number."

"I do, indeed," Erik murmured.

Double entendre, she thought. I walked into that one.

Erik pressed the button, then unexpectedly reached out and shook her hand as the elevator door opened. "Deal," he said.

Felicity nodded, then fled the building.

Chapter 12 – Practice Makes Perfect

Victor and Agnes, dressed in workout clothes, were trying their best to retain their balance on a variety of moving obstacles as they worked their way through a progression of balance exercises in the Foundation gym, perched atop the Truvenge building.

The entire rooftop was set up for exercise and diversion. Plants and small trees added a natural element to walking and running paths. Scattered benches offered an opportunity to sit and observe the skyline, or read in the shade,

Skylights allowed golden shafts of light to penetrate and brighten the walled interior. Observer stands and handball courts were located on either side and at either end of a basketball court; there was an indoor pool with a retractable roof for warm summer days, converting it for outdoor swimming. A small movie theater was equipped with a popcorn machine and posters of coming attractions. Nautilus machines in another windowed room allowed for circuit training. Victor and Agnes were in the Pilates/yoga/aerobics room, with its matted floor to cushion falls.

Balance would be crucial in the coming moment of truth, when Mr. Fitz and his karma would make their acquaintance. In this particular exercise, Victor and Agnes were to jump onto the flat platform attached to a medicine ball, and gain equilibrium. It was tough, and they had already suffered a few falls. Once they achieved balance, they were now to remain on the moving platform for a full 60 seconds, and work up to two minutes, balancing on a level plane.

Once that goal had been achieved, they would begin practicing in their street clothes.

Victor's sales background was proving quite useful in engineering an initial meeting with Mr. Fitz, who belonged to many of the same civic organizations Victor had utilized in his insurance sales practice. The fellowship enjoyed by members of such organizations as Rotary International, the Lions Club, Kiwanis International, and Optimists gave one immediate entre to affiliated clubs in any city. Victor was also a Freemason, Scottish Rite.

"My job was one of constant prospecting," he told Tracey, Joe and Agnes. "My schedule was filled with breakfasts, lunches and community projects. Meeting people was my way of finding those who could use my services and products."

Agnes queried, "Can you find out which ones this Fitz character might belong to, Victor?"

"That I can. They are all international service organizations, and they actively promote networking. Membership rosters in any city are available to all members, and every chapter publishes their meetings and welcome visits from organization members in other cities or countries. I'll find some way to connect with this character. If he's a Mason, my Lodge will have to be 'in amity' with his in order for me to attend closed meetings, which is where real connections are made."

Tracey was curious. "What does that mean, 'in amity'?"

"Well, let me see how I can explain this. Each Lodge has its jurisdiction, and each Masonic jurisdiction keeps a list of those other jurisdictions it recognizes formally.

Now, if another "recognized" jurisdiction reciprocates the recognition, the two, or more, are said to be 'in amity'- and each jurisdiction keeps a list of the other jurisdictions that it formally recognizes. Only members of jurisdictions that are in amity are permitted to attend each other's closed meetings.

"So, if this Fitz fellow belongs to a Lodge, I may or may not be able to make the connection. The other service organizations are more open, but less valuable in terms of making a solid contact with the guy. I plan to ask him for a donation to Truvenge. Maybe help us with the carnival as a sponsor. An acquaintance of mine told me Jason Fitz is reputed to have an enormous ego. Bet he'll fall for it if I can promise him lots of publicity."

Whoa!

Victor took a tumble. Agnes and Tracey, who had been timing Victor's balancing act as they chatted, rushed to help him up to his feet. He was visibly embarrassed, but Tracey reassured him, apologizing for distracting him with conversation.

"My fault. I should have known that neither of you is ready to balance and converse at the same time. This kind of exercise requires all your attention until you can do this blindfolded. We cannot allow either of you to be injured pulling this off. And we have to keep pushing forward, so get some water or a soda, Victor. Take a break." He nodded, and moved off of the practice gondola, to do as she instructed.

"By the way, that is a terrific idea," Tracey called after him, as he walked away. "Let me see what I can do to make that possible. And take a break while I put Agnes through her paces," Tracey urged him. "Go ahead. Take a few minutes. Take a short walk, go outside to drink a soda, if you'd like. Then get your ass back in here to try again."

Agnes took her workout in stride, and managed her 60 seconds of balance. "Not flawless, but adequate at this point," was Tracey's comment.

Agnes beamed.

Victor returned, determined to conquer the device and maintain his 60 seconds of balance. That accomplished, they broke for lunch.

Tracey ate quickly and excused herself, but urged Victor and Agnes to have a leisurely lunch, remarking, "Take you time. I promise you this afternoon will be brutal! I've got some stuff to do."

Back in her office, she picked up her phone and called her father. "Hey, you," she greeted Erik cheerfully, although she dreaded the confrontation to come. "All good on this end. Agnes and Victor are doing exceptionally well with today's physical challenge, and Joe's got his nose to the grindstone, but is loving every minute of it.

He's in his element, happy as a clam. But I need a few minutes of your time. Can I come on up in 15?"

She hung up, sighed, and planned her speech.

April showed her into the sanctum sanctorum, and Erik stood to greet his daughter. "To what do I owe this honor? Thirsty? Coffee?"

"Nothing, thanks. I left my pupils finishing lunch and have to get back to them. Cannot let them slack off."

"I thought you said they were doing well."

"They are. But we are on a timeline, and they have to be perfect for this to work." "So, what did you need to speak to me about?" he asked.

Tracey took a seat across from him and leaned forward. Her brow furrowed, and then she said, "I know you find Felicity attractive, but I cannot have you screwing – wrong choice of words. I cannot have to interfering with the professional relationship Felicity has had, and must maintain with this organization, and with Kriya Project. She is the most reliable and trustworthy source of referrals that we have, at this point. And the folks she refers are in the best physical and mental shape of all our referrals. She know exactly the types of individuals we are looking for and she is discrete with our information, and responsive when we are the ones who need information. We cannot lose her because you are putting the moves on her and making her uncomfortable."

"Did she complain to you about my behavior? That would be surprising." "Not exactly. She was concerned about any stress you might be under." "Did she mention she gave me a neck massage?"

"She did. She also said you were carrying a lot of tension, and that you'd complained you were not sleeping well, of late. She notice your rubbing your neck and volunteered to work with your neck and shoulder muscles to see if that would help. She is trained, apparently."

"All true. However, Felicity seemed very interested in my welfare, and I must admit, I certainly have been interested in the lady, since the moment I met her. We have a date Friday after work, so I can't imagine what the problem might be." "Well, I know you, Dad, and I know you're a charmer when it comes to the ladies. I also know faithfulness is not your strong point, to put it bluntly. I recognize you consider yourself single now, and I do not want to interfere with any sparks between you two. But I consider Felicity not just an asset to Truvenge, and to the Kriya Project, I also consider her a friend. I do not want to see her hurt. And I assuredly do not want to watch you poison the well and drive her away!"

"I have no intention of doing that."

"You'd better be serious, for if I even catch a hint that you are messing with her feelings, or doing what you usually do..."

"Love 'em and leave 'em?" "Exactly!"

"You don't have much faith in me, do you," Erik shot out, irritated. It was a statement, not a question.

"You have not merited much faith, I'm afraid. You were a rotten husband, and your background is littered with a trail of broken hearts, including my mother's. She talked with me you might an adult; a friend. I know a lot about you that you and I have never discussed. And I would not bring any of this up now, if I were not so concerned."

Tracey stood. "Just know that if I have even a passing doubt about the kind of relationship you're developing with her, I will have to mention my concerns to the Bodhi. You know that I'm closer to them than you are. They respect my observations and value my opinion. I will not stand by and let you destroy that woman, or her value and relationship with this organization. So you had better be on your best behavior. and I suggest that you develop more than a nodding acquaintance with the truth, when you make promises to her. Have a good afternoon, Dad. And get some sleep tonight."

Tracey was shaking as she pushed the elevator button. Erik still had that effect on her. He did not have to raise a hand against her to leave her trembling. Their interactions had been friendlier of late, but she had just felt the heat of his rising anger, hidden behind smooth assurances that all was on the up-and-up and that his feelings for Felicity were real.

She sighed as the elevator doors opened. She knew that her confrontation would set them back months, back to the former status quo that she knew too well; the guarded truce. But she'd understood from Felicity that Erik had pushed himself on her unexpectedly, and also sensed that her friend was unprepared for what had happened, was confused about her feelings toward him, and had - unfortunately – assumed undeserved responsibility for prompting his advances. Felicity was a strong woman, but at this moment she seemed vulnerable to Tracey; disarmed by Erik's looks, charm and position. Understandable. But Felicity did not know the snake that he was. Or could be.

Yeah, yeah, yeah . . . They're adults, she thought, and it was really none of her business, at this point. Tracey was still convinced, however, that intervening early on and giving Erik a stern warning not to act on his worst impulses, as she had, was something she'd simply had to do.

As she exited the elevator on the top floor of the Truvenge building, where she was to meet up with Agnes and Victor, her cell phone vibrated in her pocket. Pulling it out, she didn't recognize the number that was calling.

"Not now," she muttered; "leave a message, and maybe I'll get back to you. I'll be busy with Victor and Agnes for the rest of the afternoon."

Chapter 13 – Pain Revisited

It was late that evening before it occurred to Tracey to check the message left by her inconvenient caller. Relaxing on the sofa in her room, watching some idiotic sitcom on TV, she remembered the call and hunted for her cell phone. It was still in her jacket pocket, but its dim face warned her it needed juice. She plugged it into the charger on the desk in her room, and – yawning and stretching, returned to her program while the phone charged enough to be usable.

She was startled awake two hours later, blinked, checked her watch, saw it was past midnight, and headed to the bathroom to prepare for bed. Done with her preparations, she passed the desk, took her cell phone off the charger, and glanced at the phone log for a moment. A message blinked at her. However she still did not recognize the number and was in no mood to deal with whomever and whatever the call was about. It was late, and tomorrow was a full day. Tracey shut off the TV set. Time to hit the rack for some shut-eye, she thought. No way she could respond now, anyway, right? Time for lights out. Tomorrow is another day.

Waking in a panic several hours later, Tracey realized she had failed to set her alarm and was going to be late to meet her students for breakfast. She would have to skip her daily conversation with Joe about his progress, but could catch him later. Dressing hastily, she ran from the room, leaving her phone still on the desk.

It was not until late in the morning that she could escape to her room for a few minutes to collect her cell phone and listen to the message.

The very moment she heard the caller's voice, Tracey wished she had responded immediately. The caller was her step-brother.

Mark Bradford, Tracey's older half-brother, was the son of Erik Walker and his first wife, who'd died in a freak accident shortly before Erik became involved with Tracey's mother, Marilyn. Or so Tracey had been told.

Tracey was never particularly close to Mark when she was younger, because of their difference in age, and due to the fact Mark had managed to become emancipated just before his 17th birthday and left home, never to return. It was only in recent years that Tracey had grown closer to him, and they communicated more frequently, at least several times a year.

Tracey was only five or six when he left, but she recalled the raging arguments between father and Mark that often got physical. Her mother, Marilyn, had called police once, when she became terrified that Erik would kill his son. State child abuse investigators became involved, and when family counseling failed to ameliorate the situation, assisted Mark in filing for emancipation.

Mark had always been industrious and independent. A high school Junior at the time, Mark had held a job for over a year, and his best friend's family stepped forward and offered to take him in until he reached maturity at 18. Mark was a natural athlete, and his grades were stellar, assuring him scholarship money to help with his education. The Family Court judge hearing his case did not think twice before granting permission for him to move out of the Walker household. As soon as Mark reached age 18 he also appealed to the court at his final hearing to change his surname, Walker, to his mother's maiden name, Bradford. The judge assigned to his case acquiesced, and Mark Walker became Mark Bradford.

When Tracey herself reached adolescence and began having problems with Erik – including a strong suspicion that Marilyn was being physically abused by her father, but was hiding (or trying to hide) the abuse from her – she began calling Mark for advice in how to deal with the situation.

That was when Mark first told her of his suspicions about the death of his mother. The more he researched her death, the greater that suspicion had grown. He had been greatly distressed on learning from Tracey of Marilyn's disappearance.

Tracey knew of her mother's unhappiness with their dysfunctional marriage. Her father was verbally and emotionally abusive to her mother in many ways that were hardly hidden. However, Tracey had a strong feeling his abuse included physical elements, which her mother had always denied. Her mother had few skills and little self-confidence, and felt trapped in the marriage, with few friends to support her. After the death of her good friend, Tracy's godmother and namesake, when Tracey was in her early teens, Marilyn turned increasingly to her daughter for support. Tracey was convinced her mother was ashamed of her weakness in dealing with Erik, who had started accusing her of entrapment, early in their marriage. Accusations flew that she had intentionally become pregnant to ruin his first marriage so that he would marry her.

Erik's bizarre claims were far from the truth, Mark had later informed her.

Mark was now a lawyer in private practice. He had contacts with a number of private detectives that he relied on to collect evidence in the many divorce cases that he handled, and when Marilyn disappeared, he had promised Tracey to have her disappearance investigated. Tracey's hand shook as she keyed in his number. There was a chance – however remote – that he had learned something.

She held her breath and only breathed once again when he picked up.

"Mark! Hi! I am SO sorry to get back to your this late. Long story. And I just got to a spot where I can pay full attention. What's up? Have you heard something? Do you have news about Mom?"

"Hey Rabbit! No, not really. I was hoping that you had heard something?"

"Why in the world would you think that, Mark? You know I would have been on the horn to you immediately, if so! Dad and I are in New York City. But I told you that when we moved, some months ago. Tampa police have our number – well, Erik's number. But we've had no contact."

"We?"

"Well, Erik's number. We both landed jobs with this private foundation. Yeah. We're working together for this foundation. Long story, but I needed work, and was helping him a bit with his assignments. But the folks for whom he works took a shine to me, and gave me a position in keeping with my degree."

"So you finally graduated! I knew you were in classes before your mom ... well, I never knew whether you had graduated or not. And it never came up in our conversations at the time. Congratulations! What is the job?

"Chief Detective for the Truvenge Foundation, Kriya Project," Tracey informed Mark proudly.

He whistled. "Impressive. But it is just an AA in Criminal Justice, right? Are you continuing? Getting a four-year degree? That's a pretty big title for such a little girl."

Tracey laughed. "I'm waiting to acquire residency to enroll. That will happen in just four more months. I'll probably complete a four-year degree at some point, attending night classes. But the Bodhi – the fellows who own the Truvenge Foundation, took an interest in me and we have lots of long conversations. They saw particular skills and talents in me, they said, that they know would be perfect for a position that had wanted to create within the Kriya Project.

"They actually met with Erik with their recommendation, and told him to hire me for this job, so I guess I must have some innate skills they recognized would make me a good detective. I *am* organized. I *am* relentless. And I *am good*, if I say so myself. But really, why did you call – just to chat?"

"It had been a while since we'd talked, and I just wanted to see how you were getting along. I've had some of the detectives I know and trust nosing around on Marilyn's case, as I said I might. Met with two of them last week. They seemed hopeful; they have some leads they're following, but nothing has panned out yet. I just wanted to see how you were coping. And how Erik's coping."

"I am destroyed every time I think of her, Mark. You know how close I was to my mom, and she to me. That's why I am still convinced she would never use the money she'd so slowly managed to accumulate, and just take off without me. Not telling me, or taking me with her. And certainly not without contacting me at some point afterward to let me know she was safe. She knows my email address. Forwarding from the Tampa Post Office is still active. And I get the Tampa Bay Times/St. Pete Times online daily. But nothing.

"Meanwhile, Erik is hot to trot – he has started seeing a woman we both work with here. Not here, exactly. She actually refers possible employees to us for screening. Pretty lady, considerably older than I am. And that news is very current. Would he tell me, if he had heard from TPD? Good question!

"The police have *his* contact information, not mine. I guess it would depend on the nature of the contact - *if* they did reach out to him for any reason. They cleared him of any blame or complicity in her disappearance. And if they actually found something, anything . . . even as good an actor as he is, I doubt he could hide it. I certainly couldn't!!!"

"So his behavior hasn't changed in any way?" Mark asked.

"No. Should it have? Wait a minute!

"His lady friend did tell me yesterday that he'd mentioned recently he's been sleeping poorly. Now, Mark, you know Erik as well as, or better than I. When has he ever had a problem sleeping?"

"Never," Mark answered. "And that does make it unusual."

"As to his new lady-friend, I did immediately read him the riot act about taking advantage of her. This individual – this woman - is an asset to the organization. I don't want Erik's being an absolute boor to her screw up her relationship with me, with Truvenge, and with the Kriya Project. That what I work on, mostly.

"But you're right. I do not trust that Erik would tell me a damned thing, if it did not benefit him to do so. I should try to find out what this new problem is. That man has ice water in his veins, and no ability for introspection. That anything would disturb him is pretty much unheard of. But he does have a great ability to manipulate perception. Perhaps he *has* heard something. I'll ask.

"Where are you living now?"

"Well, I do finally have my own apartment - now that I'm earning a decent paycheck. And I try to have as little to do with the man as possible. He's a snake. Trust me, there is nothing he can do that will change or improve my very low opinion of him! I'll definitely nose around to find out more, and get back to you, Mark, if I learn anything."

"I'll let you go now. It's the middle of the morning, and I'm sure you have lots to do.

You know how to reach me. And, Tracey?

"Yes?"

"I want you to realize that I understand how you feel. I fell to pieces when my mother died. And you know of my great doubts about what happened – I have my suspicions, and reasons for them. If I can get to New York any time soon, let's go to dinner – someplace where we can have a real conversation, rather than these telephone hits and misses. I've never told you everything that happened at the time. Or all that I've learned since; everything that I know. And maybe, just maybe, I'll have some news about your mother by then."

"You're planning a trip here?"

"I have a case that will very likely take me to the City in a few weeks, but I'm not sure when. I'll call when I know, and you can pencil in the date. Take care, Rabbit!"

Tracey smiled on hearing the pet name he used to called her when she was very little. It had stuck, and she realized just how much she'd missed hearing it. Then she pulled herself together and headed back to check on her charges. They should be working with Azar by now, she estimated, practicing on the mock-up of the Ferris wheel car that had been set up. She hadn't seen it yet ... Good time to return.

She pushed the elevator button and wondered about Mark's call. His questions led her to believe he was trying to learn something from her. But what? Did he really think Erik would rush to tell her that Tampa Police Department had contacted him, and that she would keep it a secret? Or didn't he *get* the fact that she wouldn't tell Erik a single thing in warning, if she knew detectives would be waiting in the parking garage to arrest him? Assuming, of course, that he could be tied to her mother's vanishing.

She had initially thought Mark might have learned something new about her mother's disappearance, but it seemed more as though the call was purely a fishing expedition.

Naaah, she thought. Now *I'm* getting paranoid!

She chided herself, counseling: You're reading far too much into every word, every gesture. Your interpretation is, no doubt, way off. And *can* the suspicion! It's more likely that Mark realized just how long it's been since we last spoke, and was simply being nice. We are, after all, related. And we share the same difficult father. *If* he's really my father!

But what was the real point of the call? To let her know his detective friends had a lead, after these many months? They'd had so many leads that hadn't panned out, Tracey no longer got excited, or felt that upswelling of hope that somehow, her mother was still alive – perhaps lost and disoriented, or, or even kidnapped!

A kidnapping gone wrong, perhaps? She had often considered that. Erik *was*, at the time, the highly paid Director of a renowned and popular charity – so it was not beyond imagining. But no demand for ransom, or note to any other effect, had ever been received. There had been so many called-in leads, possible clues, and thousands of "hot tips!" All hundreds fruitless, however. After so many disillusionments, the thought of ever seeing her mother again no longer excited a reaction from her from her for any length of time. With every passing day, it became a less reasonable assumption, although she would have given anything for it to be otherwise.

"But hope springs eternal," she muttered, exiting on the top floor to monitor the progress Victor and Agnes were making with Azar.

She had been tickled pink on learning Azar had been a trapeze star in the Florida State University Flying High Circus at the Ringling Circus College. He'd been a gymnast par excellence with the U.S. Men's Olympic Team in his youth, and was a 10-year veteran of the Kriya Project. FSU had a superb forensic pathology professor, and a great lab in its Criminal Justice program. That was where she'd hoped to complete a four-year degree and move into a career in law enforcement, her choice of specialization inspired by her addiction to the multiple CSI programs on TV.

Pushing open the double doors to the complex that included the Kriya Project's laboratory and engineering facilities, Tracey was astounded by the realistic Ferris

Wheel model of the single suspended car, or gondola, that had been constructed. Azar was working with Victor and Agnes on controlling their movements and the movement of the aluminum car. The point of the exercise was to induce a maximum swinging movement of the seating area with the minimum of visible effort, while remaining safely stable on their feet.

From recent photos and a video of Jason Edward Fitz that had somehow been located, Azar was able to guesstimate his weight. Photographs of the man in business attire and on the golf course had revealed a currently tall, thin male in his late forties, who appeared to have little muscle tone and limited coordination, as evidenced by a coaching video that had been taken for Jason Fitz by the Golf Pro at Fitz's Golf & Country Club, and posted on his social media under a typed banner that read, "Steadily improving, Jason! Keep practicing! Best regards, Walter." From the photos, one could see that Jason, once rather pudgy and bespectacled, had undergone a transformation as he aged, and now had assumed the persona of a hardworking bachelor, dedicated to his company, and proudly driving a stable of exotic cars.

Tracey was proud of herself for having found that short video. But social media searches were one of her many forensic skills. Azar had been delighted when she showed him. That one current video clip was invaluable, in his calculations.

Victor, too, had been effective. Contacting his large client base over several afternoons and evenings had turned up a fellow Freemason and loyal client of long standing who actually knew their target and was more than happy to help his life insurance agent, make the necessary introduction, and vouch for Victor's bone fides. Recent tax law changes involving inheritance gave Victor an excellent pretext for soliciting a referral and an introduction from those in his client base, and after two days of fruitless calls, a Mr. Robert Toomey had been happy to oblige. Not only was Bob Toomey willing to make the personal introduction and sing praise of Victor's insurance and tax competence, skills and qualifications, but Bob was an inveterate gossip who was more than delighted to regale Victor with stories involving George Fitz and his son and heir, Jason, a once overweight, heavy drinker who had suddenly come around and changed a slew of bad habits.

Victor had carried a notepad with him when he and Bob met for drinks, and had studiously jotted down notes, explaining these details would ease conversation when he and Jason met. Knowledge of personal things like Fitz's hobbies and Lodge rank, the names of family members and the breed of dog he owned would also cement in Fitz's mind the friendship bona fides between Bob and Victor to fortify the value of Bob's referral.

"Whoa! Whoa, there, Agnes!" Azar called out. "You have to build up to the panic attack. Helen, one of our actors, will be taking you through your role tomorrow. She'll demonstrate the behaviors to indicate you are having a problem. Jump up from the seat onto the platform of the gondola with both feet, but keep your hand on the bar. If you land awkwardly, *you* may be the one losing balance. You almost lost it there, just now! Can't have that. Tracey told me she'd have my ass if either you or Victor suffered injury. *Always* have a grip on something, and keep one foot forward as you take that hard step onto the car floor.

"You'll be the last to enter the gondola, Agnes Marie, so you will be last to get into the car, and will be in the first seat that exits. As other riders are seated, the carny will be filling the other cars, and the Ferris wheel will rotate to accommodate the next group. So the rise to maximum height will be slow. You have to moderate your buildup to full panic when the car is at the apex of the ride. At that maximum height, your panic 'attack' will go full blown and you'll be hysterical, gasping for breath, terrified of the height, unsure of what is happening to you. Freaking out, in other words. You'll grab onto Jason Fitz's arm, convinced you are having a heart attack, can't breathe, and so on, using him to try to push yourself up, grabbing the bar and attempting to stand."

Azar continued his instructions:

"Victor, you'll be on the far side of Jason, reaching behind Fitz's back and trying to grab her shoulder to hold her down and calm her. As her panic escalates you'll suggest that Jason – seated between you and Agnes Marie – rise from the seat next to her and move carefully around you so that you can slide next to Agnes and settle her down. As he does that, Victor, Agnes Marie at your side now will stand quickly and move forward to grasp the bar. You will reach quickly to grab Agnes Marie's arm, rising in place and at this point, Agnes, you will move forward, holding the bar, hand to chest, looking down and gasping for breath, and begin rocking the car.

"I will be at the opposite end of the seating," Azar told her, "leaning forward, trying to see what's going on. Jason will still be moving toward me, passing your knees, Victor. I will suddenly cry out, 'She's going to jump!' Jason will instinctively turn to look, at which point I will destabilize him, push him over the edge, and grab his wrist, suspending him from the car until he agrees that he'll sign the necessary papers returning the trademark to Quirky, along with all recipes, and will release Lewis from the agreement he was coerced to sign so Jason could steal his candy invention.

"I doubt he'll quibble, suspended like that. But if he does, I will promise to ruin his reputation as a contract manufacturer if he reneges on the deal, or ever speaks of this event. And what will be my form of gentle coercion? Promising to let him slip if he won't agree. Very persuasive. The documents will be immediately signed by Fitz after we disembark from the Ferris wheel, so he has no chance to weasel out of the agreement.

"At this point, Agnes, Victor will have pulled you back onto the seat and will be busy comforting you, as I do what I need to do. The ride operator will start up the cars to let the next riders onto the ride, and a chastened and cooperative Mr. Jason Fitz should be ready to walk with me to my van to sign the forms that you, Tracey, are working with the attorneys to draw up.

"But you wouldn't let him really fall, would you, Azar?" Agnes was sincerely concerned.

"That is definitely not part of the plan, Buttercup," Azar responded, chuckling. "A dead man cannot sign papers. I am very good at this."

"What if he refuses?" Victor asked.

"The guilty never refuse. Most bullies are cowards, as I would wager this Jason Fitz is."

"And what do we do if there is a situation where we cannot enter the gondola in this precise order?" Agnes Marie asked.

"Then we improvise," Azar responded. "Each of us knows what needs to be accomplished. We will just think on our feet, and adapt."

After the session, Tracey spoke with Agnes and Victor. She had read their concern in the voices, their questions and their body language. Before they called it a day, Tracey took them aside to assure them that Azar was a highly trained, experienced gymnast and trapeze artist who, in his youth, was known for performing without a net. His partners trusted him implicitly, and he had never had an accident. He had been with the Kriya Project for ten years, and had never failed in any task or mission he had taken on for the Project.

Mollified, Vincent and Agnes Marie were in agreement that a well-executed plan of this kind was likely the only way to persuade a man who had been made extremely wealthy through the theft of another man's invention, and who had considerable resources at his disposal. They both declared it an extreme method of persuasion, but agreed there was no other way to impress this bully with the consequence of his deed.

As everyone separated, they all agreed to eat dinner on their own, and study their materials, ordering from the room service menu. There was work to be done by all – tonight's study was to read and memorize details of the construction and operation of the particular Ferris wheel that Truvenge would be renting and have set up at the carnival's site in Queens as the featured ride of the charitable carnival the Foundation was mounting to raise funds and entertain local families and visitors.

That carnival would be the scene of Mr. Jason Fitz's comeuppance – his Karma.

Chapter 14 – Blindsided

Tracey was wiped out. It had been a long, emotionally draining day. She was antsy about many things, and really needed the evening diversion of dining out. She really needed time away from the Truvenge Foundation, and felt that sampling local cuisine, on her own, would help to clear her mind.

The day had presented many developments for her to ponder. Truthfully, she hadn't had a moment in weeks to reflect on recent developments, and think things through.

Where to go? Someplace simple. She was in the mood for comfort food. For Tracey, go-to comfort foods included oatmeal-raisin cookies, fried chicken, ice cream sodas, and juicy Angus hamburgers. All calorically *verboten*, but soul-satisfying.

That meant just one place would fill the bill: The Diner. Close to the office, The Diner offered excellent 'traditional' American diner food – the burgers were divine, fries were always crisp, and The Diner offered highly regarded entrées of homemade mac 'n' cheese that could be ordered with any variety of cheeses and meats, in regional styles. Best of all, prices were low.

That was important. While steady pay permitted Tracey to enjoy a much improved lifestyle, her salary left her little discretionary income. Her mouth watered at the thought of their hamburger platters with fries and The Diner's perfect Cole slaw, made from a proprietary recipe no one on staff was permitted to disclose, not even to good customers.

The evening air had grown chilly, so she donned a jacket and knit cap, and headed out for a little food therapy. To occupy her time while waiting for her food, she took files containing copies of the same Ferris wheel schematics Victor and Agnes Marie would be studying that evening, along with information about Ferris wheel rentals. She knew, however, that she would scarcely look at them.

It took her no time at all to find her car in the parking garage next to the hospital. She had zoned out for most of the walk there. Lots of things to process.

Tracey deposited the files in the passenger seat, along with her handbag. The grumbling of her stomach reminded her she hadn't bothered to eat a thing except a breakfast bagel laden with cream cheese and lox.

The Diner has seemingly existed forever, and walking in was like traveling back in time. Tabletop jukeboxes were affixed to aluminum-framed laminate tables with matching chairs. The jukeboxes were also a feature in each booth. They were stocked with musical favorites that spanned nearly eight decades.

She settled herself on the bench seat of a booth at the back of The Diner in small alcove away from the entrance, and ordered coffee, a strawberry ice cream soda, and a hamburger platter, the burger cooked medium-rare, piled with absolutely everything, with a side of The Diner's signature coleslaw and their crispy fries.

Once the usual carafe of coffee arrived, she poured a cup, took a sip, and opened the file on Ferris wheel rentals. But she couldn't focus her attention on the words; her mind kept returning to her conversation with Mark early in the day. And she wondered if Victor and Agnes would actually be able to pull off the fine-tuned maneuvers necessary to accomplish their plan for Mr. Fitz. She pushed the rental folder aside, still open, and instead unfolded the Ferris Wheel illustrations with explanations that Victor and Agnes would be studying tonight. Azar, too, had his own copies.

Lost in the details, a tap on her shoulder startled her. She quickly refolded the illustration sheet while looking up to find a vaguely familiar man standing next to her, holding two plates of food. He addressed her by name, and asked if he could sit with her.

As her mind refocused after the unexpected intrusion, Tracey recognized the interloper from the photographs of him that she had in his case file. She was shocked at his sudden appearance at her side.

What was he doing here? How could he zero in on her so easily? How had he known who she was?

Petitioners were prohibited from interacting directly with Kriya Project staff, and the reverse also applied. How had he possibly known she would be there? Her decision to eat at The Diner had been a spontaneous one. She wondered in horror, was he *stalking* her?

"Mind if I join you?" he asked politely, still standing before Tracey with a full plate in either hand. "I saw you come in, and this is better than a phone call – to converse, I mean. I'm so sorry! I didn't mean to startle you!"

"May I sit?" he repeated.

Still somewhat startled, she nodded, and motioned to the seat across from her. She quickly refolded the diagrams, tucked the folded paper into its folder, then closed the Ferris wheel rental folder and set the two aside, tabs down, drawing the two folders to her far side. She watched as the man slid into the seat across from her, and steepled her fingers as she rested her hands on her placemat.

Once he set down the plate of chicken tenders and bowl of soup that made up his meal, he fished his wrapped cutlery bundle from his overcoat pocket, he stood again to take off his overcoat. As she watched, Tracey idly wondered how he had managed to get served while wearing his overcoat, and whether his waitress was still wondering where he had gone, food in hand.

It took Tracey a moment to find her voice. "You're …"

"Just call me Quirk. I'm Quirky Lewis, inventor of the Rainbow Gummy Drop, the world's most *delicious* candy treat. In the flesh!" he proudly announced, and laughed, shyly rubbing the back of his neck. "And *former* 'Candy King'."

His laughter was filled it with regret. "Things today are definitely not as sweet as they once were. But you already know that, don't you, Miss Walker?

Friendly as a puppy dog, and smiling broadly, Mr. Lewis stuck out his hand to shake hers, but Tracey did not reciprocate, and kept her hands folded and resting on the placement before her, so he awkwardly withdrew the extended hand and casually shoved it into the pocket of his slacks. To break the awkward silence that ensued, he attempted light-hearted conversation, and blurted, "You know, I never actually considered that someone like you would eat real diner food, like any normal person. I figured you more for a vegan. Or into haute cuisine."

She ignored that last remark.

"Please, eat," she urged, figuring a full stomach might send her uninvited guest on his way.

She was agitated, but still more, she was puzzled by how he knew who she was, and how to find her. And why in the world was he even discussing what he thought she might eat?

Tracey motioned to his own plate of chicken fingers and French fries, and the cup of bean soup he'd brought with him from wherever he'd been seated, when he spotted her. "Eat, please," she commanded.

"Food? I already had my dessert first, and I'm not that hungry. "Hey – I just want you to know I am *not* stalking you, in case *that* is what you're thinking. I recognized you over here because I'd seen your photo on the Foundation website. I eat here a lot. I do. I'm addicted to burgers and shakes."

"But you ordered chicken fingers," Tracey pointed out.

"Well, a guy's got to mix it up once in a while. I eat out *a lot*. Or order in. Never did get the hang of cooking a complete meal. Eggs and bacon and toast is about it."

"I thought you were married."

"Was. Past tense. Long story, not suitable for this venue, or for my purpose." "Which is . . ."

"To meet you, of course. Once my petition to Kriya Project was accepted, I wanted to know who would be handling it. So I googled The Truvenge foundation website. And there you were. That was, of course, after a few phone calls to the 'Truvenge Foundation" as a prospective donor got me the information I needed to identify you. They finally sent me their formal brochure – you know, what they keep out in the lobby? They sent one to me after I actually talked to the President of Truvenge. Nice man. Hey, his name is Walker, too. Are you his daughter? The brochure identifies you as Miss, and you have the same last name."

Tracey, still rattled and further unnerved by his bluntness, remarked wryly, "*That's* certainly a bit of news! I didn't know I had a photograph on the internet. Nor did my father ever indicate he'd spoken with you directly."

"Your online picture on the Truvenge web page, Miss Walker, is the same photo that is in the Truvenge brochures at the front desk in the lobby."

Tracey looking around nervously, who at Truvenge would believe her, if someone were to spot her sitting with an actual petitioner?

She now had a job she loved and a decent salary, but could lose both if they were seen together. The "non-fraternization" rules were very strict. So much depended on anonymity when working with a Petition! The Bodhi had drilled that into her. What would they think? Letting Quirky Lewis sit had, to Tracey, seemed to be way to resolve the scenario that was sure to draw eyes their way.

Lewis was making himself eminently noticeable, by standing and talking to her with food in his hands, and gesturing with his plate of chicken tenders. His persona definitely fit his name as well with his brightly colored attire.

In her mind's eye, she could envision the crunchy tenders flying off the plate with a sudden gesture. That was all it took to persuade her she should wave him to a seat and indicate he could sit and eat.

Without waiting for a reaction, Tracey began explaining to him, lowering her voice after a few people turned to look their way. "Yours is a highly atypical situation, Mr. Lewis. First off, very few of our clients self-refer. And the majority of self-referrals do not meet our rather stringent criteria for acceptance. There are strict rules about contact between petitioners and staff under any circumstance, but particularly when an Applicant *is* a self-referring Petitioner.

"A certain distance between the two parties is desirable, given the sensitive situations we often find ourselves in – and the fact that professional distance is a necessity in order for all staff to do our best work for the subject of a Petition. We must maintain that distance at all times. I, for one, can affirm that I find your unexpected presence here, under these circumstances, to be highly concerning, and not appropriate. I cannot allow cases to become personalized. I hope you can understand that. To do my best job for you, or any of our clients – and I do think I am very good at what I do – I must ask that now that we have made our acquaintance, you finish your meal, and leave the restaurant – please. I have work to do anyway. And I promise to do my best to provide a satisfactory resolution to your petition."

"When?" Lewis asked.

Tracey was brief. "At some point in the next three months. You will be notified when resolution has been achieved. Notification will be by mail, in writing, with a number for you to call to learn - verbally. Just as we would do with any other Petitioner.

"Well, pretty lady – Miss Walker - I certainly appreciate meeting you. This seemed to be a fortuitous opportunity, that I suddenly decided to take advantage of, and I thank you for your time. All those rules and regulations must have been in the fine print, which I never read. Don't know anyone who does – except lawyers. I will try my best to stay out of your way henceforth, Miss Walker. Please excuse the intrusion.

"Uh – by the way, was that a rental agreement for a Ferris wheel that I saw there? I have this acquaintance who can probably get you a great deal on a rental. He works for ..."

"Thank you Mr. Lewis. But, you need to eat and leave. We cannot be seen together! There are rules. And I like my job too well to risk losing it. We're already in discussions with a company regarding rental of a Ferris wheel for the fundraising carnival we intend to hold. I am researching. We are planning a community carnival, sometime around the beginning of this next quarter - date and location to be announced.

"That sounds swell," Quirky Lewis said, before digging into his meal.

Tracey's burger platter arrived. But she was feeling nauseous, her appetite had fled.

The rest of their conversation - idle chit-chat – went quickly as they finished their food. Various topics of conversation arose, and were dealt with. She had taken her first bite of burger when Quirky shifted the conversation and unexpectedly started an explanation of his grievance.

Quirky, explained that his creation was his baby. It might seem odd to say, but he put everything into building a treat that would make the world happy at all kinds of celebrations of happy times or just when they felt the need to have a taste sensation brighten their day to turn it around. He was so proud of what he created and the success he made it. "I had no alternative, but to hand over my trademark when put into the position I was put in. People don't realize that Miss Walker. There was no choice I was given." When I saw the Fitz family receive awards for a candy I created and marketed to the moon, it was so disheartening.

"Are you done yet?'" she asked. "Eating. Are you done? I'll flag down the waitress. Where is our waitress?

I need this boxed. I'll eat it at home. Tracey felt ashamed for not showing the emotion she had welling up inside her, but she needed to not make this personal. She could feel her sympathy start to speak out loud with the blurry vision was starting to notice.

Lewis mumbled apologies, but Tracey was short. "Let's go."

Once they had paid for their meals, Quirky Lewis offered to walk Tracey to her car, a courtesy she grudgingly accepted. At her car, Mr. Lewis opened the driver's side door for her, once she had unlocked it, and stood, like the gentleman he was, until she was seated, then closed the door and waved good-bye, turning away once Tracey started the engine.

Neither of them heard the repeated soft clicks of the cell phone camera on someone's older cell phone, nor noticed the dark shadow at the corner of the parking lot, leaning casually against the stucco wall that enclosed the parking and delivery areas of The Diner.

Chapter 15 – Taxes Can Be the Death of You; Just Ask Al Capone

Joe Belton met Victor, Agnes and Tracey for breakfast the following morning, pulling his suitcase and oxygen tank behind him. He was flying to San Antonio later that morning to stay for close to a month and tie up some of the work he had been quietly doing from his office down the hall from Tracey.

He had kept to himself most of the time, joining them only occasionally for Breakfast, and dinner, but had his lunch – usually a sandwich or personal pizza - preferring to work unflaggingly until he arrived at a natural stopping point to take a break and stretch. He was an early morning riser, and swam daily in the heated pool, doing very leisurely laps and then stopping for a while to simply float on his back and stare into the morning sky. Winter was on its way out, and it was warm enough for the retracting roof above the pool to give way to the sun and blue sky above.

Joe had researched his prey diligently, calling on a number of old acquaintance with whom he had worked in years past to pull in favors. They were all glad to hear from him and asked if he had reopened his office. He had been missed, and that made him swell with happiness. He was actually whistling a tune as he entered the dining area where a breakfast buffet was laid out and an attendant stood at the ready to make omelets or crepes, if desired. Crepes were Joe's choice, with turkey sausage. He also loaded up on a few goodies to take with him for the several-hour, business- class flight,

237

and asked for a box to carry the snacks. He'd been grateful when Tracey handed him the ticket for a direct flight, with no changes or layovers. Joe was grateful there were no stopovers, or changes of plane.

"I want you unstressed and well rested when you arrive," Tracey told him. "You will need all your energy to nail that sucker. And here is a ticket for your assistant, Edgar. I assume you have found his assistance useful?" Tracey asked, although she was well aware that Joe and the young man she'd hired to assist him had instantly hit it off and that Belton frequently lauded Edgar's thoroughness, his eagerness to learn, and his attention to detail.

For Edgar's part, he'd been educated at his father's alma mater and was following in his footsteps, planning to eventually take over his dad's hum-drum accounting practice, until Tracey had hired him on the recommendation of one of Truvenge's accounting staff, who'd taught Edgar in night class and was very impressed by his diligence and enthusiasm. Taxation was the lad's forte and primary interest. He had hopes to intern with the IRS, and was taken on by the service on the basis of exceptional references. Edgar had an easy-going manner and warm personality. When talking to Edgar, people seemed to open up, and that was a rare characteristic that was approvingly noted by his immediate supervisor, who recommended that Edgar be moved to an investigative unit for the duration of his internship, where he could hone his talents. When his internship was over, he returned to university to finish working toward his graduate degree and was considering a return to the IRS on a career basis before

Tracey brought him on to assist Joe. Edgar was perfect for the job.

Not only was he a quick learner with a love of people and talent for numbers, Edgar saw accounting as both a discipline and a puzzle, and had been leaning toward some type of advisory practice until he met Joe and learned about forensic accounting. He listened, rapt, as Joe recounted some of the more interesting and exciting cases he'd worked on that had involved embezzlement, divorce settlements, business restructuring, seeking ownership of shell companies, locating offshore accounts, and the like.

Edgar was hooked. And he took to the case of Ace Hollander like a fish to water.

It did not hurt that Edgar was strong and amiable, and served Joe well as a traveling companion and able assistant. He had an instinct for research and investigation that was truly remarkable in one so young. Joe had taken him on not only as an assistant, but also as his protégé, making introductions of the young man as a budding talent in the field of forensic accounting analysis. And Joe knew all the right people to whom he wanted to introduce Edgar.

The relationship was good for both of them. Joe appeared reinvigorated and eager to face each day. His mood and self-confidence had improved, and he seemed unrelentingly cheerful, most days. When Edgar called him "Boss," Joe absolutely beamed. Tracey could see the difference in him, and made sure to tell Felicity how well Belton was doing. But Felicity had already noticed the improvement.

"I'm thrilled, Tracey. As are Joe Belton's doctors. Even his lab results are on an upswing, and he is responding very well to treatment. They are already regarding him as a success on the new regimen, which they hope they can begin promoting for those with his breathing problems. I wish everyone of our patients could have an Edgar in their lives. And I am noting significant progress with Agnes Marie and Victor. What are you doing with those people over there that has so invigorated them? I wish we could bottle it and sell it. Remarkable."

Tracey had wanted to ask Felicity how things were going with Erik, but she knew from watching him around her friend that he was enthralled with the woman. That was a good thing. But for how long? Felicity seemed a pretty cool character, and perhaps that was what Erik needed to turn him into a decent human being, Tracey mused: Someone who was not about to put up with his crap. Someone he could not win over though seduction, or control through manipulation. Felicity was quite level- headed and independent; not emotional like her mother, Marilyn, had been. And, hopefully, not as much in love with Erik as her mother had been.

In her loneliness after the cancer death of Marilyn's childhood friend, Alison McGregor, Tracey's mom often turned to her daughter for companionship, and treated her as she would an adult friend – a confidante. Tracey's mother had grown up in a rough home situation, and her relationship with her own parents was hardly the best. Even before learning of her mother's traumatic childhood, Tracy disliked her grandparents and hated their holiday visits. Her maternal grandparents always argued, and Marilyn's dad - a big, muscle-bound man, a trucker - was always putting his hands on his daughter in a way the young girl thought was awkward and embarrassing for her mother, although Erik – for all his jealousy and possessiveness - did not seem to mind, which confused Tracy. Her Grandmother was an alcoholic, and family dinners always ended badly.

Tracey hated the holidays, and never celebrated any but New Year's Eve. She saw every new year as an opportunity to start over, to improve. To strive toward her goals in life.

Her mom had dated a guy named Adrian Eckert, a Senior, off and on during her Junior year of high school, but had a heavy crush on Erik Walker, who was at the time a popular Senior. He was Class President and Captain of the football team, but also, someone who barely noticed her - even though she was one of the prettiest girls in the entire school.

Marilyn's feelings for Adrian ran hot and cold, even though they dated fairly steadily despite the breakups, that she usually initiated.

Adrian was an acknowledged nerd, an attractive, but a skinny track star, and while not disliked, kept to himself a lot and studied, or ran track after classes. However, Adrian had proved himself a true friend, time and again, whenever Marilyn needed a shoulder to lean on; he was always there for her, as support.

As pretty as she was, Marilyn was fickle, constantly distracted by the interest expressed by cuter, more popular guys, whom she would notoriously entrance, date, and then drop. Marilyn earned the reputation as a heartbreaker and a tease; she never lacked for a date or party escort. Unfortunately, as is a common occurrence with someone like that, her fascination centered on the one fellow she could not get – Erik Walker.

Early on, Adrian had asked her to Senior Prom, but Marilyn, a Junior at the time, put him off until the last minute, then finally accepted when it seemed Erik was not going to ask, and she had already turned down everyone else who had. Resigned to going with Adrian, Marilyn, she bought a dress, told Adrian she would go as his date, and even gave him the color of her dress for the corsage, but then was greatly distressed when Erik called at the last minute to ask her to the Prom. Faced with a dilemma, and fearing Erik might be playing a trick on her (he was a great prankster in H.S. – and an often cruel one) – and really not wanting to hurt Adrian after putting him off for so long, she turned Erik down and told him he had waited too long, and that she was going with Adrian - which she did.

But Erik had made a pest of himself during the dance, cutting in when she was dancing with Adrian, giving her compliments on her appearance that Adrian could hear, bringing her punch – as if Adrian had forgotten to take care of her - and at one point in the evening, when Adrian excused himself to go to the restroom, Erik asked Marilyn for a dance, in her date's absence. He'd slipped vodka into the several glasses of punch that he'd brought Marilyn all night long, and her head was buzzing. She was thrilled to be around Erik, who whispering all kinds of 'sweet nothings' in her ear as they danced.

Adrian, however, had run into friends on his way back from the bathroom, and was nowhere to be seen, so Erik saw an opportunity, and spirited her out of the room, taking her to an empty classroom. There, he seduced her, and – her willpower dissolved by both his importuning and her intoxication - they had sex. They were gone about a half hour, and then slipped back into the room and onto the dance floor.

By the time Adrian reached their table, after a lengthy conversation with his friends, he spotted Marilyn dancing with Erik, but was oblivious to their brief absence.

It was only when rumors reached his disbelieving ears that Adrian became aware that Erik and Marilyn had disappeared from the dance for a time. Still later, rumors that reached Adrian carried with them Erik's boast that he "had melted the Ice Queen" and enticed her to give in to him. Adrian was at first horrified, then in deep denial.

Marilyn was not a virgin, and had been intimate with Adrian on several occasions over their long off-and-on-again relationship. She managed to allay his fears by convincing him that rumors had always circulated among the cliques in their school, and rarely proved true.

But she was hooked on Erik, who was now playing it cool and avoiding her much of the time. That only increased her eagerness to be with him.

Summer was around the corner, and Marilyn discretely dated both Adrian and Erik, who was now a bronzed lifeguard, making sure to keep each from knowing about the other.

By early August she realized she was pregnant. The question was, by whom? Marilyn felt certain Erik would never acknowledge he might be the father, and so gathered her courage and approached Adrian with the news. Adrian had heard enough consistent rumors by then to conclude the validity of the rumors that she was now seeing Erik, as well as him. And he had heard the Prom rumors months earlier, but had resisted confronting Marilyn, for fear of having those rumors confirmed. He was deeply in love with her, and dreaded losing her.

When Marilyn finally did approach Adrian with the announcement she was pregnant, and he was the father, he repeated the rumors and refused to even consider it was his, since he'd taken such care to avoid any consequences those times when they'd had sex.

She reminded him there had been one occasion, however, about two weeks after Prom, actually – when the condom broke. Marilyn burst into tears and told Adrian that had to have been the occasion! But she had feared just that – his denial.

Adrian had been horrified, his destroyed future flashing in front of his startled face - and he then told her all the rumors he'd heard, many repeatedly. As Adrian watched her face carefully, he determined the rumors he'd heard were likely true. At that point, they argued, and he left, swearing to have nothing to do with her any longer. Those were the days when pregnant girls did not finish school, for the most part. They dropped out. They went to visit relatives, and gave the child up for adoption. They visited back room abortionists. Or they somehow kept the child, and rarely finished their education.

Marilyn was terrified, hoping her father never noticed; knowing her mother never would.

Adrian, his best buddy, and Erik had all graduated. Erik's friends were off to prestigious universities in other states, Erik, whose grades were less than stellar, enrolled in the local Junior College, but moved into his own apartment. He kept seeing Marilyn, who was going through hell at home, and when she could no longer handle the abuse at home, moved in with him.

Early that August, she told him about the baby she was carrying and her suspicions that it was his. Surprisingly, Erik was puffed with pride about the pregnancy. "Just one time without protection, and bingo!" he would brag, as if that proved his masculinity.

He had been scouted by B-grade college for a football scholarship, and in late August, received an out-of-state scholarship to play. When he learned his tuition, books and housing would be covered, he accepted. On the heels of Marilyn's announcement of her pregnancy, Erik figured he would need a wife to take care of him while he studied and played football, and so married her, much to her family's delight and his family's dismay.

Marilyn had told Tracey this story as a cautionary tale, during a mother-daughter conversation warning Tracey to be careful about pre-marital sex. But it was enough to plant the seed that perhaps Erik was not her father, after all. She had seen photos of Adrian, and decided – based on appearance and intellect – that she was his child, and not Erik's. Escapism? Perhaps. But her resemblance to Adrian, as opposed to Erik, was uncanny.

Erik had always had an obsessive, possessive, and controlling personality. He behaved the same way about people and relationships as he did about his possessions. It would only take one chance meeting, an innocent reply to a seemingly innocent email, or a 'touch base' phone call from anyone outside the family, for him to get obsessive again about Marilyn or Tracey, and start with the interrogations, the accusations, the attempts to restrict their outlets, their interests, their friends. Obsessive behavior had been a weakness all his life, and cost him money, his marriages, and his personal and business relationships.

Marriages? Yes, marriages. It was only after several years that Marilyn learned that Erik had been briefly married the year before she became involved with him. Late in his sophomore year, he had impregnated a cheerleader from another high school in town. She was the daughter of a prominent attorney, and both sets of parents forced a marriage that lasted only months before Erik beat up his young, pregnant wife shortly before she was to give birth to their son – Mark Evans Walker, now Mark Evans Bradford.

Their divorce was filed immediately and was uncontested. His wife's parents, good Catholics, appealed to their bishop for an annulment, which was eventually granted. Marilyn had been unaware of this situation, which had been successfully hushed up by all concerned, until years later, when young Mark came to live with them as a ten year old, after his mother committed suicide. At least, that was the story at the time. When he was emancipated in his late teens, after a turbulent few years in Erik's care, Mark changed his surname from Walker to Bradford.

That musing led Tracey to think about Mark's call earlier in the week. Why did she keep thinking it was peculiar? Why did he think she might have heard something about her mother after all these months since her disappearance? Odd.

"And so," Edgar and Joe were explaining, alternating their commentary, "we've learned Ace Hollander has failed to file taxes in about six years – ever since he refined his grift and began moving from town to town, preying on the young and inexperienced, and the elderly and disabled. Hollander's scam was to start advertising in advance of his arrival, enter agreements for repairs as soon as he got to town, then completing the job and skipping town as soon as he'd been paid. Payment was deposited into a local bank account, which was promptly reduced to zero and allowed to close naturally upon remaining at zero balance for a month or two, when he was off to his next scam."

"Making money without paying taxes for six years will surely bring the heat down on him," Joe said. "And a private detective who is a good friend of mine has been building the fraud case."

"Which is a tougher case to build than tax evasion," Edgar interjected. "Remember, Al Capone was brought down because of tax evasion – not his criminal record, nor the multiple murders he ordered his henchmen to commit."

Joe addressed her directly at this point and broke into her revery, saying, "I told you this kid was crackerjack, Tracey! You sure can spot talent." He looked at his watch and pushed away from the table. "Hey, kid," Joe said, addressing his assistant. "Grab the suitcases. San Antonio calls. We have a Hollander to catch!"

It took Tracey a moment to reorient herself to the present. "I'm sorry, Joe. I was zoning out, lost in a past conversation that was on my mind. Joe, Edgar, have a great stay in San Antonio. Best wishes for getting this wrapped up quickly. Your limousine is downstairs. The driver is in April's office. Go get Hollander! And stay in touch. Let me know if any problems crop up. Safe flight, guys."

Tracey, Victor and Agnes Marie watched as the duo departed.

"Okay, kids," Tracey said to them. "Finish your coffee and let's get a move on. The Ferris wheel gondola has been raised substantially, and we are doing this from a considerable height today. Ready?"

They nodded.

"I've made contact with Fitz," Victor informed her as they walked toward the elevator. "Friendly guy. We talked about a charitable donation to enable us to hold the fundraising carnival. He is definitely open to it, as long as we give him a large booth to sell his candies. This is going to be a piece of cake."

"Excellent, Victor! I never doubted you. Get a move, on, peeps. This is going to be a long day. And you have a lot of work ahead of you."

Chapter 16 – When the Past Calls, Do You Answer?

When April forwarded the telephone call to Erik, she hesitantly apologized. "I am *so* very sorry, Mr. Walker, but I could not get this fellow to give me his name! He said you were old friends, and he wanted to see if you would remember his voice, since it's been a while. I wasn't sure quite what to do. Shall I put him through?" Erik's brow furrowed, and he hesitated a moment, trying to think who might be on the line.

Who could it be? Who had he not talked to in "a while" that he had been so close with that that person might expect him to still recognize their voice. . ...

"It *is* a man, right?" he queried.

"Right. I thought I said that," April responded. "Should I put him through?"

"Yeah. Go ahead. I'll take the call." Erik tapped a finger against the desk while waiting, obviously irritated, but curious, as well.

The gruff voice on the other end of the line was, indeed, recognizable. Erik suddenly stopped tapping. He had developed a knot in his stomach.

How the hell had they found him?

The images that flashed through his mind on hearing that gruff voice were not pleasant ones. He had successfully pushed them out of his mind for months now, but they came rushing back. Along with the knot.

"H-how are you two doing? '*Que passa*'?" he croaked. "I thought you understood that our business had concluded. And you were well paid. Both of you. You should have no complaints." There was silence on the other end of the line. Erik felt beads of sweat on his brow. His free hand was shaking as he tried to wipe it away and regain a calm demeanor, and strengthen his voice.

"To what, then, can I attribute this call?" Erik inquired of the voice on the other end of the line. He involuntarily cleared his throat before asking, "What do you want?" – then hated that the way it had made him sound nervous.

"Settle down, champ. You were good to your word. But I'm calling about something else entirely. You see, I've learned some stuff. And I've got something you might want to know about. Something very interesting. I just happened to know some stuff I found out just last night from a very interesting conversation. Seems you have apparently worked your way into something big. Something that could be a very profitable new gig for us: you, me, Barney."

"Oh? How so?" Erik asked.

"Well, I heard a few things last night. Took a few photos. Been doing a little digging since I found you and your daughter, a little digging that I discovered was pretty fascinating. Interesting young lady you've got there. You really might want to meet me, take a look at what I have. And then we can talk a little business – new business, of course."

"Look, I don't care what you have, or what you think you've learned. You came highly recommended, we negotiated, you did what I asked you to do, and you and your associate - what's his name?"

"Barney."

"Barney – you were both paid in full. Over and above, actually. I was very grateful. Let's leave it at that. We're done, get it, Gottfried?"

"Excuse me, Mr. Walker. We are done only when I say we are done, and not one minute before. Must I remind you? I know where your wife is. And so does Barney."

Heart plummeting, Erik drew a slow breath before responding to Gottfried, whose gruff tone indicated he was not fishing for a reaction, nor in a mood to play games, but felt certain he held all the cards.

"Gotcha. Look, Bert. I've already had lunch today, and my afternoon is filled with meetings. I can meet you at lunch tomorrow. The Battery. We can grab a sandwich, sit outside and talk. Can I use this number to reach you?:

"Affirmative."

"I'll call you on my cell phone around 11:00 tomorrow. We can agree where to meet. That way, you'll have my number. And incidentally - don't call me here again. Not if you want to be taken seriously."

Erik was dismayed to see his hand shaking as he moved to replace the office phone in its cradle. His hesitation, though, kept the phone on speaker just long enough to hear the second click, of another landline being hung up. He bounded up from his chair, raced to the door, and flung it open to regard April busily typing 'thank you' letters to contributors.

"Was that you?" he asked brusquely, startling his assistant.

"Was that me? Doing what? I'm working on the donor letters you asked me to write, Mr. Walker. Did I do something wrong?"

"No. No. Not at all. Carry on. Is Tracey in this afternoon?"

"Yes. She's upstairs in the gym working with Victor, Agnes, and their trainer – she's been with them all afternoon. But she's got her cell phone with her. Need me to call her?"

"Don't bother, April. I need to stretch my legs anyway. I'll look in on them and see how they're doing.

"Oh, and please block that last caller, April. It was my old broker, pestering me to get my investment business back in his control. Irritating fellow. That was why I moved my account. That, and the fact I no longer trust his advice. Thank you."

Erik was driven to find out if Tracey had been on the line, listening. The gym area had no landline phones – only the wall phone which directly dialed 911 in the event of a medical or physical emergency, and was exclusive to that purpose. Everyone used mobile devices on the rooftop to communicate. Her office was two floors below. Had she somehow picked up an active line and just stayed on to hear the call as it came in from April's switchboard? Erik didn't even know if that were possible. And April appeared to have been totally absorbed in her task when he'd opened the door to his office.

But who else could it have been? Barney?

"Barney the toothless wonder" is how he used to refer to Herbert Gottfried's assistant whenever thinking of the man, who seemed to have little education, few teeth, and no last name.

They had worked for him, but Tracey had never met either man.

Erik was unnerved. This duo's reappearance was the last thing he ever thought would happen, particularly since their move to New York City, a metropolis of nearly 8.5 million permanent residents and around 38 million overnight tourists each year.

How had they found him – and Tracey? Gottfried had specifically mentioned Tracey. But he had never met her – or had he? Had Erik talked about his daughter? Had she come home from classes while Bert and Barney were still around? Erik racked his brain. He was mystified. How would Gottfried know about his daughter – and know her by name?

When the elevator doors slid open, Erik headed for the area where most of the scale models were constructed and used for training, mind still churning with questions.

It was about time that he paid more attention to what the girl was doing these days, he decided. She no longer went through him to speak to the Bodhi, which was both good and bad. Her relationship with the triplets was excellent. Far better than his, in fact. Erik was nervous around the three of them. They creeped him out, actually. They seemed to know far more about him and Tracey than they let on, and he found that quite disturbing.

Had one of them been on the line? He had no doubt they had access to all the landlines through a separate switchboard. And he had no doubt they listened to calls as a means of monitoring their foundation, since they never left their dedicated floor in the building, except when they were taking the limousine to a meeting, or leaving town on those very rare occasions when they returned to their homeland to attend a wedding or funeral, or visit relatives, and were heading to the airport to catch their flight.

I'll bet it was one of them, he muttered. The Investigator. What was his name? Alivesh Abrer. The nosey one. Always asking questions unexpectedly. It was a technique to throw you off guard, to catch you unaware, and without time to think how to answer. All the while, he fixed you with his beady eyes.

No, he was happy to let Tracey meet with them alone. If he had completed reports to deliver, or was able to follow a written agenda with specific matters to address, those seemed to be the only situations in which he felt comfortable around the triplets. As Tracey had grown closer to them, Erik found it safe to withdraw, But he also wondered what they might be telling her things that he was missing out on – important tidbits of potentially helpful information.

When Erik walked into the huge room where the mockup of the Ferris now nearly reached the ceiling far above, he had to stop a moment to take it all in. The framework holding the car had been increased in height until it now reached a height of 50 feet, the altitude close to what they would be working with, when the retribution was planned. Erik was deeply involved with the planning of the fair, since it was intended as a fundraiser for Truvenge Foundation, but he had steered clear of the activities of the Kriya Project in that regard.

Tracey was standing atop a scaffold at an equal height with the Ferris wheel car that held Agnes Marie, Victor, and the trapeze artist, who, Erik noted, was listed on the employee roster as Stephan Burovich, but who went by his preferred name, Azar. She waved at Erik and hollered, "Glad you could join us! You need to see this! We've been at it a while, but I think it will work great to achieve our purpose!"

Well, Erik thought. That shoots that theory. There is no way that Tracey had been on the line.

Again, he wondered if the listener had been one, or all of the Bodhi. That was his greatest fear.

"Hi, everyone!" Erik greeted them. "I had a few minutes and thought I would just look in and see what all of you were up to. Practicing, I see!!"

Tracey carefully climbed down from the scaffold. It took a few minutes, confirming to Erik that she could not possibly have been the stealth listener. Once down from the height, Tracey walked over and stood beside her father, remarking, "They are doing really well. I thought today's adjustment to almost full height might be daunting, but the team is on top of it. I think they could do this in their sleep. I am very proud of Victor and Agnes. And Joe Belton, who is off for the month in San Antonio, pursuing the errant building contractor by using the full weight of the IRS against him. Did you know that if you blow the whistle on a tax scofflaw, you can get a reward for turning them in, if and when delinquent taxes and interest are assessed against that person? Joe apparently has done this a lot, and very effectively," she told him.

"Ace Hollander will be ruined, if not jailed, and we plan to scare the *merde* out of this Fitz character to get him to arrive at a suitable settlement with Mr. Lewis."

"Ace Hollander?" Erik laughed. "My lord, that sounds like a stage name." "I know," Tracey laughed. "But Joe verified that is his given name." "Who's Lewis again?" Erik asked.

"Quirky Lewis. The 'Candy King' is how he was known, until Fitz cheated him out of any claim to the incredibly popular candy Lewis invented."

"Ahh, That fellow. I recall the petition now. Filed it himself, did he?"

"Yup," Tracey responded, eyes glued to the four figures above. Azar had brought an assistant with him to stand in for the absent Jason Fitz.

"I know Azar. But who's the young guy with him?" Erik asked.

"We were introduced, but I didn't catch his name," Tracey said, eyes glued to the scene far above the polished wood floor. "Watch this. Don't look away, or you'll miss it."

She and Erik watched intently as the figures moved silently high above them, and the car of the Ferris wheel mockup began to sway sickeningly as the occupants changed positions.

"Oh my God!" Erik gasped and stared forward as, suddenly, the nameless young man – who was moving to the far side of Victor - was bumped by Azar, lost his footing, and dove through the lower central barrier of the car, flipping over the edge and – flailing and grasping desperately upward to grip the side of the car and stop his fall. Azar found his wrist and expertly gripped it. He dangled the young man over the edge for a minute or so as Azar said something to him. The young fellow nodded vigorously and was quickly pulled back into the car, where he promptly sat down, stunned, and wiped his brow with the handkerchief Azar handed him.

"Are you okay?" Tracey and Erik called up to him. He shouted down, "No matter how many times we go through this, I still can't stay cool and collected. It always feels like the first time!"

"Let's call it a day," Tracey called up to the group. "Good job, gang. We'll start again tomorrow."

"Want to take a short walk?" Tracey asked Erik. "Here, on the rooftop. Just a quick stroll."

Erik looked at her quizzically, and followed her outside. "I just thought I needed to alert you, as President of Truvenge Foundation, to a protocol breach. It just happened last night, and I have not yet had a chance to speak to the Bodhi about this. Besides, I thought that you needed to know about this, as well."

"What's the deal, Tracey? How concerned should I be?"

"I think it will be okay. He promised not to follow me around, and swore last night's meeting was unintentional."

"Who are you talking about?"

"Quirky Lewis. I had to take a break last night, so I went out for food. I chose to get a hamburger platter at The Diner. I know you think it is a dive, but I love their burgers and fries, and they make the best ice cream sodas! Quirky Lewis somehow ended up in the same place for dinner, and recognized me from my online photos."

"From the Truvenge website?"

"Yeah. It might be a good idea to take my photo off of the site. To maintain confidentiality and avoid a repeat situation. I cannot afford to be recognized."

"Agreed. I will take care of that his afternoon."

"He said he was just looking at our website online. Wanted to know a little about our organization after he filed his petition, and it was granted. He claimed he loved to eat at The Diner and had just stopped in for a bite to eat when he recognized me from my photo. He picked up his food and came over to my booth, then asked if he could join me. What was I supposed to do? Send him away, food in hand? He's a nice enough fellow. I told him he was breaking protocol and we could never be seen together again. We chatted briefly as we ate, like strangers do, and I let him know to not do that again. He walked me to the car, since it was late, and we said goodbye. Worst thing is, now I can never go back to The Diner. That really bums me out."

"Do you think he has been following you? Does he know anything about what is going on?" Erik asked.

"He swore that was not the case – that he did not realize he was doing anything wrong, but since he recognized me he thought it would be okay to come over and introduce himself. Have a little company while he ate. He did not intend to break any rules. He did see the Ferris wheel rental contract, I'd brought with me to go over. And he did mention it. I told him about our fair to raise funds for Truvenge – just a routine fundraiser that we had done in the past. He bought it.

I did not mention a single thing about his case except that it was rare for anyone to be accepted on a self-filed petition and that I could not discuss anything about it. He bought it. Was very apologetic. Very nice. But we cannot afford accidental meetings like that. I need to keep a very low profile."

"Well, I'm glad you told me. I think it will be all right," Erik told her. "But I fully agree that we need to keep you out of the limelight."

"Thank you. I'm headed to see the Bodhi now. Need me to carry any messages?"

"Only that I send my best regards, Tracey. I have a full afternoon. Meetings, two donor appointments today should be successful. You can pass that on to them."

"Will do."

Chapter 17 – An Unpleasant Meeting

It was overcast when Erik left Truvenge and started walking the several blocks to The Battery, at the south tip of Manhattan. Once known as Battery Park, the 25 acre park on the Hudson River faced New York Harbor at its southernmost point. He had arranged to meet Herbert Gottfried and Barney at the East Coast Memorial, but didn't bother to stop to buy a sandwich. There was no way the lump in his stomach would permit him to eat a bite. He did have the foresight, however, to bring an umbrella, which he paused to open as drops began to fall steadily from the leaden sky. He prayed it would not lead to a downpour.

His mood was somber, but his mind was searching for the best way to confront and cope with this unexpected development.

Erik arrived at the statue before the two men he was to meet and was amused when, nearly ten minutes later, he saw them approach. Barney was carrying a large bag of sandwiches, and it appeared that Gottfried sprang for a sub for Erik, as well.

Barney was also struggling to hold a large golf umbrella over his significantly broader and taller Boss. Erik tamed a smirk, watching Barney hustle behind Gottfried while clutching the umbrella and the bag of sandwiches, careful to extend his reach far enough to cover Gottfried's head, his little legs pumping madly.

Greetings were awkward. To say the least.

They found relatively dry seats under the branches of a large tree and settled in for a damp and unpredictable encounter.

"Here. An Italian sub with everything on it," Barney abruptly announced, pulling a crisply wrapped foot-long sandwich from the no-longer-crisp white bag. He quipped, as he handed it to Erik, "Don't say we never gave you nothin'."

"Hmmmm," Erik replied. "A lot of interesting negatives in that sentence. Thanks for the sandwich, fellows. I'll take it back to the office with me, if you don't mind, Barney.

"Now, I do need to get back to the office as soon as possible, so let's cut to the chase. I assume, Gottfried, that you have a purpose for this little meeting?"

"We do," Barney declared confidently, openly checking this bold assertion with Gottfried by glancing at the older man for approval.

Gottfried nodded his assent, explaining to Erik. "I've taken Barney under my wing. Kind of like a protégé, to help me with my businesses."

"Businesses?" Eric questioned.

"Yeah," Gottfried responded, holding up a hand to warn Barney to be quiet. "Barney and I have developed a unique business idea for a new start-up, a side business to what we usually do. And it involves you, Mr. Walker."

"Yeah, that's what I was going to say," Barney piped up, ignoring Gottfried's raised hand. "You're involved, Walker. And me and Gottfried will be your partners."

"Hush, Barney. Let me do the talking," Gottfried commanded. He took a bite of his sandwich, chewed thoughtfully, and swallowed. He popped the top on his soda, took a swig and finally turned to address Erik.

"We learned something very interesting last night. Barney wasn't actually with me, when I overheard a very interesting conversation. He was on camera duty outside, waiting for your lovely daughter and her client, friend, or whatever to leave one of my favorite burger joints – The Diner. You should try it some time. Great place."

Erik's first thought was, Thank God Tracey mentioned this to me! I would have been blindsided, and at a complete loss.

Under the circumstances, he managed to keep a bland expression, and said nothing.

"Funny, Barney and I thought the first thing you'd ask about was how we found you two. It would have been the first thing on my mind when old friends turn up, unannounced – friends I'm sure that you felt confident you'd conveniently left behind when you and your daughter hightailed it out of Tampa. But you see, I am a man of few prospects, so I value anything I see as an asset.

"After doing the work on your house, just as you ordered, I didn't give a thought to the peculiarity of your instructions. I mean, it's none of my business what you plan to do with a narrow, windowless and doorless addition to your home, with a very narrow entry. Closet? Extra storage space? Not my job to worry about your intentions. You paid well, and paid on time.

"But then your wife's disappearance hit the news. I never met her, so I didn't pay attention to it until they interviewed you on TV, and then everything fell into place. As the weeks went by, and the news coverage continued, I became increasingly more certain of what had happened." Gottfried took another huge bite of his sub, gulped more of his canned soda, and continued.

"What to do, what to do? I discussed my thoughts with Barney here, and as the investigation of your involvement wound down, he suggested you would leave town the minute you were cleared by police. He also suggested we should keep an eye on you. See how we could work our suspicions to our advantage. Brilliant idea, kid!" Gottfried reached over and patted Barney's sallow cheek.

Barney beamed, his face framed by dripping wet hair. The umbrella was not large enough to cover but one of them, and Gottfried's girth had won out.

"It made so much sense! So we started keeping an eye on you, and your daughter. Barney watched you going in and out of Kinko's, did a little sleuthing, and learned you were sending out resumes, looking for work. When you stopped mailing them out, I figured you'd found something, and we started watching the house, checking with moving companies. When you left the house one day with an overnight bag, we correctly figured you'd landed an interview out of town – or out of state. Long story short, we tracked you to New York City, and figured, correctly, that you'd soon be working for another charity. So we went online and used *Guidestar,* or some such, to search all the New York City charities, then went through all their websites to find announcements of new hires. Bingo! Truvenge announced a new Director, new President, and soon, a new Chief Investigator for a thing called Kriya Project.

"So, we knew you had moved to New York City. Odd thing was, you kept your house. We kept waiting for a For Sale or For Rent sign to go up, but nothing. Apparently, you had a reason to keep the house, even when you both were working so far away. That was peculiar. So we decided to take a field trip. And here we are."

"I can see that," Erik commented acerbically. "Look, that was a nice story. Hope you are both enjoying your visit to New York. Can we get to the point of this meeting? I am trying to accommodate you, but I have a job to get back to before the end of the day."

"The point is, Mr. Walker, that we have a strong hunch you were directly involved with your wife's disappearance. A very strong hunch. And we have been debating between us just what we should do with that suspicion, given that we may have unknowingly assisted you in disposing of her – uh – person. Her body. And we have had serious discussions, wondering how interested the police might be regarding the work we did at your house."

"And your decision?" Erik asked brusquely.

"We haven't arrived at a decision yet," Barney added, glancing at Gottfried for approval.

"Barney's right. We have not arrived at a decision yet. Coincidentally, we ate at The Diner last night. And who was within hearing distance of us? A certain Miss Tracey Walker. We both grew beards before making this trip, and we both were wearing knit caps. It was no surprise that she failed to recognize us. She sat in a booth nearby, kind of out of the main dining area, and had two folders with her, which she started to read after ordering. Then this fellow showed up, his food in hand, and asked to sit down. She looked shocked, and seemed very upset that he was there.

"We didn't think it was a boyfriend. He was too formal with her. Then he said who he was, and apologized that he had recognized her. Turns out he is a big fan of The Diner, too – who knew it was so popular?"

Barney piped up again. "Don't you want to know who it was?"

"I know who it was. Quirky Lewis. Tracey and I spoke about it this morning. Your point?" Erik said. He'd always considered Barney to be extremely annoying, and had never hidden his disdain for the man.

"The point is," Gottfried told Erik, "that irked as she was, she still permitted Mr. Lewis to join her, and we were able to hear their entire conversation. Seems like there is a part of your organization that deals with settling old scores that still need settling. Seems like that would be a lucrative business."

"It's not," Erik snapped. "Truvenge is a nonprofit, charitable organization. And the Kriya Project is part of that organization."

"As I said, seems like that could be a lucrative business. We could sell what your organization is giving away. Split the proceeds," Gottfried remarked. "There are lots of people – very influential people – people with a lot of cash – who could appreciate a service like that. What does it take, a petition? We could do that. You see that it is approved. And then you do whatever you see fit to settle things. What did Lewis call it, Barney, 'delivering karma'? There are quite a few people who could benefit from a 'karma' delivery service, and would pay very well for it."

Erik stood abruptly, his still-wrapped sandwich falling from his lap onto the pavement, and opened his umbrella with a snap. His unopened soda was on the bench and – with a smirk – Herbert Gottfried handed it to him. "Think about it, Mr. Walker. Give our proposal some serious thought. We'll be in touch."

"Yeah, we'll be in touch," echoed Barney. The little man with the crooked teeth and missing teeth grinned and nodded at Erik as he repeated Gottfried's words, and picked up their waxed paper and cans. Barney noticeably stepped around Erik's wrapped sandwich, still on the concrete where it had fallen when Erik had stood abruptly. Taunting him, Barney exposed his snaggled teeth in an overly-broad grin as he used elaborate movements to stuff their trash in a bin, while pointedly gazing at the dropped sandwich. That ugly gnome then opened the golf umbrella and skittered after his stout boss.

The stone eagle, forever poised as landing atop the East Coast Monument with talons extended, glared down at Erik who – after a moment of absolute fury - strode away in the opposite direction. The rain had tapered to a fine drizzle, almost a mist, so he didn't bother with opening his umbrella, but clutched it in his fist so tightly his knuckles whitened. He was livid with anger.

Anger at the two men, of course – grotesque connivers that they were! But, primarily, Erik was angry with himself for hiring them. That, and being so heedless in the casual conversations he'd had with Gottfried, to let slip personal information; information that helped them track him and Tracey to New York; to the Truvenge Foundation. To the Kriya Project

Damn!

His mind raced as his feet pounded against the pavement. The rain had stopped, but he still had to dodge the occasional puddle.

Erik was gratified Tracey had given him a heads up about her encounter at The Diner with Quirky Lewis, the gummy drop creator and Candy King. He pondered the situation as he strode along. The problem was two pronged, and delicate, involving both his and Tracey's positions at the Foundation, as well as Kriya Project, the Bodhi's dearest endeavor. Undercutting his double dilemma was the major issue of managing and diffusing the workmen's suspicions, now that they'd recognized the monetary value of their knowledge. Dealing with this unexpected development would certainly require deep thought, and some careful gaming of his options, and their potential outcomes. Right now, however, was not the time to tackle such a huge challenge.

Breathe, Erik silently coached himself. Take slow, deep breaths.

And remember, this is a just one more problem in a very long series of problems, every one of them tackled successfully. That's been my life, Erik thought. Nothing has ever been easy.

The best thing about problems is that they eventually have a solution, he mused. Yet all solutions have consequences, both good and bad. Risk/reward. He would have to carefully weigh his choices.

Erik decided to set aside some time to deal with it this weekend. But for this afternoon, his first task was to find someone to redesign that damned website!

He shook the water from his umbrella outside the entrance to the Truvenge Building, entered and rode an empty elevator to his floor. As the door slid open and he entered the President's office suite, April - typing rapidly, and never breaking rhythm – told him, "Before you get settled in for the afternoon, the Bodhi would like to see you."

Erik stopped in his tracks. "About anything in particular?"

"Didn't say," she replied. "Do you have any reports due? I can whip something up if you have to bring them something. They said for me to call and let them know when you were on your way up."

"Thank you April. It was drizzling on my walk back. Misty. I need to dry and comb my hair, make sure I don't look like a drowned rat."

Great, Erik thought as he entered his office and made his way to the bathroom. Just great! Exactly what I didn't need to happen after that fiasco.

He towel dried his hair and combed it, checked his teeth and smiled at himself in the mirror.

Buck up, Walker, he urged himself.

Smile. Breathe. Can't lose confidence.

It's showtime.

Chapter 18 – Life is a Carnival

It was a glorious New York day. Crisp air, warm sun, puffy clouds in a baby blue sky, with just the barest of breezes riffling the leaves. Along the streets, on the corners, and in the parks of the City, the scent of roasting nuts and caramel popcorn filled the air as vendors' toasty wares advertised their goodness and availability to passersby. It was that time of year.

Victor, Agnes Marie, Azar and Tracey strolled through the landscaped grounds of Astoria Park in Queens after enjoying an early walk along the Park's Shore Boulevard on the East River. While enjoying the views, they'd consumed the breakfast sandwiches Victor had picked up for them on his way to the Park, and they were headed back to watch the huge parking lot undergo its transformation into a fairground, and supervise the way in which the Truvenge carnival was being set up.

It was just under a day until D-Day. Since early morning, trucks with extended beds had been arriving, driving into the Astoria Park parking lot and pulling up to their assigned area beneath the RFK BRIDGE – once known as Triborough Bridge - then unloading their cargo: steel and aluminum poles, platforms, painted arcs, cushioned seats, spans, cars, and gondolas or capsules – all the crucial parts belonging to the various carnival rides which, once assembled, would thrill and entertain festive crowds of visitors for four full days.

Astoria Park was an eminently suitable location on the west shore of New York City's huge borough of Queens, adjacent to the picturesque middle-class neighborhood of Astoria, founded as a village in 1839, and named in honor of John Jacob Astor, a wealthy fur merchant. The park extended along the shore of the East River from Triborough Bridge (more recently renamed RFK Bridge) that connects Queens to Randall's Island, and to an area just north of Hell Gate Bridge.

Vistas to the south displayed the mid-Manhattan skyline, while to the north one could view the treacherous waters of Hell Gate Channel - New York Harbor's deepest water - with its dangerous reef and extreme depths resulting from deep faults that had long ago scarred the earth's crust. The RFK Bridge linked Queens with Randall's Island, directly across the East River from Astoria Park.

In response to public pressure demanding better access to the East River and its shoreline, the first 56 acres of what later became Astoria Park in the Village of Astoria were purchased by the City of New York in late 1913. In 1937 a parcel of 4.5 acres under the Triborough Bridge was purchased to expand the park, which was further enlarged in 1969 with the purchase of a 5-acre strip directly on the East River, bringing the Park's size to 65.5 well-maintained acres. Astoria Park was among the largest parks in NYC.

This park boasted six tennis courts, two large playgrounds, a fully equipped comfort station, a bandstand, enormous wading pool, athletic field, and three baseball fields, plus walkways and trails that meandered for miles through its manicured, hilly landscape.

Astoria Park had first hosted a carnival in 2011. It was the first demonstration of the large parking lot's ease of adaptation into a fairground capable of supporting thousands of visitors while offering the usual gustatory delights, rides appropriate to different ages, and sizable game booths typical of county fairs and carnival midways, with lots of room for much larger rides, including the Ferris wheel Truvenge had rented, which would soar 65 feet above the ground at its highest point, once fully assembled, inspected, and authorized by the City.

The four of them were planning the day at the park, to witness its assembly and become acquainted with the venue as the other rides were erected, the midway was laid out, and the Truvenge Carnival finally began to take shape. The carnival had been made possible by its leading sponsor, Mr. Jason Fitz, the recently appointed President of the George Fitz Candy Company, Inc., Quirky Lewis' nemesis.

The serendipitous site was now committed to the annual Astoria Park Carnival, which took the site over, for a four-day period each June. The Astoria Park Carnival had quickly grown in popularity after its founding and took place at the Park's large parking area off 19th Street and Hoyt Avenue North, and set up under the RFK Bridge, which assured dry entertainment, even in sudden spring rainstorms.

With a little cajoling and a personal visit from the Bodhi, the carnival location was also made available to the Truvenge Foundation and the numerous smaller local charities that would be joining together with Truvenge in a mutual fundraising effort. with potential to renew the Carnival annually.

"I thought you'd settled on Flushing Meadows-Corona Park as the carnival's venue, a few months back," Victor commented to Tracey as they walked. "What made you change your mind and switch to

270

Astoria Park? I've lived in the City for decades, and never even knew this was out here. Isn't this area part of Long Island? It seems pretty far out, a good distance from the City."

"What do you consider 'the City', Victor? New York City is huge! It's comprised of five boroughs, and some of those boroughs encompass as many as three counties. This is still Queens. Queens is the largest borough in New York City. It's a big chunk of land, with both urban and suburban neighborhoods. You're correct, Queens *is* in western Long Island – Brooklyn, too – although most people only think of Long Island as holding only Nassau and Sussex counties.

"But you asked what induced me to go with Astoria Park as the locale for our carnival, instead of Flushing Meadows? Let me give you a list: Pricing, availability on short notice, proximity to our client base, ease of transportation – Flushing Meadows is more difficult to get to, and Astoria Park is actually easier, especially for families using public transportation. Plus, I happen to know someone who's very active with the Astoria Park Alliance, and helped Erik and me in dealing with the Alliance objections, as well as negotiations with the New York Parks Commission."

Agnes Marie remarked, "It's not *what* you know, it's *who* you know. That's a credo I've been very aware of since I was a child."

"Yup, it's a hard truth," Tracey noted.

That was not all that she noted. Azar and Agnes Marie appeared to have hit it off splendidly. It was apparent that sparks were flying between them.

Tracey paused to question... Should she be worried? Could romance throw a monkey wrench in what promised to be a smooth operation?

She'd have to think about that – when she had the time. For now, their interest in one another presented an opportunity to release the lovebirds for an hour or two and assure that they were out of sight.

They had reached the parking lot that was to be the site of the carnival. The Ferris wheel had arrived at least an hour earlier on a huge semitrailer pulled by an enormous cab and accompanied by a large service truck pulling a big diesel generator. Tracey had driven out early to meet the drivers and point out the planned location, which would be prominently situated to attract attention. The mobile generator was to be located in a grassy spot within 150 feet of where the Ferris wheel was to be erected, since two metal grounding rods had to be driven into the terrain to electrically ground the generator. The surrounding trees and grass would also absorb the aggravating sound of the generator as it produced the strong current necessary to drive the Ferris wheel.

The Ferris wheel itself would be sturdily mounted on asphalt and positioned in a busy section of the fair to attract maximum attention, surrounded by popular rides that would also invite the most interest.

Prominently visible. Fitz will love that, Tracey had thought when deciding on location.

The site was around 27 feet wide and a little over 60 feet long.

Once all parts had been unloaded, Tracey was assured, setup of the Ferris wheel would only take a surprising three hours or so to erect.

"Look," she told Agnes Marie and Azar, "you two kids will soon have to skedaddle for a couple of hours. Go to a movie, an arcade or a sports bar. Have a long conversation. Just stay far from this park. We cannot risk

Jason Fitz spotting you here before you meet him tomorrow when you sit in the gondola. Victor and I will meet with him in front of the Ferris wheel while it's being assembled. He wants to follow its progress for a while, as it's being built, and I need to get the rental, insurance, and fundraising paperwork signed."

Victor explained, "Jason is apparently fascinated by the idea of having the ride named after him and his company. Something about how he loved riding Ferris wheels as a child. It was a big selling point. Fortuitous choice of rides to use in our plan!

"He'll have a professional photographer with him," Tracey added. "And he wanted the ride sign for the Ferris wheel to be *huge* and carry his name in large print. He demanded that we had to paint "Under new management" beneath the George Fitz Candy Company name. Not much ego involved in his charitable giving, is there? What do you want to bet he's already working with lawyers on a name change for his candy company."

"When is the sign to be delivered?" Agnes Marie asked.

"Any minute," Tracey responded. "So I want the two of you to leave. Go find a place for lunch, preferably many miles away from the park. We can afford no accidental meetings with anyone who might later recognize the two of you."

Azar spoke up. "You've got it, boss. I'll keep this young lady amused for a while."

Agnes Marie giggled like a schoolgirl.

She was obviously quite taken with Azar's chiseled physique and handsome face. His hair was starting to thin just a tad, but all in all, Tracey mused, she could see why Agnes was attracted to him.

Victor grinned at her reaction, and teased, "Get out of here, you two. Fitz absolutely cannot see either of you prior to tomorrow morning. My good buddy and fellow Mason, Jason Edward Fitz, *absolutely cannot lay eyes on you* until tomorrow when the Carnival opens. Only then will Azar and Agnes Marie join us. Fitz wants to be the very first to ride on the Ferris wheel."

"We'll be back late in the day," Agnes advised. "I haven't seen a matinee movie in ages. How about taking me to the movies, Azar? And to get an ice cream cone.

Tracey clapped her hands at the two of them. "Okay, kids. Hustle, hustle. Get out of here. See you around 5:00, back here. Jason Fitz is coming out on his lunch hour, and will be here *precisely* at 1:15. I have all the Truvenge and rental docs, and Astoria Park paperwork ready for him to sign as a major sponsor of the Carnival, and as sole sponsor of this ride. I want the three of you to examine the gondola. That will take about a half hour, and the ride should be assembled by the time we are done – or nearly so. Then the rental company will take over, and operate the ride, On the last day, at closing, the rental company will have this Ferris wheel take apart and loaded onto the truck within 4 hours, and then they will haul it away.

The site was noisy, with trucks arriving and unloading steel beams, motors, generators, and the like. Beeping cranes were lifting the parts into place and roustabouts where shouting to one another.

Victor and Tracey intended to watch as smaller components of the Ferris wheel were unloaded from the truck and construction work began. Victor had driven alone to the site, bringing their supplies for the day. Tracey had driven alone to Astoria Park, to be there when the trucks began to arrive. Azar and Agnes Marie had arrived together. Victor had brought enough folding chairs for everyone, plus a cooler of beverages and a few bags of snacks. He had prepared well, since they intended to spend the entire day onsite.

Tracey was watching the men unloading the trailer chassis, which had been unhooked from the cab after its placement in the desired location she'd pointed out for them to erect the Ferris wheel.

The roustabouts working all around them were of all ages. Some were seasoned carnival pros who worked for the companies from which the Ferris wheel and a number of other rides had been rented by Truvenge. Others appeared to be temporary hires - young men just out of high school, or unemployed men at loose ends who were willing to take day jobs.

"Here we go, Tracey, all the comforts of home!"

Victor arrived on scene carrying three folding chairs and dragging a wheeled cooler behind him. Tracey, ready for something to drink. rummaged for a soda.

"What!?" she exclaimed in disappointment. "No Orange Crush?"

"Sorry. I couldn't find that specific brand. But if you dig, I think I did pick up some kind of orange soda," Victor responded. Mollified, Tracy found one, popped the top, and settled into the chair next to his.

They watched and sipped their sodas as they marveled at the variety of structural steel shapes that had rested between the wheel support towers attached to the chassis, remarking at the way all parts of the Ferris wheel had been nestled tightly together for transport.

Tracey told Victor, "Over the past months I've learned an incredible amount about Ferris wheels, both to understand how the ride itself was constructed and operated, for our planning, and to be able to have a credible initial conversation with Fitz, and persuade him to fund the effort. Which is the ultimate irony."

"Karma," Said Victor, nodding.

They watched as the wheel spokes, tubing - both round and square - the wheel's crossmembers and wide-flanged beams were unloaded and stacked on the asphalt pavement. Separate stacks were created for the aluminum parts – heavy aluminum plates with diamond treads for the entrance and exit walkways, as well as the platform for the ride operator; aluminum seats, and sections of the wheel's drive rim which – once attached to the spokes – would form a circle about 10 feet smaller than the outermost wheel rim from which the seats would be suspended.

Tracy explained that a pair of rubber drive wheels would be set up and would push against the aluminum drive rims, causing the wheel to rotate. The wheel's persistent rotation would quickly rub any painted steel bare, exposing the drive rims a vital element of the Ferris wheel, to rust. Therefore, aluminum was necessary.

"Most components are specifically manufactured by the company building the Ferris wheel. Other necessary parts – especially electrical ones like drive motors and the copper rings that bring electrical power from the hubs to lights on the rotating spokes, the brushes supplying power to the rings, electrical cables and wires, and the bulbs and sockets for the electrical lights are all made by other manufacturers, as are the tires, brakes, axles for the chassis, and the cab that pulls the whole lot, plus the plastic-covered support cables, protected as they are from inclement weather. The plastic covers also work with the themes and colors of the particular Ferris wheel.

"Can you believe that everything necessary to erect a this, and every traveling Ferris wheel is required to conform to specific measurements? That's what restricts their size. Believe me, I was ready to rent the biggest Ferris wheel that I could – bigger than this one!

"Ferris wheels designed to for road transport from one location to the next have to conform to the height, width, and length restrictions mandated for highway vehicles. Restrictions can, and do vary from state to state. But most states limit trailer width to just eight feet, six inches, with a maximum height of thirteen and a half feet. Length is restricted to 55 feet, which is two inches longer that the restriction on semitrailers."

"Why is that allowed?" Victor asked Tracey.

"I think the exception is because it is considered a piece of machinery that cannot be reduced in size. But that's why you can't rent a Ferris wheel much over 55 feet high. When fully erected and in operation, the wheel Truvenge rented will be about 60 feet in diameter and it will be about 65 feet above the ground at its apex, when you consider the chassis supporting the wheel, with the steps and operation platform."

"How many will it carry, when filled to capacity?" Victor asked.

"When full, our Ferris wheel has a capacity to carry up to 64 riders in 16 seats. That's four people - or two couples – per gondola."

Looking around at all the activity, Victor commented, "Can you imagine what this place will look like when its filled with amusement park rides, booths of games and the scent of carnival food in the air?

"Yum! I live for the dreadfully unhealthy food you can buy at carnivals," he declared. "I can never resist, even though my doctor doesn't approve, and my stomach and bowels generally complain well into the next day! Somehow, though, I can't fight the temptation presented by a deep-fried candy bar or Polish sausage on a grilled bun, piled high with sauteed peppers and onions." He laughed.

They fell silent and watched as a pair of hydraulic tubes on either side of the anchoring chassis began to extend, pulling with them the two hinged Ferris wheel support towers – each with a narrow ladder at the edge to enable access to the wheel's electrical drive motors, the drive rim wheels and other essential parts for repair or maintenance.

When Victor queried, Tracey explained that the purpose of the square -tubed support arms on each side of the towers, which were slowly extending in length as the two towers rose to upright position, was to provide the large wheel with the side-to-side stability it required. Anchored by the length, breadth, and weight of the chassis, these supporting arms would be pulled to each side and solidly locked into place. The cavity in the tubing would protect the electrical and hydraulic lines.

The operation platform and the steps were installed next.

Victor then asked, "What are the safety restrictions? What's the accident protection like? You know, with the Ferris wheel's safety measures?"

"Well, the design of every Ferris wheel has to take into account the precise calculations necessary to be certain that the horizontal and vertical forces of the wheel, when the ride is fully loaded, can be supported by its structure. Once it starts to rotate at full speed, the forces are enormous. So, that is a form of safety restriction. Safety interlocks have to be specifically designed to prevent the wheel from starting to revolve, or moving unexpectedly when loading and unloading riders. And to prevent accidents.

"The safety interlocks are what keep a distracted or inexperienced operator from inadvertently doing something stupid, or operating the Ferris wheel unsafely. As to operation, I don't think it can be too complicated. 'Start/Stop – Rotate -Full Rotation'. Not exactly rocket science, you know. I don't think many amusement ride operators are Rhodes scholars! What time is it, Vic?"

"We have about another fifteen minutes before Fitz is due to show," he answered, displaying to Tracey, what appeared to be a very expensive watch. But then, Victor didn't mind bragging that he was a hard worker and a *really* friendly guy who had done exceptionally well in his business.

Good for him, Tracey thought. He had certainly been effective in getting Jason Fitz to become a major sponsor of the Carnival event. Better yet, Fitz was footing the entire bill for the Ferris wheel.

"Let me get my briefcase out of the car – keys, please, Victor? I have all of Fitz's paperwork in it, and I have to get his signed forms to the right people, pronto," Tracey told him. "I'm riding the grace period. Be right back."

She had no sooner returned from the car when Victor spotted Jason Fitz parking his own car.

Tracery followed his fixed gaze and turned to see what he was staring at, then whistled. "Aston Martin. Wow. Fitz knows his cars."

"It must be a new purchase," Victor remarked. "He used to drive a black sedan. Big car. I forget the make. But it was definitely not a sports car. New position, you know. And I think he talked the company Board into authorizing a pretty significant raise when he took over his dad's position. This looks like a splurge."

"Is he married?" Tracey asked, purely out of curiosity.

"No," Victor said. "At least, not at present. Not sure if there's an -ex. He's never mentioned anyone."

Tracey smirked. "It figures! No one to object to the purchase - or demand equal treatment. No baby carrier; no car seat to strap into the back seat. If there even *is* a back seat."

"Jason, hello! Over here," Victor called out, standing as he waved to the tall, thin man hurrying in their direction.

Tracey stood to shake hands. "Hi, Jason! It's great to meet you in person, at long last," she greeted him.

"Yeah, hi there. Tracey, right? Good to be here. Is that our Ferris wheel in pieces over there? And there? And there? Whoa!! How tall is that thing!? And they are still unloading? Damn, how long will it take to put that together?"

Fitz talked fast, and his questions were rapid-fire, offering Tracey scant opportunity to respond to any of them. He seemed, to her to be as nervous as a Chihuahua - a fact Victor later explained was Jason's normal state.

Although Jason had told Tracey how eager he was to watch the installation of the Ferris wheel, he quickly lost interest and seemed impatient to move business along as he jiggled one knee for a minute or so while watching, then sharply tapped the other knee with two fingers of his right hand and said abruptly, "You have some papers for me to sign? Where are they?"

Tracey reached for her briefcase and clicked the locks to open the case and produce the papers.

"Oh, and isn't there supposed to be a sign? For the Ferris wheel, and at the Carnival entrance? I'd like to see those signs. Now, if you don't mind." He was already standing as he said this, looking all around as if they might be nearby, and he had simply overlooked their presence.

Tracey snapped the locks shut once again, celebrating the fact that she had not had to remove the three folders of documents from the hard case, and stood. Glaring for a moment at Victor, who wore a bemused expression and suppressed a smile.

"It's this way, Jason. Please follow me. Victor, will you please keep an eye on my briefcase?"

Jason followed her to the grassy area in the shade, near the silent generator. The large signs lay flat on the wrappings that had been pulled apart to permit Tracey's early-morning inspection and approval. Jason saw them immediately and rushed to see the sign changes that had resulted from his instructions. He stared at the sign, examining every inch, up close, then stepped away to get a better view.

Tracey bent down and lifted each sign with both hands, angling it just enough for Jason to get a better look.

"It's not heavy," she commented when she saw his expression, "But then, for just four days' use, it doesn't have to be. What do you think?"

She watched as he looked at it, walking back and forth in front of the sign. Fitz then retreated a few yards, turned, and came at the sign straight on, as if he were walking up to it as an attendee might, and stood directly in front of it, staring. Jason walked from one side to the other and stopped every few feet to look at it for a good while from every angle.

All this while, Tracey held her breath, waiting for the complaint that would send the sign back to its maker for a last-minute alteration, or an addition.

At last, Fitz uttered his approval. "Superb!" he called out, as though she were twenty feet away, rather than ten. "Now, where were those papers?"

Victor had a soft drink waiting for each of them when they returned. He declined to sit and poured some savory snacks into a shallow bowl that he placed on the seat of the empty chair, instead. "I'll leave you two to your paperwork. "I'm heading over to watch the assembly close up and personal, maybe ask some questions, if they'll tolerate me pestering them.

As Tracey retrieved the folders of contracts, waivers and agreements from the briefcase, she noticed a single typewritten sheet and, thinking it had fallen from the last folder, stuck it at the back of the papers to be signed. Dealing with the man unnerved her, but she was dismayed to see that her feelings reveal themselves in the trembling and fumbling of her hands.

She pulled herself together with some effort, donned a smile, and rapidly introduced him to the nature of each folder, the purpose of each form, and pointed out where he was to sign. Tracey assured Jason she would email a copy of each signed document, and proceeded to have him sign more than a dozen documents, as she took him through the folders to the last paper she intended for him to sign, but hesitated a moment, staring at the paper in her hand while he consulted his watch.

"I have to go," he said, setting the pen atop her briefcase.

"I thought you might want to stay around to watch the operational and safety tests of the wheel, Tracy urged.

"Can't stay for that. I have to get back for a meeting."

It was then Tracey made an executive decision.

"One last page. Sign this one page, so we don't run into problems. – I think we got the docs out of order. I'll have my assistant put them in sequence when I get back. Last signature of the day!" she cajoled. "This is it, and you can go. We'll see you first thing tomorrow, 9:00 a.m. sharp, to take the first ride on your Ferris wheel."

"I will want to say a few words about my company," Jason asserted. "Talk to the people about our products."

"You can have as much time as you need, Mr. Fitz – Jason. You'll be the one determining when the first turn of the Ferris wheel to open the Carnival occurs. And as our major sponsor, you will be on that first ride." Tracey picked up the pen and handed it back to him, pushing the last paper in front of him. "And I hope your photographer gets some great publicity shots."

Jason inked his final signature of the day without a glance at the paperwork, and left, with a farewell wave to Victor, who had just returned.

"Have I scared you away?" Victor joked.

"Not at all," Jason Fitz replied, while walking toward his car. "Everything is as promised. And I have a meeting to get to."

"Until tomorrow!" Victor and Tracey called out as he walked away.

"Nine in the morning! I'll be here," was his reply. And, with a flippant, backhanded wave, Fitz was gone.

Chapter 19 – Karma Has a Mind of Her Own

It was D-Day at last, and a brilliant, crisp Autumn day it was! The carnival rides spread beneath the RFK bridge in a carpet of fun that Tracey hoped would be profitable, as well, while achieving the ends that Kriya Project needed to occur that day. Final plans had been reviewed with Erik, and with the Bodhi, who had given their final approval of all arrangements and plans.

Erik had been unusually glum when Tracey spoke with him at some length toward the end of the previous day. She wondered if his romance with Felicity had hit a snag. He seemed nervous and out of sorts, which she found highly unusual. Tracey was convinced the man she increasingly disliked and sought to avoid, whenever possible, had ice water running through his veins.

To see him distraught for any length of time was unusual, although he had put on a superb show of emotion following the disappearance of his wife – Tracey's mom – and throughout the police investigation. A real Academy Award performance, she thought, deserving of an Oscar. So his apparently real disquiet over anything was highly unusual. Had he actually fallen in love with Felicity?

The Ferris wheel, prominently poised at the entrance to the carnival, bore signage that properly named all contributors, with the name of Jason Fitz, major Carnival sponsor and President of the George Fitz Candy Company – now under new management – writ large on the colorful sign. He should be pleased, Tracey thought.

The Ferris wheel was positioned to capture the best views of New York City and the waterway when the gondolas reached their apex. It should be a very popular ride, she decided with satisfaction.

Vendors, carnies, and ride managers had been arriving in droves to prepare and to finalize details since the first rays of sun began to glitter on the surface of the river, just minutes after sunrise. Tracey had been among the first to arrive, and watched as the cooktops and popcorn machines in the many food kiosks were fired up and began to produce the enticing odors of the staple carnival foods Victor had raved about. Scents of popcorn, candy corn, spun sugar, and fried onions and peppers and pizza filled the air as cooking began for the day, in anticipation of the large weekend crowds that were expected.

Tracey bustled about, checking with vendors, visually inspecting the rides. She fielded a call from Joe that caught her up on his progress nailing Ace Hollander for his crimes through the IRS, and spoke with her friend with the Astoria Park Alliance. This was the first major event she had ever been responsible for, and Tracey was a bundle of nerves. Her stomach growled. She had failed to eat breakfast, so she bought a pretzel to fill the void, but declined the customary German mustard that usually accompanied the treat. Even so, she could only finish half of it.

Victor was the next to show up, sans Agnes Marie.

"Where is she?" Tracey asked him. "I thought you were bringing Agnes?"

"Change of plans. She called me before I left, to tell me Azar would be driving her here this morning."

Tracey was chagrined. "Does that mean they spent the night together?" she inquired.

"Don't know - and didn't want to ask. I have noticed Agnes Marie guards her privacy very closely. Habit, I suppose. Military secrets and all that," Victor commented. "She does not open up much around me, either," he commented, eyeing Tracey for a reaction.

"She does not confide in me, either, Victor - if that's what you are fishing for. I know only her professional history and reason for being involved with the hospital. That is all Felicity told me. And I doubt Felicity knows much more than we do. A woman as lovely as Agnes Marie, employed as she has been in a field dominated by men would likely have a few tales to tell, but she never discusses her personal affairs. And I assume she is not a stranger to romance."

"What kind of romance, I wonder? Victor mused.

Yesterday she and Azar were getting kind of flirty, and they seemed eager to take off together for the afternoon."

"Who knows?" he shrugged. "As long as they both get here this morning with clear heads, I'm good with whatever their relationship is."

"Me, too, I guess. I don't usually pry, but we are engaged in some pretty serious business here today, and I can't help but wonder about the depth of their involvement, and what it might mean to the Kriya Project – and to their performance today," Tracey said with a frown.

"Just chill, Tracey," Victor suggested, "you can't worry about things you cannot control. Not today. You have enough other anxieties to keep you busy!"

"And here they are," Tracey commented as Azar drove into the parking lot, found a space, and the two of them approached the Ferris wheel, waving to Tracey and Victor.

"When is Fitz supposed to arrive?" Azar asked as they shook hands all around. "Great day for the opening!"

Agnes Marie sniffed the air. "Caramel corn. Smell it? I love the smell, and the taste. I skipped breakfast for this – the food."

"Jason Fitz is due to arrive around 9:30 this morning, the official opening time. But the two of you do need to disappear until then," Tracey told them. That is when he is supposed to meet Victor and me. The two of you need to arrive separately, slightly before and immediately after 9:30. You know your cover stories?"

"I work for a company that is responsible for the side shows," Azar chimed in, "and I want to ride the wheel before my gig starts, a little later."

"And I am friends with one of the food concessionaires – helping her out - and want to ride the Ferris wheel before things get really busy and I lose the opportunity," Agnes Marie piped up. "I've never ridden a Ferris wheel before, but a friend told me about the spectacular views from the top, and so I slipped away for a ride. Yesterday, Tracey, I befriended the woman who owns the kettle corn concession. She does all the fairs and carnivals, and she did in fact tell me that. Gonna go visit her now and ask how I can help out later – and I'll load up on a bag of the stuff to munch on. I made sure to travel light – no handbag, just this small purse for cash, my I.D., and a lipstick. The long strap lets me wear it securely, like this, see? Crossways from shoulder to waist, so it won't get in the way."

"Excellent," Tracey remarked. "I'll wait here with Victor for Jason Fitz to arrive. He should be here within the half hour, photographer in tow. I imagine we'll spend a good twenty minutes on a photo shoot, and then

Fitz wants to address the crowd that gathers - before they're allowed onto the Ferris wheel for its 'maiden voyage.' We'll see you both in about 40-45 minutes. Remember to arrive separately, but meet in line to get your tickets. And then, Agnes, you will need to wait near Jason. Chat him up and get friendly with Fitz while Victor pays for both of them and brings back the tickets. Azar will get carnival courtesy and won't have to pay. I checked on that. He just has to name the sideshow company he is with – it is one he knows. He'll ride free; professional courtesy. Now skedaddle, you two," Tracey instructed. "See you soon."

She and Victor watched as Azar and Agnes walked away, keeping a suitable distance from one another as they did so. Tracey found that reassuring. This was going to work. She and Victor had time to waste, so they strolled down the midway and back, arriving in time to spot Jason Fitz emerging from an SUV driven by his photographer, who was unloading his equipment and cameras from the back of the vehicle.

Jason strode over, waving at Tracey and Victor, and was elated when he saw the large sign with his name prominently displayed above that of his company. Another vehicle drove up behind them and parked nearby, unloading boxes of candy manufactured by the George Fitz Candy Company. They set up a display table and cash register beneath the sign Jason Fitz had so proudly just admired with approval. "Good spot to make some sales," he commented to no one in particular. "Should be a profitable day!"

They engaged in idle talk until the photographer had been introduced to Tracey and Victor, then took Tracey aside to propose taking photos of the entire carnival for Truvenge records, and publication in any fundraising materials. Tracey was thrilled when he made the proposal; she had entirely forgotten to engage a photographer, and the fellow's offer was more than reasonable.

They shook hands on the deal, and the photographer – Greg by name – began posing them for pictures both organizations could use.

Once out of sight of Tracey and Victor, Azar caught up with Agnes-Marie and clasped her hand. He bent to whisper in her ear, "I'm glad you made arrangements to stay last night, dear girl. You made me a very happy man. Did you enjoy . . ."

Agnes Marie cut him off, replying, "I did Now hush and get away from me, handsome. We absolutely cannot afford to be identified together. We'll meet up at the ticket booth, shortly. I am going to see my new friend the kettle corn lady, and get a bag of the yummy stuff. My stomach is starting to growl. Now, get – and no parting kiss!"

"Your wish is my command, Mademoiselle," Azar mocked. "See you later!" They parted company and went their separate ways.

For all their planning, no one had counted on Murphy's law coming into play, and for Jason Fitz to be enchanted by Agnes Marie as they talked after they'd introduced themselves once she'd purchased her ticket.

Jason was at the head of the growing line of ticket holders, in front of the gate that prevented waiting passengers from rushing onto the platform. He was waiting for Victor to join him, after paying for their tickets, and planned to stand on the platform to give a brief welcome to those in line, to tout his sponsorship and recommend his company's candy, being offered for sale at first-day reduced prices. It appeared, however, that Victor had been caught up in conversation with an unrecognized individual on his way back from the cashier's box after paying for two tickets for the ride. He continued talking for several minutes.

Tracey, too was on her way back to the Ferris wheel after having been called away to attend to another matter.

All eyes were on Victor.

Jason and Agnes Marie had enjoyed getting to know one another after introducing themselves and sharing some of Agnes Marie's remaining caramel corn. They laughed at a few carnival jokes, told to them by the ride operator, with whom they'd started a conversation while waiting for Victor. When introducing himself to the operator, Jason had explained his intention to formally address the crowd from the platform, before loading the ride. All was ready, and the crowd was growing antsy at the delay. The operator suggested that Agnes Marie and Jason join him on the platform so Mr. Fitz could begin talking to the restive people, who were starting to wonder loudly just what was going on.

He opened the gate, and Agnes and Jason stepped onto the platform, with Agnes Marie standing in the background as Jason was handed a microphone and addressed the waiting families and individuals. He explained to them that he was a major sponsor of the Truvenge Carnival, and that the Ferris wheel ride was being brought to them by the George Fitz Candy Manufacturing Company. He said a few words about the great humanitarian work that was undertaken every day by the Truvenge Foundation, committed to helping New Yorkers build stronger families and better lives for themselves. Then he spent a few minutes talking about the family-owned candy company, told the growing crowd what growing up around all that candy was like for a young boy, and wound up his talk by promoting the wide assortment of his company's candy, available for sale at special pricing as a first-day special for Carnival attendees.

Victor noticed what was happening, cut short his conversation, and hurried toward them, waving the tickets he'd purchased. With arm raised high, tickets in hand, and muttering litany of "Excuse me, please" as he elbowed his way through the crowd.

When Victor arrived at last, the impatient people burst into applause.

Trying to speed things along, the operator told Agnes Marie and Jason to get into the first gondola, so the Ferris wheel could be loaded, and the ride started. He then opened the gate to let in Victor, who was bowing to the applause of the crowd. But as he rose from the bow and turned to take his place as planned, Victor became concerned. The seating was going to be all out of whack!

Jason, being a gentleman, had offered Agnes first entry onto the gondola, and followed her on. To complicate matters, Azar had appeared, seemingly out of nowhere, dressed in trapeze tights and wearing soft shoes, and flashed a badge of some sort at the operator as he quickly explained he was a trapeze artist making an appearance with the sideshow and had to be in the first car in order to get back in time for his performance. He then slipped into the gondola beside Jason Fitz, leaving the final last-in-first-out seat for Victor, who was flummoxed by the change in the order of seating, but could say nothing.

Tracey, watching from afar, had duly noted the friendly chit-chat between Jason and Agnes Marie while waiting for Victor. It seemed to her that Azar had been watching the same very friendly exchange between the two of them as well, and had moved swiftly to protect his interests. It was just as she had feared: Cupid was paying a part in his decisions! On second thought, however, Tracey realized the change in seating order could actually work to their benefit, though it would leave Victor with no role to play now that he had lost control of the situation.

After pausing for a moment to consider what had just transpired, Tracey continued walking toward the Ferris wheel that was being loaded, gondola by gondola, still wondering how this was going to play out. She blamed herself, in part. Leaving to take care of another, lesser problem had prevented her from riding herd on Victor – who had he been talking to for so long, anyway?

Her absence had also kept her from intervening as Agnes took an unexpected spot in the gondola. Well, Tracey rationalized, she's still in an end position, so this might work out yet.

She was still a good distance from the Ferris wheel, so she quickened her steps, eyes glued to the tableaux in front of her. The chaos at the gate had settled, as people lined up in an orderly queue. Tickets were being taken, each 4-person gondola was slowly being loaded, and the operator was then rotating the 16-spoke wheel another $1/16^{th}$ of the way to the apex 60 feet above the platform.

Tracey had checked her watch when she first saw Agnes and Jason take their seats next to each other, and watched as Azar jumped in front of Victor to sit beside Jason. After Victor was seated and the safety bar hooked in place, the Ferris wheel had slowly rotated. The entire process had taken nearly two minutes.

As other riders were seated, the assisting carny organized the next group to fill the following gondola, and the 16 Ferris wheel gondolas were then rotated again to accommodate the next group. She calculated quickly that, at a rate of one to two minutes per loading, the rise to maximum height at the wheel's apex would be slow enough for her to arrive at the base of the Ferris wheel just as the gondola carrying the four people with whom she was preoccupied reached the wheel's apex, where the action was to take place.

The third gondola was now being lifted, as yet another took its place. Five gondolas to go. Music, and the increasingly interesting views as each gondola rose into the air kept riders entertained and patient, chattering amongst themselves.

Organization of the crowd had paid off, however, and Tracey noted with some alarm that the loading time had decreased. She picked up her pace, now striding rapidly in the direction of the wheel. The fourth gondola had lifted, and now the fifth. Three left to load. Her adrenalin kicked in and she found herself jogging, furious with herself for not doing so earlier. Just two gondolas were left to load.

She began to run.

Jason had been trying to charm Agnes Marie, describing his business, his good fortune, his inspiration and the privilege he felt in being able to sponsor the Carnival and Ferris wheel for Truvenge, and the joys of tearing down a highway in his Aston Martin, wind in his hair. Wouldn't she enjoy a ride?

Victor could practically see the steam emitting from Azar's ears. He kept interjecting observations and trying to distract Jason from his focus on Agnes Marie. She, in turn, began to appear visibly more uncomfortable, continuously staring down and gripping the bar. She had begun hyperventilating, and place the hand not on the bar on her heart.

Jason was oblivious, although Azar was staring intently at her.

Man, he has it bad! Victor thought. And if he doesn't pay attention to what this ride is doing, we're screwed.

Victor elbowed Azar, as if by accident, and said loudly, "Look at that view! And we're almost at the top!! Just one more turn of the wheel."

He could tell that he had done the right thing when Azar became immediately alert, and Agnes began gasping, to the point that Jason finally recognized she was in deep distress. Victor had to admire her acting ability.

One more turn of the wheel brought them to the top, 65 feet above the ground below.

Victor glanced around, trying to find Tracey, and spotted her running, still about 50 feet from the platform steps.

Agnes Marie suddenly jumped to her feet. Holding onto the safety bar with her left hand, she seemed to struggle to breathe, and loudly declared, "I can't breathe! I can't breathe! Oh, God, my heart! it's beating so very fast! I – I feel dizzy . . ."

Agnes Marie was gripping the protective bar tightly, knuckles whitened with the intensity of her grip, but began swaying as she clutched her chest and fought for breath. Watching her intently, Victor was equally uncertain whether she was still acting, or truly in physical distress.

Jason reached out to hold onto her waist and upper arm, in order to steady her - rising slightly as he did so.

His clear intention was to help guide her to a sitting position once again.

Then, to everyone's horror, the Ferris wheel – which had begun its slow ascent, to move the gondola upward – abruptly jerked to a full stop, throwing riders forward, then back, with some violence.

Agnes Marie shrieked as she pitched forward, over the railing, followed closely by Jason – who had still been in motion, rising to his feet to help her, when the Ferris wheel unexpectedly lurched without warning. His forward motion was unstoppable, and he dove over the protective bar at the front of their gondola.

Cries of dismay filled the air as all gondolas jerked to a stop, then violently swung forward.

Quick as a shot, Azar was at the safety bar and had grabbed hold of Agnes. But when he caught her by her wrist, he heard her shoulder dislocate and her head collide with metal of the swinging gondola, silencing her in mid-scream. He groaned, fearing the worst.

Jason Fitz had managed to grasp the black metal bar as he dove over the raised front of the gondola, but found that the glossy paint finish that added an attractive touch to the overall appearance of the vibrantly colored Ferris wheel weakened his grip, and one of his hands slipped as he hung on to the bar, and dangled over the side of the now-still car.

Seeing Jason's hand slip, Azar unwisely reached for Fitz and grasped his thicker wrist while still trying to raise an unconscious Agnes Marie. A tall man, Azar was leaning over the rail as he did this.

Victor, fearing Azar would slip over the bar himself if he tried to bring Agnes Marie to safety while holding onto Jason's jacket-covered, dapperly cuffed wrist, had the good sense to quickly tackle Azar by his lower legs, anchoring Azar with his weight while the well-muscled trapeze artist attempted to lift Agnes Marie back into the gondola, trying to raise the slender woman with the strength of one arm, while keeping a grip on Fitz's wrist.

Fitz whined in fear and began panting and gasping as he tried to bring up his free arm to grasp the painted safety rail. Azar noted how weak Jason was. "Desk jockey," he muttered. "Just my luck!" Fitz was unsuccessful in latching onto the rail for support, and Azar could tell that Jason's arm was slipping lower in his sleeve. Azar feared he might wind up holding nothing more than Jason Fitz's jacket as the one hand with which Jason grasped the black railing began to slide, one heart- pounding quarter inch after another over what seemed to Azar to be hours. Victor, who was crouched at the floor of the car, and still clutching Azar's legs, was necessary to anchoring the man, and both men agreed he should not move and attempt to assist, since Victor's weight was essential to keeping Azar in the gondola.

Azar was exerting every effort to save both Agnes Marie and Jason Fitz, and his face was turning purple with the strain. Beads of sweat from his physical exertion had popped onto forehead and were in serious danger of dripping into his eyes.

By now, the plight of the two individuals who were dangling from the uppermost gondola was known to everyone riding the Ferris wheel, as they craned their necks to see. The buzz of frightened conversation engulfed the Ferris wheel. On the platform, frantic activity ensued as a rescue ladder was sought to assist in bringing the injured down from the apex, while a 911 call was made to summon two ambulances, and police, to the scene.

Still panting from running the last yards to the Ferris wheel, Tracey's heart was pounding with fear. What had gone wrong? How had this happened? She questioned those around her, but got no answers. No one had actually seen how it happened.

Tracey's eyes were glued on the uppermost gondola where the drama was still occurring. She realized she was holding her breath and silently told herself, "breathe." She shut her eyes and filled her lungs.

A scream rent the air, and then another, followed by a huge outcry of horror.

She opened her eyes, just as Tracey heard a resounding 'thud,' and was met by the sight of a crumpled body lying in a heap on the stamped steel platform of the ride.

It was the body of a man.

Tracey was not one to faint, but the blood drained from her face and she felt as though she were going to be sick. She grabbed the shoulder of a man standing nearby to steady herself, and he supported her to the platform steps, where she sat in a daze.

"He's got her!" the cry went up from the crowd, and was repeated from gondola to gondola, along with huzzas and at least a dozen iterations of "Thank God!"

Tracey strained, looking up into the sun, trying to see the occupants of the gondola. Victor and Azar had lifted the limp body of Agnes Marie onto the seat, but the two of them were visible, sharing a hearty handshake, and both cocking their heads, as though speaking to a third person – presumably talking to a supine Agnes Marie.

"That's good. She's conscious," Tracey murmured gratefully. Her cell phone rang, and she automatically answered it while staring at the now-rotating wheel that was lowering the gondola holding the Kriya group. Sirens announced the simultaneous arrival of two ambulances, an EMT wagon and a police car.

"Hello," she spoke into the phone. "Who? Oh, Mark! Listen, this is the worst time possible. I can't talk. I'm up to my ass in alligators, and they're snapping at me."

She listened for a moment and responded, I don't care how important it is, Mark! I have a really serious situation on my hands. I'll call you tonight. You can tell me then. Yes, I promise. Gotta go!"

Medics were working on Agnes Marie, cleaning away blood, bandaging her head wound, stabilizing her neck, taking vital signs, and talking with her to gather what details they could. As shock set in they covered her with a blanket and loaded her into the ambulance. Azar climbed in beside Agnes Marie. He had suffered cuts, as well, and had a blood pressure cuff on his arm as Tracey and a police detective walked to the ambulance they were in, hoping to learn her condition and speak to Azar. Victor joined them.

As the second ambulance drove away with the body of the deceased, a more senior EMT technician walked over to them to get essential information and signatures. He announced to Tracey and NYPD Detective D'Onofrio that "the gentleman" had died from multiple injuries in his 60-foot fall, including a broken back and neck. Fitz had evidently died on impact.

Victor and Tracey followed the ambulance carrying Azar and Agnes Marie to the closest hospital. Tracey had no idea where they were going but Victor had assured her and Azar that he could vouch for the hospital where Agnes Marie would be admitted. He patted Tracey's hands as she twisted the handkerchief he had leant her to catch her tears. Victor recounted his story as he drove.

His chief concern, however, was that their first mission for Kriya Project had been a total failure.

"We never got Quirky Lewis the return of his trademark. And now Jason Fitz is dead. We've failed in our task. And we've created a real legal mess for Truvenge. I never should have stopped to talk with that old client I ran into after buying the tickets! The lineup got screwed up because of me. It's my fault. Mine and Azar's. He's so smitten with Agnes Marie he couldn't take his eyes off her. And Azar was breathing down Jason's neck once he saw how they were getting along. It's just one massive screwup! Worst of all is that I was left in a crouch on the gondola floor, hanging on to Azar's legs like my life depended on it, and could not move to help him hold on to Fitz. And you never got the paperwork signed. Total failure, all around."

"We don't know that yet. We have to speak with the Bodhi first. I will make the call and put you on speaker phone. You are the only real witness to everything that happened, Victor. But don't blame yourself. The entire wheel came to a sudden stop. All the gondolas were set swinging. I understand there were other injuries among the riders. The first aid station looked busy. I saw that a crowd had gathered there while we were involved with the Detective. I'm glad he came with a uniformed officer to keep order. There will be an investigation, of course, but from what you have told me, and what I saw with my own eyes, the real culpable party was the ride operator. Did you hear an explanation from anyone as to why he abruptly stopped the wheel like that?"

"I heard something along the lines that something obstructed the gears, Victor replied. It was not a voluntary stop. That is what I overheard the operator telling Det. D'Onofrio. That would explain why the stop was so sudden – not smooth at all, like it would have been if the operator merely stopped the wheel in the normal course of operation."

"Well, I was still too far to see anything but a general view of what happened with the wheel and the gondolas. My Lord in heaven, you all must have been terrified!" Tracey exclaimed.

"We were. But why did you say that we don't know yet if we failed? Fitz is dead, and we did not get him to sign the release. Why do you have to talk to the Bodhi to find out anything?

"Because, my friend, on the day Jason came out to see the assembly of the Ferris wheel, I brought all his paperwork in my briefcase. When he was in such a rush to get back to work, I had him sign the stack of papers I'd taken out of the briefcase, which he did, without allowing me to go through them with him, He never asked to read a one of them!

"While waiting, I had signed for Truvenge wherever I needed to, before putting the forms back in the case. The signature lines were all color tagged, and I pulled everything out, together, and placed the pile of documents in a stack atop the hard briefcase I was forced to use as a table of sorts, so Jason would have a hard surface on which to sign or cosign the forms – most of which were for the lease of the Ferris wheel, and his sponsorship agreement with Truvenge – a dozen multi-page documents, at least. I called over a young man who was standing around watching the work on the Ferris wheel, and asked him to be a witness to Fitz's signatures. Thankfully, I had the foresight the take a snapshot of his driver's license, to have his address and proper identification, and gave the fellow a twenty for his time. Jason was so rushed, neither of us read the documents before he signed them," Tracey explained, then paused.

"And ...?" Victor queried, prompting her.

"And he was *very* distracted - in a major hurry to get back for an appointment - and in the rush, I had pulled out and he had inadvertently signed the quit claim to Lewis' trademark and recipes! And it is all witnessed by me, and by the young man I mentioned. I did not realize it until, back at the office, I photocopied and separated all the documents.

"When I saw what had happened, I decided to keep the signed document and its copies, thinking it would be useful as was a fallback in case the document he was to sign after the ride was spoiled in some manner. You know, as a backup. Should we be able to use it, it will of course have to be filed as a claim. It would now have to be filed as a claim against either his estate, or the George Fitz Manufacturing Company. I assume it's a corporation. If so, the claim will doubtlessly be fought by the corporation's lawyers. But given that the date of signature was BEFORE the date of the accident, and there is another witness – and yes, I got the young man's email and cell phone number.

"I mean – how can anything be tied to Truvenge besides our general corporate responsibility In having organized the Carnival and co-leased the Ferris wheel that cause his death? There is no question of a motive. So, Victor, *IF* the Bodhi say we can use it – and that is a big if – we will have succeeded, after all."

"Got it," Victor said. "You are one smart cookie, Miss Tracey. Let's hope the Bodhi agree."

"I have to make the call to inform them of this mess, now, and we'll see what they say. You will have to do most of the talking, since you are the best witness of what occurred."

She dialed the Bodhi's direct line, and an assistant put the call on speakerphone, so all could speak and listen to the call. Tracey took a deep breath, and began to explain the situation to the triplets. Then Victor spoke to them at length, explaining everything except what Tracey had told him about the signed release.

Tracey then took over the conversation, and while Victor turned into the hospital entrance and found a place to park, she explained that she had Jason Fitz's signed release and transfer of the trademark and all recipes, which had been signed and witnessed the previous day. She explained the circumstances of the signing, and asked the Bodhi what she should do, and whether the signed agreement should be – could be – used. She held her breath, and Victor nervously drummed his thumbs against the steering wheel as they waited for a reply.

After Tracey's and Victor's presentation of the tragic developments of the day, the Bodhi conversed for a few minutes in a language neither Victor nor Tracey could understand.

Then Aadil Adish – 'he who delivers the message of Justice' – gave his measured response, and rendered his decision.

"We will have to see your copy of the release document, Miss Tracy Walker, and examine the sufficiency of the identification of the witness to the signatures of this Mr. Fitz, who has been released from this earthly plane of existence to review his recent life, and what lessons he has learned from it.

"I hear in your voices that you are both naturally quite distressed, as his death was never your intention. But I promise you, Karma often has a mind of her own, and it appears – as it often does - that true Karma overtook your plans and rendered her own decision. You must understand that we at the Kriya Project are not the ones who effect retribution. We merely set the stage, as it were, to hurry Karma along so that the injured can rest easy, and live the remainder of their lives with a greater sense of peace. That the release was signed and witnesses in the manner that it was, is a most fortuitous happening. The stars were properly aligned for that to happen."

"You make it seem that very little in this life is of our own planning," Victor joked. "Very little is," Aadil Adish replied.

Tracey did not get back to her own apartment until nearly 1:00 in the morning, and flung herself on the bed in exhaustion.

Agnes Marie was in intensive care. Her internal injuries required surgery, and her concussion was being monitored. The good news was that she was groggy and mentally confused due to her head injury, but conscious. She would fully recover. Azar was thrilled, and promised to stay the night in the visitors' waiting room so he would be available to see her as soon as was permissible. Referring to his own injuries, he had said, "These are mere scratches. I have suffered worse. The important thing is, I was able to save the right person."

The Truvenge legal team had been advised of events, so they would be ready to pursue matters in the morning.

The Bodhi had approached the entire fiasco as if it were 'business as usual.' No one was going to get fired – or even scolded.

Quirky Lewis would have his retribution, and Joe and the IRS were hot on the trail of Ace Hollander, scoundrel extraordinaire.

Tracey was emotionally drained. Whipped.

Then she remembered the urgency in Mark's voice when he'd called at the most inopportune time with what he had described as "extremely important information." She hadn't called him back, and it was too late to initiate a conversation that she really did not want to deal with, after the grueling day she'd had.

She rolled from back to stomach and propped herself on her elbows to quickly scan text messages for those that would have to be dealt with, first thing in the morning.

Sure enough, there was a brief text from Mark. Brief as it was, it might well have been a bullet from a gun, for the impact it had on Tracey.

Her cell phone trembled in her hand, then dropped to the floor after as she read his message:

"You never called, but I need to tell you this: Your mother is alive & has told me everything. She's recovering & asked to see you. Call me ASAP!!!!"

Tracey screamed, and then broke down sobbing.

Karma does, indeed, have a mind of its own.

*****

CPSIA information can be obtained
at www.ICGtesting.com
Printed in the USA
BVHW041602190422
634706BV00017B/996